THE CONCEPT OF A PERSON

By the same author

THE FOUNDATIONS OF EMPIRICAL KNOWLEDGE
PHILOSOPHICAL ESSAYS
THE PROBLEM OF KNOWLEDGE
THE REVOLUTION IN PHILOSOPHY (*with others*)

THE CONCEPT OF A PERSON

AND OTHER ESSAYS

BY

A. J. AYER

Fellow of New College and Wykeham Professor of Logic in the University of Oxford

LONDON

MACMILLAN & CO LTD

NEW YORK · ST MARTIN'S PRESS

1964

First Edition 1963 *Reprinted* 1964

MACMILLAN AND COMPANY LIMITED
St Martin's Street London WC2
also Bombay Calcutta Madras Melbourne

THE MACMILLAN COMPANY OF CANADA LIMITED
70 Bond Street Toronto 2

ST MARTIN'S PRESS INC
175 Fifth Avenue New York 10 NY

TO

DEE AYER

PRINTED IN GREAT BRITAIN

PREFACE

Four of the nine essays which make up this book have not been previously published. They are the essay on 'The Concept of a Person', which gives the book its title, and those on 'Names and Descriptions', 'Truth', and 'Fatalism'. An earlier, but in many ways very different, version of 'Names and Descriptions' appeared in a Polish translation in *Studia Filozoficzne*, 5.20, in 1960, and some parts of the essay on 'Truth' are based on an essay with the same title which was published in 1953 in No. 25, Fasc. 3, of the *Revue Internationale de Philosophie*.

Of the other essays 'Philosophy and Language' was delivered as an inaugural lecture at Oxford in November 1960 and subsequently published by the Oxford University Press: 'Can There Be A Private Language?' appeared in the *Supplementary Proceedings of the Aristotelian Society for 1954*, as the first paper in a symposium in which the other participant was Mr. R. Rhees: 'Privacy' was delivered to the British Academy in 1959 as one of the annual philosophical lectures provided for by the Henriette Hertz Trust; it appeared in the *Proceedings of the British Academy* for that year and was separately published by the Oxford University Press: 'What is a Law of Nature?' appeared in 1956 in No. 36, Fasc. 2, of the *Revue Internationale de Philosophie*. Of the two notes on Probability, 'The Conception of Probability as a Logical Relation' appeared in a volume entitled *Observation and Interpretation*, which records the proceedings of the Ninth Symposium of the Colston Research Society held in the University of

Bristol in April 1957, and 'On the Probability of Particular Events' was published in No. 58, Fasc. 4, of the *Revue Internationale de Philosophie* in 1961.

My thanks are due to the editors, institutions, and publishers concerned for permission to reprint this set of articles, and also to my secretary, Mrs. Rosanne Richardson, for her help in preparing this volume for the press.

A. J. AYER

NEW COLLEGE,
OXFORD
24 October 1962

CONTENTS

1

PHILOSOPHY AND LANGUAGE

OXFORD philosophy has changed very much in the course of the present century. In so far as it has changed for the better, a large proportion of the credit must go to my predecessor in this Chair, Professor H. H. Price. Certainly the philosophers of my generation are very greatly in his debt. It is now nearly thirty years since I listened, as an undergraduate, to his lectures on *Perception*. Professor Price was, and is, an extremely good lecturer, but more than the form, it was the matter of those lectures that excited us. In the sombre philosophical climate of the Oxford of that time, here was a bold attempt to let in air and light: a theory of perception in which the principles of British empiricism were developed with a rigour and attention to detail which they had in that context never yet received. The book which grew out of the lectures remains a classic in its field. It is true that there has been a reaction against its doctrines. The theory took sense-data very seriously, and the prestige of sense-data is no longer what it was: Professor Price himself has wavered in his loyalty to them. Nevertheless the use that he then made of them enabled us to obtain a much clearer grasp of the problems which they were designed to meet. There may be better ways of solving these problems, though I am not at all sure that they have yet been found, but hardly a more effective way of bringing them to light.

In his more recent work, including his book on *Thinking and Experience*, Professor Price has addressed himself always to difficult and important questions, and he has treated them with the open-mindedness and the fertility of invention which are characteristic of him. I hope it will not be thought impertinent if I say that one of his great virtues as a philosopher is that he does not suffer from an over-dose of common sense. He is inclined to think that the world is a much stranger place than we ordinarily take it to be, so that even the most fanciful theories about it may be found to contain an element of truth. This results in a width of philosophical sympathy which I wish that I could emulate. But this tolerance is never lax; the theories are subjected to a very rigorous scrutiny. Neither is there anything slipshod about Professor Price's methods. He does not deal in riddles. Whatever the subject of his investigation, his treatment of it is thoroughly systematic. With his manifest enjoyment of philosophy, there goes a belief in its seriousness and importance. I only hope that I can prove myself worthy of his example.

I

It is notorious that philosophers disagree not only about the truth of particular theories, or the answers to specific problems, but about the character and purpose of their whole activity. To some extent this is due to the vagueness with which the word 'philosophy' is used. In a bookseller's catalogue the works which are listed under this heading may legitimately range from a treatise on formal logic to an assemblage of copy-book maxims, or a romantic disquisition on the destiny of man. But there is more at issue here than a question of vagueness. It cannot always be assumed that when philosophers disagree about the nature of their subject they are merely contending for the possession of a title. For even when they are addressing themselves to the same questions, to the conflict of realism and idealism, for example, or the problem of negation, or the investigation of the nature of truth, they may still take very different views of the character of these problems, of the kind of answer that they call for, and of the standards of proof which the answers are required to meet.

In recent years, however, there has been a tendency, at least in English-speaking countries, for this range of disagreement to be narrowed. There has been talk of a revolution in philosophy; and one of its main results is thought to be that philosophers now take a more sophisticated view of their own procedures: they have become more clearly aware of what they are trying to do. The conclusion which they have reached is that philosophy is, in some special sense, an inquiry into language. How this inquiry is to be conducted, what purposes it serves, how its progress is assessed, are questions which still need to be clarified. We shall in fact see that diverse answers can be given to them. But however uncertain they may be about the details, there is now a fair measure of agreement among philosophers that theirs is what is technically called a second-order subject. They do not set out to describe, or even to explain, the world, still less to change it. Their concern is only with the way in which we speak about the world. Philosophy, it has been said, is talk about talk.

This conception of philosophy is derived from various sources. In part, it is a legacy of logical positivism; it owes something to the example of G. E. Moore, still more, perhaps, to the later teachings of Wittgenstein. But these influences work in rather different ways. The logical positivists were anxious first of all to purify philosophy of metaphysics: it would then be left free to develop as a branch of logic. The language in which they were interested was the language of science, and the rôle which they assigned to the philosopher was mainly that of explicating terms which belonged to scientific methodology; he was to bring the resources of modern formal logic to bear upon such concepts as those of testability, or confirmation, or probability, or truth. He could also serve the cause of science in more specific ways, by exhibiting the structure of scientific theories, defining the expressions which occurred in them, and showing how they were formally related. If he had the technical ability to remodel scientific language, whether by redefining terms in current use or by introducing new expressions which would be scientifically fruitful, so much the better. Thus philosophy was seen as merging into science. Only the methodological problems were strictly its own perquisite: and it might be expected that they would soon be solved.

The part played by G. E. Moore is less straightforward. He himself was always careful to say that the practice of what he called analysis was only one of the functions of philosophy. Moreover, he did not conceive of it as an inquiry into language. It was concerned, in his view, not with linguistic expressions, but rather with the concepts, or propositions, or facts, for which they stood. Nevertheless, the reduction of philosophy to an inquiry into language was a reasonable consequence of the position which he held. It could be traced indirectly to his defence of common sense. For if he was right in claiming that he knew for certain that 'the common sense view of the world' was wholly true, it followed that the propositions which comprised it were not vulnerable to philosophy: since they were known to be true no philosophical argument could show them to be false. Neither did they have to appeal to philosophy for any warrant of their truth. Admittedly, Moore did try to give a proof that there is an external world, a belief which undoubtedly figures in the common sense view: but since his proof consisted merely in deducing that there were external objects from the fact of his knowing that he had two hands, it did no more than underline the point that the common sense view of the world could safely be left to justify itself. But if this applies to the empirical propositions which are accepted by common sense, there seems to be no reason why it should not also apply to the empirical hypotheses of science, or to the formal propositions of mathematics and logic. They, too, have their appropriate standards of proof; and when they satisfy these standards they are accepted without being made to earn a philosophical certificate. Neither, on this view, can there be a philosophical foundation for any of our normative judgements; for the upshot of Moore's 'naturalistic fallacy' is that judgements of value are autonomous. But if all these domains of discourse are closed to the philosopher, in the sense that it is not his province to decide the validity of any of the propositions that occur in them, what is there left for him to do? The answer is that he can occupy himself with the analysis of these propositions. It is not his business to tell us whether they are true, but it is his business to tell us what they mean.

To conceive of philosophy as the practice of analysis is not, however, necessarily to regard it as an inquiry into language. It would seem that Moore himself was inclined to reify meanings: the concepts or propositions which philosophers sought to analyse were given the status of non-natural objects. No doubt it was not possible to apprehend them unless one understood the appropriate words, but this applied equally to many of the objects of the sciences. A philosopher who had no mastery of language would be as helpless as a mathematician who could not handle numerals: but just as the mathematician was not concerned with numerals as such but rather with the numbers which they represented, so the philosopher's command of language was merely a necessary means to the investigation of the objective properties of concepts. If this was Moore's view, it was one that he shared with philosophers of other schools. It is found among the followers of Cook Wilson, with their talk of apprehending necessary connections between universals, and also among the phenomenologists who would make philosophy consist in what they call the intuition of essences : for these essences turn out to be meanings, regarded as objective entities.

This view of meaning is still very widely held ; but it has been locally discredited through the influence of Wittgenstein. The turning-point was the shift in Wittgenstein's philosophy from the metaphor of treating words as pictures to the metaphor of treating words as tools. Linguistic signs are meaningful, but there are no such things as meanings. Instead of looking upon the meaning of a word as something which it acquires by its relation to an object, we are to content ourselves with asking how the word is used. I shall argue later on that this identification of meaning with use is neither so radical nor so fruitful a step as is commonly supposed. It is doubtful even if it does, in any interesting sense, turn questions of meaning into questions of language ; but, because it is thought to do so, it completes this line of development of the notion of linguistic philosophy.

There is another important point in which Wittgenstein's idea of philosophy differed from Moore's. Though he was open-minded about questions of method, Moore clearly looked upon philosophical analysis as a source of knowledge. He believed that it issued in propositions which were true or false. To take only one example, he thought it certainly true that a proposition like 'this is a human hand' had for its subject some sense-datum, and he thought that the question what, in such a case, was being asserted of the sense-datum was one to which there was a valid answer. He did not think that anybody knew what the answer was, but he firmly believed that it was ascertainable. Once it was ascertained we should have discovered the analysis of an important class of propositions about physical objects. This would be a most valuable item in our stock of philosophical truths. For Wittgenstein, on the other hand, the idea that there could be a stock of philosophical truths was dangerously naïve. He thought that people made difficulties for themselves by failing to understand how their language worked. This led them to raise problems to which they could see no issue, to construct dilemmas which they could not resolve. In their efforts to escape from these perplexities they relapsed into talking nonsense. The remedy was to trace the muddle to its source by exposing the linguistic misconception from which it arose : and this was the rôle assigned to the enlightened philosopher. Thus the success of a philosophical inquiry would consist, not in the acquisition of a fresh piece of knowledge, but rather in the disappearance of the problem on which it was directed. We should have been made to see that our puzzlement was gratuitous.

This is an accurate account of what Wittgenstein mainly says about philosophy in his later works, but the implication that he came to look upon it merely as a form of intellectual therapy is in some degree misleading. For it must be remarked that the therapy takes the form of argument. If we fall into confusion through misunderstanding the logic of our language, it has to be shown that the assumptions which we have made about it are mistaken : and the statement that they are mistaken is itself a philosophical thesis. If it is true, it is an addition to our knowledge. In such cases, indeed, the thesis is negative in form. We are told that a view which had seemed to us plausible is false. But the theses are not always negative. It is hardly possible to say what the logic of our language is not, without making some suggestion as to what it is. Some analysis is offered of the meaning of those types of expression that are thought most likely to deceive. It is not called analysis, and it is not conducted in a systematic fashion ; to a very considerable extent the reader is left to draw the moral for himself. The point is that there are morals to be drawn. What their nature is and how much they really have to do with language are among the questions which we now have to examine.

II

It should already be clear that talk of linguistic philosophy does not take us very far. The activities which the term can be made to cover are much too disparate. Not only is there a distinction to be made between the formal and the informal methods of approach, but the informal methods, in particular, comprise a number of different procedures. If I concentrate mainly upon them, it is not that I think that the use of formal methods is uninteresting or unfruitful; it is rather that the aims which it can be expected to achieve are much more easily discernible. It applies to languages of which the syntax and, if necessary, the semantics can be formalized; that is, to languages with regard to which it is possible to specify what combinations of signs count as sentences of the language; which of these sentences are derivable from one another; and, in the case where the language can be used to make empirical statements, what are the observable states of affairs which certain of these sentences designate. For a natural language, such as English, these conditions cannot be met; perhaps not even in principle, and certainly not in practice. The forms of its sentences are too multifarious and too elastic; the rules of derivation are not delimited; neither are the observable states of affairs which its most simple sentences can be used to designate. Nevertheless fragments of it can be formalized; or at any rate models can be made in which certain features of it are ideally reconstructed. By this means light can be thrown on such matters as the scaffolding of scientific theories, and the methodological conditions which they are required to satisfy.

The merits, as well as the limitations, of this way of doing philosophy can best be brought out by considering what is perhaps its most conspicuous achievement: Tarski's formal treatment of the concept of truth.[1] For various reasons, including the threat of the semantic paradoxes, Tarski makes no attempt to define the term 'truth' as it is used in any natural language. His much quoted formula, '*s* is true in *L* if and only if *p*', which yields such sentences as '"snow is white" is true in English if and only if snow is white', was never meant for a general definition. It was put forward rather as a condition of adequacy which any definition of truth for a given language had to meet. The definition must be such that every sentence which was obtained from the formula by putting a sentence of the language in the place of '*p*' and the name of that sentence in the place of '*s*' should follow from it. Tarski sought to show that definitions which satisfied this requirement could be supplied for formalized languages of a special type. The restrictions which he had to place upon them in order to maintain consistency are very significant, but an account of them is not necessary for our present purpose.

The example which Tarski chose to illustrate his thesis was that of the language of the class-calculus. His method was to specify, in a formal way, the combinations of signs belonging to the language that were to be taken as its sentential functions, and then to define, within this universe of discourse, the notion of the satisfaction of a sentential function. This was achieved by specifying the relations of class-inclusion which the values of the variables in the elementary functions had to bear to one another in order that these functions should be satisfied, and then by defining the satisfaction of more complex functions recursively. Now sentential functions are not sentences: they become

[1] A. Tarski, 'The Concept of Truth in Formalized Languages': reprinted in *Logic, Semantics, Metamathematics.*

sentences only when the free variables which they contain are quantified, or replaced by constants : but sentences can be treated as limiting cases of sentential functions with the peculiarity that they are satisfied by every relevant object or by none. The way was then laid open to defining a true sentence of this language as any sentence which is satisfied by every infinite sequence of classes.

On its own ground I do not think that this definition can be faulted. It has been criticized for making truth a predicate of sentences instead of propositions: but the only serious objection to making truth a predicate of sentences is that token-reflexive sentences, sentences which contain pronouns, or spatial or temporal demonstratives, or tensed verbs, may have different truth-values on different occasions of their use. Since none of the sentences in a formalized language, such as that of the class-calculus, are token reflexive, this objection does not here arise. But we do not ordinarily talk of sentences as being true. If anyone insists, even in this case, on speaking with the vulgar, his pedantry is easy to accommodate. All we need do is to say that a proposition of the class-calculus is true if it is expressed by a sentence which is true in Tarski's sense. The reason against doing this is not only that it is unnecessary, but that it is methodologically out of place. Truth is being defined for a language of which the sentences can be formally specified, but what it is for a sentence to express a proposition has yet to be made clear.

But even when we allow that, in cases of this type, truth can legitimately be ascribed to sentences, it is not at all evident that Tarski's achievement has much to do with any question of language. What he has primarily done is to exhibit the structure of a logical theory, with reference to its truth-conditions. This has a bearing upon language only in the trivial sense in which the description of any theory may have a bearing upon language. The account of what would make the theory true can always be represented as an account of the truth-conditions of the sentences in which the theory can be expressed. There is, however, a wider implication with regard to what is meant by truth in general. The moral which can be drawn from Tarski's definition, as well as from the schema which supplies the definition with its test of adequacy, is that to establish that a sentence is true amounts to the same as establishing the sentence itself. This means that there is, as Ramsey put it, 'no separate problem of truth',[1] but only the problem of assertion. If we understand how sentences can be used to refer to facts, and how we are justified in accepting them, we do not have to worry further about the nature of truth. The question with which philosophers have really been concerned when they have tried to develop 'theories of truth' are questions of testability and meaning. It is because it leaves these questions unanswered that they have mostly been dissatisfied with Tarski's account.[2] But this merely shows that when they asked 'What is truth?' they were not looking for a formal definition. In that line there is nothing better than Tarski has to give.

Very much the same applies to the attempts that have been made, by Carnap and others, to develop formal theories of confirmation. It is possible and useful to work out a system for measuring the degree to which the content of one proposition is included in that of another: and it can then be stipulated that a proposition is to be said to confirm any proposition the range of which is included in its own. But if anyone is worried by Hume's problem of showing how any inductive argument can be justified, this procedure will not help him. Neither will it protect us from Goodman's paradox which purports to show that the evidence

[1] F. P. Ramsey, 'Facts and Propositions', *The Foundations of Mathematics*, p. 142.

[2] *Vide* 'Truth', p. 162 *infra*.

which we naturally take as confirming a given hypothesis always confirms some contrary hypothesis to an equal degree.[1] We may escape from this difficulty, as Goodman does, into a form of pragmatism ; but a move of this kind is quite different in character from those that are made within a formal theory. Once more it does not appear that this group of problems has very much to do with language, except in the obvious sense that when it comes to particular instances the question whether one proposition confirms another depends upon their meaning.

A characteristic of what I have been calling the formal approach is its reliance on the symbolism of mathematical logic ; but the utility of such an artificial symbolism extends beyond its application to formalized languages. It can be employed in other fields to secure a neatness and precision which is not within the resources of ordinary prose. This holds especially for attempts at what is known as reductive analysis. From the early Greeks, philosophers have been concerned with the question of what there really is : but in more recent times this mainly takes the form of trying to show that something, which there appears to be, is not. Thus it has been alleged that there are no such things as numbers but only numerals, no such things as propositions but only sentences, no such things as classes but only individuals, no abstract entities of any kind but only concrete ones, no such things as minds but only bodies, or conversely no such things as bodies but only minds. Nowadays, claims of this kind are usually made in a more sophisticated way. 'Points are really classes of volumes.' 'Material things are logical constructions out of sense-data.' This brings out more clearly what issue is involved in these denials of reality. The thesis is always that some category of objects is dispensable. It can be presented as a linguistic thesis to the effect that sentences which contain expressions of one

[1] Nelson Goodman, *Fact, Fiction and Forecast*, ch. 3.

type can be replaced by sentences which contain expressions of another; that, for example, anything that we want to say about numbers can be rephrased as a statement about numerals, that talk about classes is shorthand for talk about individuals, that to speak of mental states or processes is a way of speaking about physical behaviour. The assumption is that certain types of entity are philosophically suspect, and the purpose is to show that references to such entities are nevertheless innocuous; they can be construed as disguised references to entities which are relatively less problematic.

Now clearly the best way to make a point of this kind good is actually to carry out the reduction; to supply a set of rules for transforming sentences of one type into those of another. And it is here that it may be found necessary to have recourse to an artificial symbolism. In the first place it has to be made clear what type of reduction is being attempted; whether, for example, the replacement for a given sentence has to be synonymous with it, and in that case what are the criteria for synonymity; or whether some weaker condition will suffice; such as its being possible to correlate one 'language' with another in such a way that corresponding sentences have, if not necessarily the same meaning, at least the same truth-value. Whatever condition is chosen the task of showing that it can be satisfied will not be simple. Even to sketch a method of eliminating abstract entities will be found to require more powerful tools than are available to those who insist on remaining within the confines of ordinary language. This applies also to phenomenalism. The view that statements about physical objects must somehow be reducible to statements about sense-data has been fairly widely held; but there have been very few experiments in carrying out the transformation. One reason for this is the lack of the requisite terms at the sensory level. If the phenomenalist's claim is to have any chance of being vindicated, a 'language of appearance' must be artificially constructed.

But while the use of formal techniques may be helpful, or even essential, to the pursuit of the stated aims of reductive analysis, the interest of this type of philosophy lies elsewhere. There is no question here of supplying definitions, or elaborating concepts, which will be of scientific value; it is not claimed that talk about sense-data is more serviceable than the talk about physical objects which it is intended to replace; there is no practical advantage in making statements about individuals do the work of statements about classes. The reason why this effort is made to eliminate certain types of entity is that it is thought that they cannot be real, or at least that their reality is dubious: and the ground for this is that they are not observable. This may seem an odd reason for wishing to dispense with physical objects, but we have here to reckon with the admittedly doubtful assumption that only sense-data are directly perceived. Thus the point of reductive analysis is that it is the product of a radical empiricism. It has a linguistic aspect in so far as it seeks to show that one sort of expression can perform the office of another, but this is the outcome not of any dispassionate study of language but of an *a priori* conception of reality. It is assumed that significant discourse must in the end refer to a limited set of objects, because these are the only objects that there can really be.

III

Reductive analysis has now gone rather out of fashion. This is partly because philosophers have become unwilling to commit themselves openly to its presuppositions, or indeed to acknowledge presuppositions of any kind, partly because the proffered analyses were not convincing. Even in the cases where it seemed obvious that the reduction must be feasible, such as the transformation of statements about nations into statements about persons, or that of statements about propositions into statements about sentences, the rules for making exact translations were not forthcoming. Perhaps some weaker type of reduction was called for ; but it was not made clear what form it should take, or even what purpose it would serve. As a result, the suspicion grew that this sort of analysis was a waste of time. Why should we labour to replace one type of expression by another ? If we find it convenient to talk about propositions, or classes, or any other sort of abstract entity, why should we struggle to eliminate them ? It is not as if we had any difficulty in understanding what was said about them. But are we not then overcrowding our picture of the universe ? Can we really believe in the existence of such Platonic entities ? Rightly or wrongly this bogey has lost its power to scarify. If the objection is not simply ignored, it is met cavalierly with a plea of metaphysical innocence.

The trouble with the reductionists, it is now maintained, is that they had too little respect for language. Though they did their best to torture it on their Procrustean bed, it proved too strong for them : they were unable to obtain the avowals that they wanted. What we must do instead is to approach language without preconceptions, to see how it actually does work.

But why should this be of any philosophical interest ? One answer, which we have already noted, is that it will free us from certain deep perplexities for which our misinterpretations of language are responsible. Another more positive answer is that a careful examination of the workings of our language will give us an insight into the structure of the world which it describes. Let us now try to see how far these claims are justified.

The principal method of catching language at work is to

study examples of the ways in which certain expressions are actually used. There are, however, significantly different manners of putting this into practice. One is to take a group of kindred terms and try, by giving examples, to show exactly how they differ in meaning. Thus one may inquire how being disingenuous differs from being uncandid, and how both of them differ from being insincere. Is it really true, as the dictionary says, that 'disingenuous' is the opposite of 'ingenuous'? Surely to deny that a remark is ingenuous and to assert that it is disingenuous is not to say the same thing. But then what is the opposite of 'ingenuous'? 'Sophisticated'? 'Uncandid'? Perhaps there is no single word. With skill and patience we may be able to construct examples which will make these nuances clear.

But what shall we have gained? If it is said that knowledge of this kind is to be valued for its own sake, well and good. Certainly the work of the lexicographer is neither trivial nor easy. But how far does this sort of inquiry take us towards the solution of anything that has ever been regarded as a philosophical problem? No doubt my actual example was not especially favourable. Moral philosophers might indeed be interested in the question of sincerity, but hardly in determining the different types or shades of insincerity that might be denoted by different English words. But are there much better examples to be found? It has indeed been claimed that examining the use of words like 'inadvertently', 'deliberately', 'mistakenly', 'intentionally', would help us to deal more effectively with the problem of free-will, perhaps even to dispose of the problem altogether. The idea is that we can learn in this way what are the circumstances in which we credit people with responsibility for their acts, and on what grounds we are ready to absolve them; and it is agreed that the extent to which they are responsible is the measure of the extent to which they are free. But while this is, no doubt, a useful way of making clear how we do in fact proceed with the ascription of responsibility, it touches only lightly on the problem of free-will. For those who are troubled by this problem are perfectly well aware that we are in fact trained to distinguish between the cases in which an agent can 'help himself', and those in which he cannot. Their trouble is that they do not see how this distinction can be justified. If all human actions are causally explicable, is there not a very good sense in which no one can ever help doing what he does ? Now it may well be that this reasoning is muddled ; and, if so, that the muddle can be shown up. But then some other method must be chosen ; it is no answer to the denier of free-will merely to pin-point ways of using language in which the falsity of his position is already presupposed.

But is it not an answer ? Surely the mere fact that we are able to employ a certain type of expression in ordinary speech is a proof that it has application. If it is ever correct to say that anyone acts freely, then he does act freely. For what can it be to act freely if not to behave in a way which satisfies the conditions under which the expression 'acting freely' is properly applied ? If an expression X is correctly used to apply to just those things that have the property Y, then for anything to have the property Y it must be sufficient that X can be correctly applied to it.

This argument is plausible, but I believe that it is unsound. It overlooks the fact that there is no sharp dividing line between the description of facts and their interpretation ; even at the level of common sense our ordinary language will be found to carry a considerable load of theory. One may allow that an expression is being used correctly if it is applied to a situation which has certain characteristic features, but one is not therefore bound to accept the interpretation of those features which the use of the expression tacitly implies. Thus in a society which believes in witchcraft it is perfectly correct in certain circumstances to say that a person is bewitched: the symptoms which are commonly regarded as the sign of demonic possession may be quite clearly marked: it does not follow, however, that demons really are at work. In the same way, when there is evidence that a man has deliberately done whatever he did, that he was in full possession of his faculties, that he was not under constraint, it may be correct to say that he acted freely and it may be in accordance with common practice to hold him responsible for what he has done. But if the implication is that his action was not causally determined, one may consistently reject it; and the way in which one expresses this rejection may be to say that the man was not really free at all. I do not say that this is the implication, or even that if it were, it would not be true. My point is only that this is the question on which the dispute about free-will has mainly turned; and that it cannot be settled merely by giving a careful and accurate account of customary usage.

The argument which we have been discussing has come to be known as the argument from paradigm cases. It is used as a weapon against philosophical scepticism in the interests of common sense. Thus when a philosopher says, as many have, that it is not certain that there are physical objects, he is asked how he thinks that words like 'chair' and 'table' came into common use. Did he not himself learn the use of these words by being shown specimens of what they stood for? Surely then the undoubted fact that we constantly come upon situations to which such words apply is an incontestable proof that physical objects exist? This is, indeed, as favourable an example as one could hope to find, but even so the argument is not conclusive. The question is how much our use of these words is taken to involve. If, for example, it commits us to the theory that there are things which exist independently of being perceived, then a philosopher may consistently doubt or reject this proposition, even though he admits that there are situations to which the words that are commonly taken to stand for physical objects are properly applied. People have been trained to use these words, and do correctly use them, when they have certain perceptions; but this is no guarantee that the interpretation of these perceptions which is involved in the claim that there are physical objects is itself correct. Again, I am not saying that such a philosopher would be right. The arguments which lead him to doubt or deny that anything can exist without being perceived may be demonstrably fallacious. All I am saying is that he is not refuted merely by the fact that words like 'chair' and 'table' have a customary use.

The reason why he is not refuted is that his doubts bear upon what Moore would call a question of analysis, rather than a question of fact. It is a matter of fact that the criteria by which we actually determine that there are such things as chairs and tables are very frequently satisfied; and if the statement that there are physical objects is construed simply as a consequence of this fact, it is not open to question on philosophical grounds. On the other hand, it may be construed not just as claiming that these criteria are often satisfied but as affirming the common sense view of what this satisfaction comes to; and in that case it is entirely open to philosophical argument. When it is a matter of interpretation, there is nothing sacrosanct about common sense.

The difficulty here is that the distinction between questions of fact and questions of analysis is not so easily drawn as most philosophers now seem to think. If one takes the view that ordinary language is perfectly in order, one will assign to the statements, which it is used to make, only such interpretations as will allow them in many cases to be true.

Thus a sophisticated behaviourist need not deny that there are what are ordinarily classified as mental facts : he does not have to claim that we are wrong in supposing that we think and feel. We are not wrong, he may say, because all that we really mean by this, though we may not know it, is that we are disposed to behave in certain ways. If our ordinary language were thoroughly animistic, then, even assuming behaviourism to be false, we should not be wrong in personifying all the works of nature, or at any rate not wrong on any question of fact ; for what we should really mean by this talk would be exactly what we now really mean by talking about physical objects. If primitive people who do speak in this way make any mistake at all, it is a mistake in analysis : they do not understand the logic of their language.

I think that this view is tenable, but it rests on a theory of meaning which its advocates commonly fail to make explicit. The theory is not new ; it is summed up in the verification principle on which the logical positivists relied for their elimination of metaphysics. In very rough terms, the assumption is that the meaning of a sentence is yielded by a description of the observations which would make it true. Thus the animists' language is translatable into our own, inasmuch as the statements which it is used to express are verified by the same observations as serve to verify the statements which we make about physical objects. The fact that they believe themselves to be talking about spirits merely shows that they are poor philosophers. Their language is burdened with metaphysical trappings from which ours is taken to be free. If we are more tolerant, we may just say that they have a different conceptual system : but the difference is then a difference in form and not in factual content.

For my part I have no wish to disown the verification principle, though it suffers from a vagueness which it has not yet been found possible to eradicate. I doubt, however, if it is a wholly effective means of distinguishing questions of analysis or interpretation from questions of fact. The trouble lies with the assumption that it is possible to supply a neutral record of facts, which is free from any taint of theory ; a common bedrock for divergent interpretations. But this is highly dubious. It is claimed, for example, that a naïve realist and a follower of Berkeley do not differ with regard to any matter of fact. Whatever they may respectively think that they mean by their perceptual judgements, they accept the same observable states of affairs as showing them to be true. But what are these observable states of affairs ? The Berkeleian describes them in a way that the naïve realist finds unintelligible : the naïve realist describes them in a way that the Berkeleian might regard as begging the question against him. It is common ground, at least for those who accept the verification principle, that in the normal way, when a man sets out to describe what he perceives, he manages to assert something which is true ; but what this is may be a matter for dispute. It has been thought that it could first be stated and then analysed ; but it would seem that in the very attempt to state it one already commits oneself to some form of analysis.

If this is right, it appears that philosophy does after all intrude upon questions of empirical fact. Once it is established what is to count as a fact, that is, once the criteria are settled, it is an empirical and not a philosophical question whether they are satisfied. But adoption of these criteria implies the acceptance of a given conceptual system, and the appraisal of conceptual systems does fall within the province of philosophy. To maintain that ordinary language is perfectly in order is to declare oneself satisfied with the conceptual system that we actually have, or at least with that part of it which is contained in the terminology of common sense. But however well the system works on the whole, it is not immune from criticism. Even among its categorial features there may be some which prove on investigation to be ill adapted to their purpose. The concept of 'cause' is a possible example. No doubt such concepts can be re-interpreted so as to escape the objections to which they were exposed. But it does not seem plausible to maintain with respect to every such redefinition that it merely records what was intended all along.

IV

Not only does the verification principle play an essential part in the vindication of ordinary language; it also sustains the doctrine that the meaning of an expression is to be identified with its use. At first sight, it is by no means clear what this doctrine comes to: for a given set of words can be employed for many different purposes, to inform, to persuade, to amuse, to deceive, to threaten, to distract, sometimes simply to show off; and yet on all these occasions they may have the same meaning. The fulfilment of the purpose depends on the meaning, but it does not constitute it. Sometimes again, there may be no connection at all between the meaning of a word and the use to which it is put, as when it is employed purely for decoration, for example as part of a *collage*. So if one is to maintain that the meaning of words consists in their use, one will have to specify what sort of use this is; and the only plausible answer is that it is a matter of what they are used to signify, of what it is that they are used to name, or designate, or state, or question, or command, as the case may be. For the sake of simplicity, let us confine ourselves to the example of declarative discourse, as expressed in indicative sentences. The thesis is then that the meaning of such an indicative sentence is identical with what it is used to state.

This seems innocent enough, indeed rather too innocent: for on the face of it, to say that the meaning of an indicative sentence is identical with what it is used to state is to say no more than that its meaning is what it means. The point of talking about 'use' emerges only when we go on to consider how we are supposed to determine what a given sentence states; and it is here that the principle of verification once more comes in. For the answer is that to specify the use of a sentence, in this sense, is to describe the situations to which it is applied; in other words to describe the situations, the states of affairs, by which the statement it expresses would be verified.

The employment of this principle, in some manner or other, is characteristic of all types of informal analysis, but it can be made to operate in various ways. Thus in the work of philosophers like Wittgenstein or Ryle, no special attention is paid to niceties of language. I do not mean by this that they are not careful in their choice of words, but only that they are not concerned with discriminating shades of meaning. They approach language not in the spirit of a collector, in search of rare or interesting specimens, but rather in that of a diagnostician. They are concerned with those concepts, or families of concepts, which, for one reason or another, have given trouble to philosophers, and their aim is to dispel the confusions which have grown around them. As I said before, this aim is not merely negative: the removal of our philosophical perplexities should leave us with a better understanding of the rôles that these concepts really do fulfil; in certain cases it may even put us in a position to amend them.

The method is simply to take a new look at the facts. Thus when Ryle sets out to destroy what he regards as the myth of the ghost in the machine,[1] he tries to make us fix our attention on the actual phenomena of what is supposed to be our mental life. He asks us to consider what actually

[1] G. Ryle, *The Concept of Mind*.

happens in typical cases when someone is acting intelligently, or working out a problem, or yielding to a motive, or doing what he wants, or in the grip of some feeling or emotion. Do we invariably find that some inner process is at work, that there is some private object or occurrence with which the intelligence, or the emotion, or the motive, or the act of will can be identified? If we do not, this is a proof that the existence of such ghostly entities is not an essential feature of these 'mental' facts. The official thesis that everything that ranks as a mental phenomenon unfolds itself upon a private stage is refuted by the production of counter-examples. Of course this is not enough to lay the ghost: it still remains possible that there are performances which do take place upon the private stage, however little part they play in what are ordinarily regarded as the principal operations of the mind. The physicalist position may also be exposed to counter-examples. But my object here is not to criticize Ryle's conclusions, but to consider the method by which they are reached.

The questions which he raises may also be put in a form which makes their character appear more linguistic. Instead of asking what actually happens when someone does, for example, act intelligently, one may ask what makes it correct to say that someone is acting intelligently: what are the typical circumstances in which we should ordinarily say that someone was yielding to such and such a motive; how do we in fact use such sentences as 'he is very angry' or 'I intend to go to London to-morrow'? In this way the emphasis is apparently made to fall upon our verbal habits. But this appearance is delusive. The question is not: when do we say this rather than that; when, for example, do we say that someone intended to do something, rather than that he meant to do it, or that he designed to do it? Neither is any interest taken in the philological or social reasons that there may be for our employing a particular form of words. The question is, given that we do make statements of such and such a sort, what are the circumstances that would make them true? In short, the emphasis is not on our verbal habits themselves, but on the situations to which they are adapted. It is true that an account of the facts which verify a given statement will also be an account of the way in which the words that describe these facts are used; but it still makes a difference where the emphasis falls. The difference is between starting with the words and then looking for the facts to which to fit them, and starting with an identification of the facts and then seeing how they can best be described.

In Wittgenstein's later work there is on the face of it a much greater emphasis on language; so much so indeed that at one point he speaks of his own investigations as grammatical: philosophical problems are to be solved 'by looking into the workings of our language, and that in such a way as to make us recognize those workings in despite of an urge to misunderstand them'.[1] But when we examine how this process of looking into the workings of our language is actually conducted, we find once again that it is chiefly a matter of the meticulous inspection of a certain range of facts. When Wittgenstein, for example, asks us to consider the English word 'reading', or the German word '*lesen*', he does not in fact direct our attention to the multiplicity of uses to which these words are put. We hear nothing about lip-reading, or reading fortunes, or reading the expression on a person's face. We are asked rather to consider what actually happens when, for example, someone reads a newspaper. Since reading words is more than merely looking at a series of shapes, we are inclined to say that reading consists in 'a special conscious activity of mind'.[2] But is this hypothesis really borne out by the

[1] L. Wittgenstein, *Philosophical Investigations*, i. 109.
[2] L. Wittgenstein, *op. cit.* i. 156.

facts ? In reply, we are given a series of examples, some of them very subtle, the moral of which is that 'in different circumstances we apply different criteria for a person's reading'.[1] Again, this can be taken as showing that what a dictionary might represent as one particular use of the verb 'to read' is in fact a family of uses ; but again this would put the emphasis in the wrong place. What is being brought to our attention is the variety of the phenomena in which reading of this sort may consist.

The effort which we are urged to make, both by Wittgenstein and Ryle, is to see the phenomena as they really are, to divest ourselves of any preconception which may lead us to distort the facts. But, as I have already tried to show, no record of the facts can be free from all interpretation. One's account of what actually happens is governed by one's idea of what is possible. To put it in linguistic terms, the way in which one construes a given type of statement depends upon one's general view of meaning. Thus when Wittgenstein declares that an inner process stands in need of outward criteria, when he denies the possibility of a private language on the ground that there can be no language without rules of which the observance can be publicly checked, he is fashioning a mould into which the facts must be made to fit. These principles are not derived from an open-minded study of the way in which the English, or the German, or any other language happens to work : they set limits to what any use of language can achieve, and so help to decree what facts are possible ; for if anything is a fact it can be stated. Since they lay down what we are capable of meaning, any account of what we do mean will be expected to conform to them.

This is not in itself an objection to Wittgenstein's procedure. There must always be some method of approach. The value of the method can be tested only by its results.

[1] L. Wittgenstein, *op. cit.* i. 164.

Here, however, there is the difficulty that the results themselves must be evaluated. If they are tested by the same criteria as are used in obtaining them, they are bound to be favourable so long as the method is consistent. But then this whole proceeding lies open to the charge of begging the question. On the other hand, it is not to be expected that one should employ any other criteria than those which from the outset have been assumed to be correct. Thus, so long as it is free from inner contradiction, it is hard to see how any philosophical thesis can be refuted, and equally hard to see how it can ever be proved. Let us take for example the thesis of physicalism ; that all statements which ostensibly refer to mental states or processes are translatable into statements about physical occurrences. The obvious way to refute it is to produce a counter-example, which in this case seems quite easy. There are any number of statements about people's thoughts and sensations and feelings which appear to be logically independent of any statement about their bodily condition or behaviour. But the adherent to physicalism may not recognize these examples : he may insist that they be interpreted in accordance with his principles. He will do so not because this is the meaning that they manifestly have, but because he has convinced himself on *a priori* grounds that no other way of interpreting them is possible. Our only hope then is to make the interpretations appear so strained that the assumptions on which they rest become discredited. As for the proof of any such thesis, it rests on the absence of any refutation of this sort. So long as we cannot find any convincing counter-example, the thesis is allowed to stand. In this respect the procedure followed in philosophy is like that of the natural sciences.

I have argued that what passes for linguistic philosophy, at least as it is represented in the work of such authors as Wittgenstein and Ryle, is concerned with language only to the extent that a study of language is inseparable from a study of the facts which it is used to describe. To use a somewhat imperfect analogy, the interest lies in the photographs, and not in the mechanism of the camera by which they happen to be taken. In Wittgenstein's case, indeed, there is a predominant concern with the general problem of the way in which language is related to the things of which it speaks; but, while they are illustrated by examples, his answers to this question are not based upon the special features of any given language. They do not so much elucidate our actual uses of words as determine what uses are possible.

The aim, then, is to see the facts for what they are. Sometimes it is enough to have them simply pointed out to us, but often reasons must be supplied for thinking that a given description of them is correct. And here we may come upon a form of argument which is straightforwardly linguistic. It consists in appealing to the fact that certain combinations of words do or do not make sense. Thus when Ryle is concerned to distinguish between knowledge and belief, he points out that whereas the English word 'belief' can be qualified by adjectives like 'obstinate', 'wavering', or 'unswerving', which are also appropriate to nouns like 'loyalty' or 'addiction', this is not true of the word 'knowledge'. We say of a belief, but not of knowledge, that it is slipped into or given up: we can say of someone that he is trying to stop believing something, but not that he is trying to stop knowing something: we can ask why people believe things, but not why they know them; we say 'How do you know?' but not 'How do you believe?'[1] The point of all this is to show that knowing, unlike believing, is not a disposition which is actualized in events: the possession of knowledge is an achievement; it marks a capacity for getting something right. If we recognize this,

[1] *The Concept of Mind*, p. 134.

we shall avoid the mistake of looking for the essence of knowledge in some special state of mind; we shall not be taken in by the philosopher's myth of there being 'acts of knowing' which mysteriously guarantee the truth or reality of the 'objects' which are known.

This appeal to what it makes sense to say is not a new device in philosophy. It goes back to the ancient Greeks. When Socrates in the *Theaetetus* is attacking the suggestion that perception is identical with knowledge, one of the arguments which Plato makes him use is that what can be said of the one cannot be said of the other. We talk of things being perceived distinctly or indistinctly, clearly or faintly, from a distance or near at hand, but these are not ways in which anything can be said to be known. The conclusion is that perception and knowledge cannot be identical.[1] It should, however, be added that while Plato is sure of this conclusion he mainly relies on other arguments to establish it. The weight which he attaches to this verbal argument seems to be relatively slight. Thus when Socrates, a little later in the dialogue, is made to deliver a speech against himself in Protagoras's name, he raises the objection that he has not dealt with Protagoras honestly. He ought to have examined more carefully the reasons which induced Protagoras to identify perception with knowledge 'instead of taking as a basis the ordinary meaning of nouns and words, which most people pervert in haphazard ways and thereby cause all sorts of perplexity in one another'.[2]

No doubt this overstates the danger of relying on inferences from ordinary usage. Even so, the most that can be established, by the fact that words which it is permissible to couple with one expression cannot significantly be coupled with another, is that the two expressions are not strictly synonymous. If it is a necessary condition of the

[1] Plato, *Theaetetus* 165 d.

[2] *Ibid.* 168 c.

identity of A with B that everything that can be said of A can equally be said of B, then it follows that the references of the two expressions are not identical. It does not follow, however, that one cannot be defined in terms of the other. The facts which Ryle adduces concerning the different ways in which we talk of belief and knowledge do not entail that knowledge cannot be defined in terms of belief. They entail only that the definition cannot take the form of simply equating them. They do not prove even that it is a mistake to talk about 'acts of knowing'. For if a philosopher is convinced that there are such things as he intends this expression to designate, he will not mind admitting that he is using the word 'knowing' in an unusual sense: he may even maintain that it is legitimate to extend its use so that it comes to refer to the processes of which it commonly signifies the successful completion. Nevertheless, if it can be shown, as it surely can, that such a view would be mistaken on other grounds, then the verbal argument does have its point. Not only does it reinforce the other arguments, but it supplies an explanation of the mistake. It shows how philosophers may in fact have come to grief through misunderstanding the grammar of their language.

V

What I have been calling a verbal argument is one in which the premisses consist of facts which relate to the special features of some natural language; such facts as that certain English words are not ordinarily found in combination, or that certain English words, which perform roughly the same function, are actually used in subtly different ways. It would be a good thing, perhaps, if the appellation of linguistic philosophy were restricted to arguments of this type. In a more extended sense, however, it may be said that most philosophical arguments are linguistic; for they mainly consist in stating that one proposition does, or does not, follow from another; and whether or not one proposition follows from another depends entirely on the meaning of the sentences by which they are expressed. The trouble is that very often when these alleged entailments are of philosophical interest, their validity is in dispute. The meaning of the crucial terms is just what needs to be settled. In such a case, there is little profit in researching into the niceties of English, or French, or German idiom; again the procedure is rather to try to look freshly at the facts. If one proposition does not entail the other, it should be possible to find, or at any rate to imagine, some state of affairs in which one proposition would be true and the other false. In short, it is once more a question of searching for a counter-example. Of course there is still the danger that what one takes to be a counter-example will be interpreted in a different fashion by those whom one is trying to refute. It is, indeed, partly for this reason that philosophical problems so long remain unsolved.

Among the most obstinate of these problems are those that relate to the theory of knowledge. As I have tried to show elsewhere,[1] these problems are best presented in the form of the need to find an answer to a certain type of scepticism. By raising the question how we know that propositions of some familiar sort are true, the sceptic tries to demonstrate that our claim to knowledge is unwarranted; that not only do we not know such propositions to be true, but we do not even have any good reason to believe them. Now it might well be thought that here, if anywhere, the solution would lie in some form of linguistic analysis. How do we actually use the sentences in question? What are the typical circumstances in which we unhesitatingly accept the propositions which they express? Suppose, for example, that the sceptic is maintaining that one has no good

[1] See *The Problem of Knowledge.*

reason to believe in the existence of other people who have thoughts and feelings like one's own. Need we do more than simply draw his attention to the familiar situations in which we do ascribe these properties to other people ? Is it not just an empirical fact that propositions of this sort are very often verified ?

Once more this is the argument from the paradigm case ; and it suffers from the weakness which we have already exposed. The situations to which we draw the sceptic's attention have to be interpreted. Are we to say that the mental life which one ascribes to others is somehow to be identified with their observable behaviour ? Are we to say that this behaviour which we point to is the basis for an inductive inference ? Or can we find another, more subtle form of answer ? In the first case, the sceptic may claim that his point has been conceded : in the second, he will want to know how the inference can be justified : in the third, he will demand to be shown what other form of answer is possible, and exactly how it meets his arguments. Neither will it help us to point out that when we talk of someone's knowing what another person thinks or feels we are using the word 'know' in a way that accords with ordinary practice. For the contention which we have to meet is that ordinary practice is here at fault ; not that the word 'know' is being used incorrectly, but rather that the claim, which it is rightly understood to make, turns out on investigation to be incapable of being justified.

It is not my purpose here to consider how in such an instance the sceptic can best be answered. The point which I wish to make is just that when it comes to problems of this kind it is not sufficient merely to reinspect the facts. If the sceptic's arguments are to be effectively challenged his presuppositions must be brought to light : if we think that he misrepresents the evidence, we must furnish some other principles of interpretation ; if it is his idea of proof that is erroneous, we must devise a better theory of our own.

In general, I think that the current philosophical emphasis on fact, as opposed to theory, has been overdone. Too often, the claim to dispense with theory is a way of masking assumptions which, whatever their merit, had better be brought into the open. But, apart from this, the distrust which is rightly felt for speculative metaphysics is not a sufficient ground for limiting the scale of philosophical analysis: there is no reason to suppose that the only concepts which are worth investigating are those that have a comparatively narrow range, or that all that we can usefully do is to describe how concepts of this kind are actually employed. It is equally possible, and perhaps of more importance, to examine the architectonic features of our conceptual system; to apply analytical techniques to the investigation of categories. There are, indeed, very welcome signs, for example in the recent work of Mr. Strawson [1] and Professor Hampshire,[2] of a movement in this direction. To some extent the movement marks a return to Kant; a revival not exactly of Kant's doctrines but of his method of approach.

There is, however, a danger in following Kant too closely. It consists in succumbing to a kind of *a priori* anthropology, in assuming that certain fundamental features of our own conceptual system are necessities of language, which is the modern equivalent for necessities of thought. Thus it may be maintained that it is impossible for there to be a language which does not recognize the distinction between particulars and universals, or that physical objects must of necessity be the primary particulars in any universe of discourse which is comparable to our own. Such theses do indeed become more plausible when they are restricted to languages whose capacities are required to match those

[1] See P. F. Strawson, *Individuals.*
[2] See S. N. Hampshire, *Thought and Action.*

of ordinary English, but this qualification also runs the risk of making them trivial. For it may then be argued that the work which a language does depends upon its categorial structure ; so that no language which differs radically from our own in this respect can be capable of doing exactly the same work. But the answer to this is that, even if they are not strictly inter-translatable, languages of different structure may still be equipped to give substantially the same information ; to every fact which can be stated in the one, there will be a correlate which can be stated in the other. For example, a language without tenses, or other token-reflexive signs, cannot be an exact model of a language which possesses them. It will have no precise equivalent for a sentence like 'I met him yesterday'. Nevertheless, if the language affords the means of describing the persons to whom the pronouns refer, if it enables us to name the date which is indicated by 'yesterday' and also perhaps, in order to get the full effect of the past tense, the date at which the sentence is formulated, then substantially the same result will be obtained. There will be a loss of economy, but no loss of information.

This being so, I see no *a priori* reason why even such an important concept as that of a physical object should be regarded as indispensable. Might not substantially the same facts be expressed in a language reflecting a universe of discourse in which the basic particulars were momentary events ? And there are other possibilities. One which is worthy of consideration is that regions of space-time be treated as the only individuals. Neither is it certain that there need be any reference to individuals at all. The main tendency of Russell's theory of descriptions, as developed especially by Professor Quine,[1] is towards the elimination of singular terms. It may indeed be contended that the attempts so far made to achieve this have not been wholly

[1] See W. V. Quine, *Word and Object*.

satisfactory, but I can see no ground for simply assuming that it is not feasible.[1]

But why should one concern oneself with questions of this kind except as an exercise in ingenuity? There may be various reasons. For example, the elimination of singular terms may be seen as the only way out of the difficulties which are attached to the notion of substance. But the most convincing answer is that there can hardly be a better way of gaining an understanding of the work that these concepts actually do than by seeing how it would be possible to replace them.

Finally, whatever view one may take of the more specialized interests of linguistic philosophy, there still remains the problem of elucidating the concept of language itself. One of the debts that we owe to Wittgenstein, and before him to the pragmatists, is a realization of the active part that language plays in the constitution of facts. If 'the world is everything that is the case',[2] then what can be the case depends upon our conceptual system. But exactly what this comes to, and how it is to be reconciled with the objectivity of fact, are problems that still need to be resolved. They also bring into consideration the possibility of devising a general theory of meaning. At the present time such questions tend to be suspect just because of their extreme generality. My own view is that this is rather a reason for pursuing them. I believe it to be the best way of preserving analytical philosophy from the scholasticism which has been threatening to overtake it.

[1] *Vide* 'Names and Descriptions', p. 129 *infra*.
[2] L. Wittgenstein, *Tractatus Logico-Philosophicus*, i.

2

CAN THERE BE A PRIVATE LANGUAGE?

In a quite ordinary sense, it is obvious that there can be private languages. There can be, because there are. A language may be said to be private when it is devised to enable a limited number of persons to communicate with one another in a way that is not intelligible to anyone outside the group. By this criterion, thieves' slang and family jargons are private languages. Such languages are not strictly private, in the sense that only one person uses and understands them, but there may very well be languages that are. Men have been known to keep diaries in codes which no one else is meant to understand. A private code is not, indeed, a private language, but rather a private method of transcribing some given language. It is, however, possible that a very secretive diarist may not be satisfied with putting familiar words into an unfamiliar notation, but may prefer to invent new words: the two processes are in any case not sharply distinct. If he carries his invention far enough he can properly be said to be employing a private language. For all I know, this has actually been done.

From this point of view, what makes a language private is simply the fact that it satisfies the purpose of being intelligible only to a single person, or to a restricted set of people. It is necessary here to bring in a reference to purpose, since a language may come to be intelligible only to a few people, or even only to a single person, merely by falling into general disuse: but such 'dead' languages are not considered to be private, if the limitation of their use was not originally intended. One may characterize a private language by saying that it is not in this sense meant to be alive. There is, however, no reason, in principle, why it should not come alive. The fact that only one person, or only a few people, are able to understand it is purely contingent. Just as it is possible, in theory, that any code should be broken, so can a private language come to be more widely understood. Such private languages are in general derived from public languages, and even if there are any which are not so derived, they will still be translatable into public languages. Their ceasing to be private is then just a matter of enough people becoming able to translate them or, what is more difficult but still theoretically possible, not to translate but even so to understand them.

If I am right, then, there is a use for the expression 'private language' which clearly allows it to have application. But this is not the use which philosophers have commonly given it. What philosophers usually seem to have in mind when they speak of a private language is one that is, in their view, necessarily private, in as much as it is used by some particular person to refer only to his own private experiences. For it is often held that for a language to be public it must refer to what is publicly observable: if a person could limit himself to describing his own sensations or feelings, then, strictly speaking, only he would understand what he was saying; his utterance might indirectly convey some information to others, but it could not mean to them exactly what it meant to him. Thus, Carnap who gives the name of 'protocol language' to any set of sentences which are used to give 'a direct record' of one's own experience argues, in his booklet on *The Unity of Science*,[1] that if an utterance like 'thirst now',

[1] pp. 76 ff.

belonging to the protocol language of a subject S_1, is construed as expressing 'only what is immediately given' to S_1, it cannot be understood by anyone else. Another subject S_2 may claim to be able to recognize and so to refer to S_1's thirst, but 'strictly speaking' all that he ever recognizes is some physical state of S_1's body. 'If by "the thirst of S_1" we understand not the physical state of his body, but his sensations of thirst, *i.e.* something non-material, then S_1's thirst is fundamentally beyond the reach of S_2's recognition.'[1] S_2 cannot possibly verify any statement which refers to S_1's thirst, in this sense, and consequently cannot understand it. 'In general,' Carnap continues, 'every statement in any person's protocol language would have sense for that person alone. . . . Even when the same words and sentences occur in various protocol languages, their sense would be different, they could not even be compared. Every protocol language could therefore be applied only solipsistically: there would be no intersubjective protocol language. This is the consequence obtained by consistent adherence to the usual view and terminology (rejected by the author).'[2]

Since Carnap wishes to maintain that people can understand one another's protocol statements, if only on the ground that this is a necessary condition for statements made in what he calls the physical language to be intersubjectively verifiable, he draws the inference that 'protocol language is a part of physical language'. That is, he concludes that sentences which on the face of it refer to private experiences must be logically equivalent to sentences which describe some physical state of the subject. Other philosophers have followed him in giving a physicalist interpretation to the statements that one makes about the experiences of others, but have stopped short of extending it to all the statements that one may make about one's own. They

[1] *The Unity of Science*, p. 79. [2] *Ibid.* p. 80.

prefer to hold that certain sentences do serve only to describe the speaker's private experiences, and that, this being so, they have a different meaning for him from any that they can possibly have for anybody else.

In his *Philosophical Investigations* Wittgenstein appears to go much further than this. He seems to take the view that someone who attempted to use language in this private way would not merely be unable to communicate his meaning to others, but would have no meaning to communicate even to himself; he would not succeed in saying anything at all. 'Let us', says Wittgenstein,[1] 'imagine the following case: I want to keep a diary about the recurrence of a certain sensation. To this end I associate it with the sign "E" and write this sign in a calendar for every day on which I have the sensation. — I will remark first of all that a definition of the sign cannot be formulated. — But still I can give myself a kind of ostensive definition. — How? Can I point to the sensation? Not in the ordinary sense. But I speak or write the sign down, and at the same time I concentrate my attention on the sensation — and so, as it were, point to it inwardly. — But what is this ceremony for? for that is all it seems to be! A definition surely serves to establish the meaning of a sign. — Well, that is done precisely by the concentration of my attention; for in this way I impress on myself the connection between the sign and the sensation. But "I impress it on myself" can only mean: this process brings it about that I remember the connection *right* in the future. But in the present case I have no criterion of correctness. One would like to say: whatever is going to seem right to me is right. And that only means that here one can't talk about "right".'

Again, 'What reason have we for calling "E" the sign for a *sensation*? For "sensation" is a word of our common language, not of one intelligible to me alone. So the use

[1] *Philosophical Investigations*, i. 258.

of the word stands in need of a justification which everybody understands.' [1]

This point is then developed further: 'Let us imagine a table (something like a dictionary) that exists only in our imagination. A dictionary can be used to justify the translation of a word X into a word Y. But are we also to call it a justification if such a table is to be looked up only in the imagination? — "Well, yes; then it is a subjective justification." — But justification consists in appealing to something independent. — "But surely I can appeal from one memory to another. For example, I don't know if I have remembered the time of departure of a train right, and to check it I call to mind how a page of the time-table looked. Isn't it the same here?"—No; for this process has got to produce a memory which is actually *correct*. If the mental image of the time-table could not itself be *tested* for correctness, how could it confirm the correctness of the first memory? (As if someone were to buy several copies of the morning paper to assure himself that what it said was true.)

'Looking up a table in the imagination is no more looking up a table than the image of the result of an imagined experiment is the result of an experiment.' [2]

The case is quite different, Wittgenstein thinks, when the sensation can be coupled with some outward manifestation. Thus he maintains that the language which we ordinarily use to describe our 'inner experiences' is not private because the words which one uses to refer to one's sensations are 'tied up with [one's] natural expressions of sensation',[3] with the result that other people are in a position to understand them. Similarly he grants that the person who tries to describe his private sensation by writing down the sign 'E' in his diary might find a use for this sign if he discovered that whenever he had the sensation in

[1] *Op. cit.* I. 261. [2] *Op. cit.* I. 265. [3] *Op. cit.* I. 256.

question it could be shown by means of some measuring instrument that his blood pressure rose. For this would give him a way of telling that his blood pressure was rising without bothering to consult the instrument. But then, argues Wittgenstein, it will make no difference whether his recognition of the sensation is right or not. Provided that whenever he thinks he recognizes it, there is independent evidence that his blood pressure rises, it will not matter if he is invariably mistaken, if the sensation which he takes to be the same on each occasion is really not the same at all. 'And that alone shows that the hypothesis that [he] makes a mistake is mere show.' [1]

Let us examine this argument. A point to which Wittgenstein constantly recurs is that the ascription of meaning to a sign is something that needs to be justified: the justification consists in there being some independent test for determining that the sign is being used correctly; independent, that is, of the subject's recognition, or supposed recognition, of the object which he intends the sign to signify. His claim to recognize the object, his belief that it really is the same, is not to be accepted unless it can be backed by further evidence. Apparently, too, this evidence must be public: it must, at least in theory, be accessible to everyone. Merely to check one private sensation by another would not be enough. For if one cannot be trusted to recognize one of them, neither can one be trusted to recognize the other.

But unless there is something that one is allowed to recognize, no test can ever be completed: there will be no justification for the use of any sign at all. I check my memory of the time at which the train is due to leave by visualizing a page of the time-table; and I am required to check this in its turn by looking up the page. But unless I can trust my eyesight at this point, unless I can recognize

[1] *Op. cit.* I. 270.

the figures that I see written down, I am still no better off. It is true that if I distrust my eyesight I have the resource of consulting other people ; but then I have to understand their testimony, I have correctly to identify the signs that they make. Let the object to which I am attempting to refer be as public as you please, let the word which I use for this purpose belong to some common language, my assurance that I am using the word correctly, that I am using it to refer to the 'right' object, must in the end rest on the testimony of my senses. It is through hearing what other people say, or through seeing what they write, or observing their movements, that I am enabled to conclude that their use of the word agrees with mine.[1] But if without further ado I can recognize such noises or shapes or movements, why can I not also recognize a private sensation ? It is all very well for Wittgenstein to say that writing down the sign 'E', at the same time as I attend to the sensation, is an idle ceremony. How is it any more idle than writing down a sign, whether it be the conventionally correct sign or not, at the same time as I observe some 'public' object ? There is, indeed, a problem about what is involved in endowing any sign with meaning, but it is no less of a problem in the case where the object for

[1] My use of a similar argument in my book *The Problem of Knowledge* has led Miss Anscombe to accuse me of committing a logical fallacy (*vide* her book *An Introduction to Wittgenstein's Tractatus*, pp. 138-9). She supposes that I argue 'from the fact that it is not possible, and *a fortiori* not necessary, that every identification or recognition should in fact be checked, to the innocuousness of the notion of an uncheckable identification'. I agree with her that this is a fallacy, but I do not think I have committed it. My argument is that since every process of checking must terminate in some act of recognition, no process of checking can establish anything unless some acts of recognition are taken as valid in themselves. This does not imply that these acts of recognition are uncheckable in the sense that their deliverances could not in their turn be subjected to further checks ; but then these further checks would again have to terminate in acts of recognition which were taken as valid in themselves and so *ad infinitum*. If the inference drawn from this is that an act of recognition is worthless unless it is corroborated by other acts of recognition, the recognition of private sensations will not necessarily be excluded. For there is no reason in principle why such acts of recognition should not corroborate one another.

which the sign is supposed to stand is public than in the case where it is private. Whatever it is about my behaviour that transforms the making of a sound, or the inscription of a shape, into the employment of a sign can equally well occur in either case.

But, it may be said, in the one case I can point to the object I am trying to name, I can give an ostensive definition of it; in the other I cannot. For merely attending to an object is not pointing to it. But what difference does this make? I can indeed extend my finger in the direction of a physical object, while I pronounce what I intend to be the object's name; and I cannot extend my finger in the direction of a private sensation. But how is this extending of my finger itself anything more than an idle ceremony? If it is to play its part in the giving of an ostensive definition, this gesture has to be endowed with meaning. But if I can endow such a gesture with meaning, I can endow a word with meaning, without the gesture.

I suppose that the reason why the gesture is thought to be important is that it enables me to make my meaning clear to others. Of course they have to interpret me correctly. If they are not intelligent, or I am not careful, they may think that I am pointing to one thing when I really intend to point to another. But successful communication by this method is at least possible. The object to which I mean to point is one that they can observe. On the other hand, no amount of gesturing on my part can direct their attention to a private sensation of mine, which *ex hypothesi* they cannot observe, assuming further that this sensation has no 'natural expression'. So I cannot give an ostensive definition of the word which I wish to stand for the sensation. Nor can I define it in terms of other words, for how are they to be defined? Consequently I cannot succeed in giving it any meaning.

This argument is based on two assumptions, both of

which I believe to be false. One is that in a case of this sort it is impossible, logically impossible, to understand a sign unless one can either observe the object which it signifies, or at least observe something with which this object is naturally associated. And the other is that for a person to be able to attach meaning to a sign it is necessary that other people should be capable of understanding it too. It will be convenient to begin by examining the second of these assumptions which leads on to the first.

Imagine a Robinson Crusoe left alone on his island while still an infant, having not yet learned to speak. Let him, like Romulus and Remus, be nurtured by a wolf, or some other animal, until he can fend for himself; and so let him grow to manhood. He will certainly be able to recognize many things upon the island, in the sense that he adapts his behaviour to them. Is it inconceivable that he should also name them? There may be psychological grounds for doubting whether such a solitary being would in fact invent a language. The development of language, it may be argued, is a social phenomenon. But surely it is not self-contradictory to suppose that someone, uninstructed in the use of any existing language, makes up a language for himself. After all, some human being must have been the first to use a symbol. And even if he did so as a member of a group, in order to communicate with the other members, even if his choice of symbols was socially conditioned, it is at least conceivable that it should originally have been a purely private enterprise. The hypothesis of G. K. Chesterton's dancing professor about the origin of language, that it came 'from the formulated secret language of some individual creature', is very probably false, but it is certainly not unintelligible.

But if we allow that our Robinson Crusoe could invent words to describe the flora and fauna of his island, why not allow that he could also invent words to describe his sensations? In neither case will he be able to justify his use of words by drawing on the evidence provided by a fellow creature: but while this is a useful check, it is not indispensable. It would be difficult to argue that the power of communication, the ability even to keep a private diary, could come to him only with the arrival of Man Friday. His justification for describing his environment in the way that he does will be that he perceives it to have just those features which his words are intended to describe. His knowing how to use these words will be a matter of his remembering what objects they are meant to stand for, and, so of his being able to recognize these objects. But why should he not succeed in recognizing them? And why then should he not equally succeed in recognizing his sensations? Undoubtedly, he may make mistakes. He may think that a bird which he sees flying past is a bird of the same type as one which he had previously named, when in fact it is of a different type, sufficiently different for him to have given it a different name if he had observed it more closely. Similarly, he may think that a sensation is the same as others which he has identified, when in fact, in the relevant aspects, it is not the same. In neither case may the mistake make any practical difference to him, but to say that nothing turns upon a mistake is not to say that it is not a mistake at all. In the case of the bird, there is a slightly greater chance of his detecting his mistake, since the identical bird may reappear: but even so he has to rely upon his memory for the assurance that it is the identical bird. In the case of the sensation, he has only his memory as a means of deciding whether his identification is correct or not. In this respect he is indeed like Wittgenstein's man who buys several copies of the morning paper to assure himself that what it says is true. But the reason why this seems to us so absurd is that we take it for granted that one copy of a morning paper will duplicate another;

there is no absurdity in buying a second newspaper, of a different type, and using it to check the first. And in a place where there was only one morning newspaper, but it was so produced that misprints might occur in one copy without occurring in all, it would be perfectly sensible to buy several copies and check them against each other. Of course there remains the important difference that the facts which the newspaper reports are independently verifiable, in theory if not always in practice. But verification must stop somewhere. As I have already argued, unless something is recognized, without being referred to a further test, nothing can be tested. In the case of Crusoe's sensation, we are supposing that beyond his memory there is no further test. It does not follow that he has no means of identifying it, or that it does not make sense to say that he identifies it right or wrong.

So long as Crusoe remains alone on the island, so long, that is, as he communicates only with himself, the principal distinction which he is likely to draw between 'external' objects and his 'inner' experiences is that his experiences are transient in a way that external objects are not. He will not be bound to draw even this distinction ; his criteria for identity may be different from our own ; but it is reasonable to suppose that they will be the same. Assuming, then, that his language admits the distinction, he will find on the arrival of Man Friday that it acquires a new importance. For whereas he will be able to teach Man Friday the use of the words which he has devised to stand for external objects by showing him the objects for which they stand, he will not, in this way, be able to teach him the use of the words which he has devised to stand for his sensations. And in the cases where these sensations are entirely private, in the sense that they have no 'natural expressions' which Man Friday can identify, it may well be that Crusoe fails to find any way of teaching him the use of the words which he employs to stand for them. But from the fact that he cannot teach this part of his language to Man Friday it by no means follows that he has no use for it himself. In a context of this sort, one can teach only what one already understands. The ability to teach, or rather the ability of someone else to learn, cannot therefore be a prerequisite for understanding.

Neither does it necessarily follow, in these circumstances, that Man Friday will be incapable of learning the meaning of the words which Crusoe uses to describe his private sensations. It is surely a contingent fact that we depend upon ostensive definitions, to the extent that we do, for learning what words mean. As it is, a child is not taught how to describe his feelings in the way he is taught to describe the objects in his nursery. His mother cannot point to his pain in the way that she can point to his cup and spoon. But she knows that he has a pain because he cries and because she sees that something has happened to him which is likely to cause him pain; and knowing that he is in pain she is able to teach him what to call it. If there were no external signs of his sensations she would have no means of detecting when he had them, and therefore could not teach him how to describe them. This is indeed the case, but it might easily be otherwise. We can imagine two persons being so attuned to one another that whenever either has a private sensation of a certain sort, the other has it too. In that case, when one of them described what he was feeling the other might very well follow the description, even though he had no 'external' evidence to guide him. But how could either of them ever know that he had identified the other's feeling correctly? Well, how can two people ever know that they mean the same by a word which they use to refer to some 'public' object? Only because each finds the other's reactions appropriate. Similarly one may suppose that Man Friday sympathizes when Crusoe's private sensation is painful, and congratulates him when it is pleasant, that he is able to say when it begins and when it stops, that he correctly describes it as being rather like such and such another sensation, and very different from a third, thereby affording proof that he also understands the words that stand for these sensations. Admittedly, such tests are not conclusive. But the tests which we ordinarily take as showing that we mean the same by the words which we apply to public objects are not conclusive either: they leave it at least theoretically open that we do not after all mean quite the same. But from the fact that the tests are not conclusive it does not, in either case, follow that they have no force at all. It is true also that such tests as the expressed agreement about the duration of the experience require that the two men already share a common language, which they have no doubt built up on the basis of common observations. It would indeed be difficult, though still, I think, not necessarily impossible,[1] for them to establish communication if all their experiences were private, in Wittgenstein's sense. But even if their understanding each other's use of words could come about only if some of the objects which these words described were public, it would not follow that they all must be so.

It is not even necessary to make the assumption that Man Friday comes to know what Crusoe's sensations are, and so to understand the words which signify them, through having similar sensations of his own. It is conceivable that he should satisfy all the tests which go to show that he has this knowledge, and indeed that he should actually have it, even though the experience which he rightly ascribes to Crusoe is unlike any that he has, or ever has had, himself. It would indeed be very strange if someone had this power of seeing, as it were, directly into another's soul. But it is strange only in the sense that it is

[1] I have come to doubt this. See footnote to 'Privacy', p. 78.

something which, on causal grounds, we should not expect to happen. The idea of its happening breaks no logical rule. An analogous case would be that of someone's imagining, or seeming to remember, an experience which was unlike any that he had ever actually had. To allow that such things are possible is, indeed, to admit innate ideas, in the Lockean sense, but that is not a serious objection. The admission is not even inconsistent with the prevalent varieties of empiricism. It can still be made a rule that in order to understand a word which signifies a sensation one must know what it would be like to have the sensation in question: that is, one must be able to identify the sensation when one has it, and so to verify the statement which describes it. The peculiarity of the cases which we are envisaging is just that people are credited with the ability to identify experiences which they have not previously had. There may indeed be causal objections to the hypothesis that this can ever happen. The point which concerns us now is that these objections are no more than causal. The ways in which languages are actually learned do not logically circumscribe the possibilities of their being understood.

If the sort of insight which we have been attributing to Man Friday were commonly possessed, we might well be led to revise our concepts of publicity and privacy. The mistake which is made by philosophers like Carnap is that of supposing that being public or being private, in the senses which are relevant to this discussion, are properties which are somehow attached to different sorts of objects, independently of our linguistic usage. But the reason why one object is publicly and another only privately accessible is that in the one case it makes sense to say that the object is observed by more than one person and in the other it does not.[1] Tables are public; it makes sense to say that several

[1] This is an over-simplification, see 'Privacy'.

people are perceiving the same table. Headaches are private: it does not make sense to say that several people are feeling the same headache. But just as we can assimilate tables to headaches by introducing a notation in which two different persons' perceiving the same table becomes a matter of their each sensing their own private 'tabular' sense-data, so we could assimilate headaches to tables by introducing a notation in which it was correct to speak of a common headache, which certain people only were in a condition to perceive. As things are, this notation would not be convenient. But if people were so constituted that they were communally exposed to headaches in the way that they are communally exposed to the weather, we might cease to think of headaches as being necessarily private. A London particular might come to be a local headache as well as, or instead of, a local fog. Certain persons might escape it, just as certain persons, for one reason or another, may fail to perceive the fog. But the fog exists for all that, and so, given this new way of speaking, would the public headache. The conditions which would make this way of speaking useful do not, indeed, obtain; but that they do not is, once again, a purely contingent fact.

The facts being what they are, we do not have a use for such expressions as 'S_2's feeling S_1's thirst' or 'S_2's observing the sensation of thirst which S_1 feels'. On the other hand, we do attach a meaning to saying that the same physical object, or process, or event, for instance a state of S_1's body, is observed by S_2 as well as by S_1. Does it follow, as Carnap thinks, that for this reason S_2 cannot understand a statement which refers to S_1's feeling of thirst, whereas he can understand a statement which refers to the condition of S_1's body? Suppose that we modified our rules for identity, in a way that many philosophers have proposed, and allowed ourselves to say that what was ordinarily described as S_1 and S_2's observing the same physical event was 'really' a case of each of them sensing his own sense-data which, while they might be qualitatively similar, could not be literally the same. Should we thereby be committed to denying that either could understand what the other said about this physical event? Surely not. And equally the fact that S_2 cannot feel, or inspect, S_1's feelings in no way entails that he cannot understand what S_1 says about them. The criteria for deciding whether two people understand each other are logically independent of the fact that we do, or do not, have a use for saying that literally the same objects are perceived by both.

I conclude, first, that for a person to use descriptive language meaningfully it is not necessary that any other person should understand him, and, secondly, that for anyone to understand a descriptive statement it is not necessary that he should himself be able to observe what it describes. It is not even necessary that he should be able to observe something which is naturally associated with what it describes, in the way that feelings are associated with their 'natural expressions'. If we insist on making it a necessary condition for our understanding a descriptive statement that we are able to observe what it describes, we shall find ourselves disclaiming the possibility of understanding not merely statements about other people's private sensations, but also statements about the past; either that, or reinterpreting them in such a way that they change their reference, as when philosophers substitute bodily states for feelings, and the future for the past. Both courses, I now think, are mistaken. No doubt it is a necessary condition for my understanding a descriptive statement that it should be, in some way, verifiable. But it need not be directly verifiable, and even if it is directly verifiable, it need not be directly verifiable by me.

3

PRIVACY

I

In spite of the misgivings of philosophers, it is still a common practice to distinguish fairly sharply between mind and matter ; and one of the principal features of this distinction is that a privacy which is denied to matter is attributed to mind. There are, however, many sorts of privacy : the word 'private' is used in a number of different ways, and the sense in which the contents of our minds are supposed to be private requires to be made clear. By making it clear we may also come to discover how far this supposition can be justified.

Since the privacy of mind is contrasted with the publicity of matter, it may be helpful first to consider what is meant by saying that the material world is public. A plausible answer is that the publicity of physical objects, or events, or activities, or processes, consists in their having to satisfy the following condition : that in whatever way their existence is detectable by any one person, it be also detectable by others ; not necessarily by any other person that one chooses to describe, since the specification of an observer may itself restrict the range of observations that it is open to him to make, but at least by other persons in general ; and not necessarily in practice but at least in principle. There may be physical objects that only one person ever in fact has the opportunity to perceive, but it must be logically possible for others to perceive them too ; it must make sense to say of other persons that they perceive the very same physical objects and perceive them in the very same manner as he does. It is sufficiently obvious that this usually does make sense, so that our condition of publicity for the physical domain is at least very widely satisfied.

I am not sure, however, that it is universally satisfied. It holds for shoes and ships and sealing-wax and cabbages, but possibly not for kings. For when we come to human bodies, the events or processes which occur in them, and the activities in which they engage, it is arguable that we find exceptions to our general rule. The argument would be that one may, through organic sensation, be aware of one's body and of some of its activities in a way that it is not even logically possible for any one else to be aware of them. Thus, walking, pushing, frowning, coughing, sighing are physical activities. They can be witnessed by other people; indeed, other people may well be in a better position to testify to their occurrence than the person who is engaged in them. Even so, it may be said, he has one way of detecting these processes or activities which is not available to others. He alone can *feel* that they are going on.

To evaluate this argument we have to decide what we are to understand by saying that something is or is not detected by different people in the same way. How is the expression 'in the same way' to be interpreted? In the sense in which I am using it here, two people may be said to detect the existence of an object in the same way, if, for example, they both see it. The fact that they see it through different pairs of eyes, or from different angles, or with different degrees of clarity is left out of account. Questions arise as to whether we are still to say that the existence of an object is detected in the same way when it is seen, for example, in a mirror, or on a screen, or through a microscope, and here I do not think that there is any general method of drawing the line. We have to take special decisions : but it does not matter for our present argument which way such cases are decided. In general, also, two people may be said to detect the existence of an object in the same way if they both are touching it, though here again one may wish to draw a distinction between the case where one explores the shape of the object and that in which one only feels it with one's finger tips. And the same applies to other forms of sense-perception, including organic sensation. For example, two people may be said to detect in the same way that an object is moving, if it is attached to a rope which they are holding and both feel the strain in their arms when the rope is pulled.

But in that case, it may be argued, there is no ground for holding that one's organic awareness of the physical activities of one's own body affords one a means of detecting them which is logically denied to others. For there is no logical difficulty in supposing that some other person is also able to detect them through kinaesthetic sensation. It is conceivable, for example, that two people should be so attuned to one another that when one of them was organically aware of some bodily state or activity, the other had a sympathetic feeling of the same kind. Or, if this be thought too fanciful, one might suppose that the condition of a person's body was recorded by a machine which was so constructed that it could be read kinaesthetically. With a little ingenuity, I have no doubt that we could find other examples. They might not be practical, but their being intelligible and free from contradiction would be enough to prove the point.

But is this all that we are going to require ? Surely, the case in which one person feels himself to be engaged in some physical activity and another detects it by having sympathetic sensations, or by reading a machine kinaesthetically, is considerably different from that of two persons feeling the pull of a rope. In the latter case one has no hesitation in saying that they each discover in the same way that the object which is attached to the rope is moving : but in the former case I think that the corresponding conclusion would not be generally admitted. I think that if it is to be said that one detects what is going on in someone else's body in the same way as he does, it is not sufficient in this instance that one should have similar sensations : it is necessary also that they play the same rôle as his do, which means that they would have to be located not in one's own body but in his.

Now it might be maintained that even this was logically possible. After all, it is known that kinaesthetic sensations can be located outside one's body : for example, many people have had the experience of feeling pressure at the end of a stick rather than in the hand which is holding it. And if one's range of feeling can go beyond one's own body, why should it not at least theoretically extend to another person's ? Might one not detect, for example, that someone was frowning, not merely by feeling the corresponding sensation in one's own forehead, but by locating it in his ? The difficulty is even to imagine what such an experience would be like.

An argument against its possibility would be that it is a defining property of 'my' body to be the locus of my organic sensations. This would not entail that these sensations could never be located outside my body, but only that any human body in which they were located would necessarily be mine. According to this argument, we may think that it makes sense to talk of one person's locating a sensation of frowning in another's forehead because we already think of the two bodies as separately identified ; but here we fall into contradiction. For what distinguishes my body from his is just, among other things, that my sensations of frowning are located in this forehead and not in that. Of course nothing of this sort is needed for distinguishing the two bodies as physical objects ; but it is needed for distinguishing them as one person's or another's. Not, indeed, that one has to observe where one's feelings are located in order to discover which body is one's own. It is not suggested that one identifies one's own body in the way that one may identify a piece of personal property. No doubt arises for me about this body's being mine. But, it is argued, the reason why no doubt arises is that it necessarily is the body in which my feelings are located. To suppose otherwise, to try to extend the possible range of feeling in the way that we have been doing, would be to undermine the ground on which we are standing ; we should be presupposing the distinction between one person's body and another's and at the same time robbing it of its usual sense.

I think that this argument has some force. One obvious objection to it is that my body is not distinguished only by being the locus of my feelings. It also supplies, as it were, the viewpoint from which I survey the world, so that even if I had no organic sensations, or located them elsewhere, it would still play a special rôle in my experience. Another most important feature is that it responds to my will in a way that other bodies do not. The control which I exercise over it when I focus my eyes, for example, or nod my head, or raise my arm is not the same, not of the same kind, as any control that I can exercise over the corresponding movements of others. I doubt indeed if it is logically possible that it should be the same. One might, through hypnosis or some other method, obtain such power over another person that he responded automatically to one's will ; even so, the sense in which one could be said to be raising his arm, for example, would still be rather different from that in which one raises one's own. But what if we took more fanciful examples ? Suppose, for instance, that when I decided to make a movement, I found as often as not that it was executed not by me but by someone else, and this quite independently of any decision that he made. Could it not then be said that I controlled his body in just the way that I control my own ? Here again, it might be objected that this piece of science fiction is inconsistent with the distinction between persons which it presupposes. And here again there seems to be no method of deciding whether this show of inconsistency amounts to a formal contradiction or not.

Perhaps, then, the most that can be said is that it is characteristic of 'my' body that it normally is the locus of my sensations, just as it is characteristic of it that it normally responds to my will in a way that other bodies do not. These rules are part of the logical framework which gives to our talk about persons and their bodies the meaning that it has. But this framework may be sufficiently flexible to allow for the abnormal case in which one or other of these rules is broken. Thus it may not be a logical impossibility that someone should on occasion be aware of another's physical state in the way that the other is himself aware of it.

I say only that it *may* not be because, as I have already indicated, this does not seem to me to be the sort of question that has a correct answer in terms of standard usage. We have to decide what attitude to take. If we admit the possibility of such abnormal cases, then we may hold that our criterion of publicity is satisfied in principle throughout the physical domain, though in the case of human bodies and some of their activities there will be a rather disturbing difference between what is sanctioned in principle and what occurs in fact. If on the other hand we refuse to give this sanction, two courses will be open to us. Either we can maintain our criterion of publicity, and accept the consequence that there are physical processes which do not satisfy it, so that if the mental activities of human beings are private in this sense, this does not distinguish them from the physical. Or if we insist that everything physical is to be public we can adopt a weaker criterion of publicity. Thus, instead of requiring of what is public that in any way in which its existence is detectable by any one person it be detectable in the *same* way by others, we might require only that it be detectable in *some* way by others. If we took this course we should again be blunting the distinction between the mental and the physical ; for we shall find that what are ordinarily classified as mental processes or activities are public in this weaker sense.

II

Returning now to the stronger criterion, I wish to suggest that one thing that is commonly meant by saying that mental happenings are private is just that they fail to satisfy it. Thus it is held not to be true of such states or processes as thinking, wishing, dreaming, intending, imagining, or feeling, that in whatever way their occurrence is detectable by any one person it is detectable also by others. It is not detectable by others in a way in which it is detectable by the person to whom these states or processes are attributed. He alone can be directly aware of their existence and their character. He knows what he thinks or feels in a way that it is logically impossible that any other person should.

This view has been contested on various grounds. An initial objection is that it is not at all clear what is meant by saying that a person is directly aware of his own mental processes or states. If it is just that he usually knows what he is thinking or feeling, then, even if this is true, it does not yield the desired result ; for this knowledge might be shared by others. Neither does this explain the use of the word 'directly'. It is not just that he knows what he thinks or feels, but that the knowledge somehow automatically accrues to him through the fact that these thoughts and feelings are his own. But what sense can we make of this?

Some philosophers, especially those influenced by Wittgenstein, hold that there is no sense to be made of it. They would say, not that a person normally does not know what he is thinking or feeling, nor yet that he does not gain this knowledge in the way suggested, but rather that it is a mistake to talk of knowledge in this case. People *have* thoughts and feelings, but this is not a matter of their knowing anything. To say, as philosophers do, that they are conscious of their thoughts and feelings is permissible only if it is just a way of saying that they have them. 'It can't be said of me at all', says Wittgenstein, '(except perhaps as a joke) that I *know* that I am in pain.' [1] But is this really so? What is true is that we seldom, if ever, find occasion to use such sentences as 'he knows that he is in pain', or 'I know that I am thinking about a philosophical problem', or even 'I know that I am looking at a sheet of paper'. The prefixing of the words 'I know that' or 'he knows that' makes what would otherwise be respectable, if not very interesting, sentences appear somewhat ridiculous. But the reason for this, surely, is not that the claim to knowledge is inapplicable in these cases, but rather that it is superfluous. We find it silly for someone to tell us that he knows that he is in pain, because if he is in pain we take it for granted that he knows it; and similarly with the other examples. But from the fact that the claim is superfluous it does not follow that it is unjustified. If, in the course of a discussion about knowledge, or as part of a game, one were challenged to give a list of things that one knew, I think it would be quite proper to give such replies as 'I know that I am thinking about a philosophical problem', or 'I know that I am looking at a sheet of paper', or 'I know that I am in pain'. Indeed this is about the only

[1] *Philosophical Investigations*, i. 246.

context in which sentences of this kind do have a natural use; as furnishing examples of what one may safely claim to know. A proof that they are legitimate examples is that the information which they convey can be made the subject of a lie. I do not think anyone would maintain that to speak of telling lies about one's thoughts or feelings was an unnatural or even an uncommon use of language. If he did, he would certainly be wrong. But to tell a lie is not just to make a false statement: it is to make a statement that one knows to be false; and this implies denying what one knows to be true.

One reason why philosophers dispute the legitimacy of such examples is that they assume that expressions of the form 'I know that . . .' must be completed by sentences which are used to make statements: and they hold that this condition is not satisfied by sentences like 'I am in pain'. Thus it is alleged that to say that I am in pain, as to say that I am bored or that I am amused, or to make any other pronouncement of that sort, is not to deliver a report about my feelings, but rather just to express them. It is as if I were to groan or to yawn or to laugh. In short these sentences are construed as having the force of ejaculations; and one does not say of an ejaculation that it is known to be true. In these instances, indeed, this argument has some plausibility: there does not seem to be much difference between saying that one is in pain and showing it by crying out. But even here the argument works both ways: whatever reason it gives for saying that the apparent statement has the force of an ejaculation is equally a reason for saying that the ejaculation has the force of a statement. And in other cases of this autobiographical type it hardly works at all. If a man says, for example, that he is worrying about his debts, it is surely very perverse to maintain that he is merely expressing a feeling and not making a report of it as well. Or, to return to one of my previous examples, if I say that I am thinking about a philosophical problem, I am surely not doing anything like emitting an ejaculation: I am making a statement which is in fact true and known to me to be so. Even in the case of declarations of intention, which there is some ground for refusing to treat as narrative statements, the fact that one can lie about one's intentions implies that one can know what they are. So if it is to be said that sentences like 'I intend to go to Paris to-morrow' do not report anything and consequently are not used to make statements, then the principle that 'knowing that' applies only to statements will have to be given up, together with the principle that it is only when words are used to make statements that they express what can be either true or false: for if I can know what my intentions are, it follows that a verbal formulation of these intentions can be true. This being so, it seems to me preferable to allow that such formulations are used to make statements, whatever expressive function they may perform besides.

I conclude then that one can properly be said to have knowledge of one's own thoughts or feelings or intentions; but it is not easy to give an account of the way in which this knowledge arises. One of its peculiarities is that it does not depend upon investigation; it is not, or need not be, the outcome of an inquiry. It is indeed possible to conduct a kind of inner research, to interrogate oneself about one's thoughts or feelings, and to learn something from the answer. But this is not an activity in which many people engage for much of their time, and as a rule it is not necessary to engage in it in order to know what one thinks or feels. It is possible also to be a detached spectator of one's mental states or processes, to stand aside from them and contemplate them as though they were being unfolded upon a stage. No doubt this has helped to sustain the view that one's knowledge of what one thinks and feels is obtained by introspection, a kind of inner perception analogous to the 'outer' perception of physical events. But, as critics of this view have pointed out, the analogy is misleading. Our thoughts and feelings do not normally 'pose' for us in the way that physical objects do. This is, indeed, a dispute in which both sides are at fault; the champions of introspection in assuming that our mental states and processes are constantly surveyed by us, their opponents in denying that this ever happens at all. The critics are right, however, on the main point; in the sense in which having thoughts and feelings entails being conscious of them, it does not entail observing them after the fashion either of an investigator or of a spectator. Therefore to say that we know what goes on in our minds by introspection is either false or trivial: false, if it implies that we are made aware of our mental states by passing them under review; trivial, if it is taken, as it sometimes is, to mean no more than that we obtain this sort of knowledge in the special way that we do.

But what difference is there then, it may be asked, between knowing what our thoughts and feelings are and merely having them? Whatever its other defects, the model of the inner theatre does at least mark out a distinction; the spectator is separated from the scene of which he is a witness. This is indeed the feature of the model that makes it attractive. If we discard this model, as I think we must, will not the distinction disappear with it? What other account of it can we give?

The distinction is all the more difficult to preserve, as there is a tendency to make the connection between having thoughts and feelings and knowing what they are a logical one, that is, to make it logically impossible for anyone not to know what conscious thoughts and feelings he has. There is an easy transition from saying that if one is in pain one knows it, to saying that if one is in pain one *must* know it. In the first case the possibility of one's being in pain and not knowing it is left theoretically open, however seldom it may in fact be realized: in the second it is logically excluded. But to take the second course is to play into the hands of those who maintain, in my opinion wrongly, that one should not talk of knowledge at all in this context. For if my knowing what my thoughts and feelings are were a logical consequence of my having them, the reference to knowledge would be otiose; the words 'I know that' in such an expression as 'I know that I am in pain' would add nothing to the sense of the phrase that followed them: and since their presence would suggest that they did add something, it would in that case be better that they should be dropped.

But if they are not to be dropped, what can they be understood to add? The answer which I propose is that knowing what one's thoughts and feelings are, as distinct from merely having them, may be taken to consist in being able to give a true report of them. The two normally go together, but they are not logically connected. Animals and young children, who have not acquired the use of language, have feelings and images of which they may be said to be conscious, but, on this view, they do not know that they have them; they may think in images but they do not know what it is that they are thinking. On the other hand it is very rare for an adult human being not to know what he is thinking or feeling. Only in exceptional cases will one be unable to give any report at all, or unable to give a correct report. It is not of course necessary that these reports should actually be made, but only that they should be forthcoming if required. Neither, on the occasions when they are made, does it matter whether they are strictly simultaneous with the occurrences to which they refer, or slightly retrospective. I shall not at this stage enter into the question whether these reports are ever infallible. For the claim to knowledge to be justified it is sufficient that they should be true. And this helps us to explain why expressions like 'I know that I am in pain' or 'I know that I am thinking about a philosophical problem' sound so odd. It is not just that we expect people to know what they are thinking or feeling. It is also that if someone *says* truly that he is in pain or says truly that he is thinking about a philosophical problem, it follows that he knows it.

This gives us the clue also to what may be meant by saying that knowledge of this kind is direct. In other cases where knowledge is claimed, it is not sufficient that one be able to give a true report of what one claims to know : it is necessary also that the claim be authorized, and this is done by adducing some other statement which in some way supports the statement for which the claim is made. But in this case no such authority is needed ; there is no demand for evidence ; the question how one knows does not arise. It would clearly be absurd to ask anyone how he knew that he was thinking about a philosophical problem, or how he knew that he was in pain. For what could he answer except that this *was* what he was thinking about, or that this *was* what he was feeling ? Our knowledge of our thoughts and feelings accrues to us automatically in the sense that having them puts us in a position and gives us the authority to report them. All that is then required is that the reports be true.

III

I have tried to show that there is a sense in which it can properly be said that a person is directly aware of his own thoughts and feelings. If this be accepted, does it follow that he alone can be directly aware of them ? Are they private to him in the sense that this is at least one way in which they are detectable by him but not by anybody else ?

Many philosophers would conclude that this was so, for the following reason : they would argue that being directly aware of someone's, say Mr. X's, thoughts or feelings entailed having them, that having Mr. X's thoughts or feelings entailed being Mr. X, and that it was logically impossible that anyone should be Mr. X but Mr. X himself.

I shall not dispute the last of these propositions though I think that it raises interesting and difficult problems about individuation. It does seem clear, however, that if you refer to people in a way which implies that they are different, you cannot consistently with this form of reference suppose that they might be the same. And this is all that the present argument requires. On the other hand, the second proposition seems to me less secure. I do not think it should be taken for granted that having the thoughts or feelings of Mr. X entails being Mr. X, if this is understood to imply that no two persons' thoughts or feelings can be the same. But I shall return to this question later on. I wish now to discuss the first step in the argument; the proposition that being directly aware of someone's thoughts or feelings entails actually having them.

It might be thought that this was a question which we had already settled. For in explaining what could be meant by direct awareness in this sense, I said that having certain thoughts or feelings put one in a position and gave one the authority to report them; and this would appear to make the possession of the thoughts or feelings in question a necessary condition for being directly aware of them. Nevertheless, I think it might still be argued that there is at least a logical possibility of being in a similar position with regard to thoughts and feelings that one does not have; that is, of being able to make reports about the mental states of others in the same 'immediate' way as one makes them about one's own, to report on them, in short, as if they were one's own. I believe that this is what psychologists have in mind when they talk of the possibility of co-consciousness. An example would be the relation of Eve Black to Eve White, and of Jane to both of them in *The Three Faces of Eve*, a much publicized account of a startling case of multiple personality. The claim of Eve Black to be conscious of what went on in the mind of Eve White, and that of Jane, the third personality to emerge, to be conscious of what went on in the minds of both Eves were in fact admitted by the doctors to be valid. It is enough for our purposes, however, that they could significantly be made.

In these cases of split or multiple personality, the several persons are indeed housed in the same body, for the control of which they compete; and it may therefore be objected that they are not sufficiently separate. We may choose to speak of the two Eves as being different persons; but we should do no less justice to the facts if we spoke of there being only one person with two or more different personalities. More justice, indeed; for the only reason there is for speaking of different persons in such a case is that the personalities appear to be so different. The only use of this example, therefore, is to show what might count as one person's being directly aware of the mental state of another, when they occupied different bodies: and it is doubtful whether this occurs. It is not established that different persons, in this sense, display the type of co-consciousness that is credited to different characters in a multiple personality.

But is it not conceivable that they should? To some extent, this idea is already favoured by the evidence which supports the existence of telepathy. The accounts which are given of telepathic experiences do indeed suggest that it is more like receiving a message than anything analogous to reporting one's own feelings: their oddity consists in the fact that the message is not transmitted by any ordinary means. But suppose that someone did claim to be 'telepathically' aware of some other person's mental states and that his reports of them were found to be consistently true: and suppose that when he was asked how he did it he said that it was like asking him how he knew what his own thoughts and feelings were; so far as he was concerned the only difference was that the other person's thoughts and feelings came to him under a different label. Might we not accept this account? And might we not then decide to say that he was directly aware of thoughts and feelings which were not his own? In the same way, if someone claimed to be able to remember the experiences of another, in the same 'automatic' fashion as he remembered his own, and was found to be generally right, might we not discard another apparent source of privacy, in this weaker sense, by allowing the possibility of one's experiences being remembered by others as well as by oneself? I do not press these suggestions, but they seem to me less fanciful than the idea of the possible displacement of bodily sensations which we considered earlier on.

There is, however, one important respect in which being directly aware of another person's thoughts or feelings would differ from remembering them, and differ also from detecting his physical movements by organic sensations in the way that he did: I am assuming for the sake of argument that all these procedures are allowed to be logically possible. As we have already remarked, the fact that I may become aware of some of my physical activities through kinaesthetic or organic sensation does not put me in a better position to testify to their occurrence than are those who merely observe them 'from the outside': their acquisition of the power to detect them 'from the inside' would not raise the level of their testimony to mine, since it is on as good a level already. The case of memory is slightly different in that one's claims to remember at any rate one's more recent experiences tend to be taken as authoritative, although in special circumstances this authority may be overridden. But if someone else were to be credited with the power of 'remembering' one's experiences, his testimony on this subject might come to be regarded as equal in value, or even superior, to one's own. I suppose there would have to be an initial period in which it was checked by one's own; otherwise his claim to possess this power would never be admitted. But once it had been admitted, his reports of one's past experiences might, in a conflict of testimony, outweigh one's own, if they were found to agree better with any external evidence that went to show what these experiences had been. In many cases, such as that of remembering one's dreams, there might indeed not be any external evidence, and here it would be natural to give preference to the subject's own reports. Even so I do not think that we should be logically bound to regard them as decisive.

When it comes, on the other hand, to a person's knowledge of his present thoughts and feelings, then I do think that there are many cases in which we logically are obliged to give him the last word. Even if we allow it to be possible for others to become aware of his thoughts and feelings in the way that he does, their knowledge of them will be subordinate to his. The accuracy of their reports will be checked by his, and where there is disagreement his verdict must prevail. Thus, even if one's mental states are not private in the sense that there is any single way in which, of necessity, they are detectable by oneself alone, they may still be private in yet another sense. One may be the final authority concerning their existence and their character.

This is, indeed, a version of the doctrine of 'privileged access' which has come in for such heavy criticism in recent years. On many points I think that its critics have been justified: but I also think that they have made things too easy for themselves by their choice of examples. They are right in maintaining that when it is a question of a person's motives, or of his being in an emotional state, such as that of anger or jealousy or fear, his word is not authoritative: he may deceive himself about his motives; he may honestly believe that he is angry when his behaviour shows that he is not, or, as more commonly happens, refuse to admit that he is angry when he very plainly is. In all such cases, some outside observer may prove to be a better judge of the facts. But these examples are weighted: in so far as the terms in which we talk of a man's motives or his emotions involve a reference to his behaviour, there is clearly no reason to regard his accounts of them as privileged. On the other hand, when it comes to simple sensations, such things as Professor Ryle calls twinges or pangs, then surely there can be no better witness to their occurrence than the person who feels them? If someone else who claimed to be co-conscious with him, gave a different report, we might suspect that our subject was lying about his sensations, but not that he was just mistaken: if we believed him to be honest, it is the other's claim to co-consciousness that would be discredited. This comes out even more strongly when it is a question not of feeling but of thinking. If I am lost in a day-dream, and offered a penny for my thoughts, I may choose not to avow them; but if I do honestly avow them there can surely be no question of anyone's word for them being taken against mine. It is not possible that any other person, whatever may be his parapsychological powers, should know better than I do what I am day-dreaming about. Or, to take another example which was suggested to me by Professor Ryle, to the detriment of the position which he took in the *Concept of Mind*, suppose that a child tells you that he is drawing a ship, you may feel that the drawing does not at all resemble a ship, a psychologist may discover that it is 'really' a symbol for something else, but in a straightforward sense the child knows what he is trying to draw; and if he himself says that he means it to be a ship, then no one else can be in a position to override him. Of course, he may be using the word 'ship' incorrectly, but that is a different question. The point is that whatever the word means in his usage, he is the final authority as to whether it applies, in this usage, to what he is setting out to draw.

There is, however, a problem here. If we maintain that in cases of this kind one is oneself the best possible authority as to what one thinks or intends or feels, does this not commit us to the view that one cannot be mistaken, that one's reports of these matters are, in the technical sense, incorrigible? For if one could be mistaken, it is conceivable that one's mistakes should be corrected by some other person, it is conceivable that he should be more often right about the nature of one's thoughts or feelings than one was oneself; and in that case there would seem to be no justification for insisting that one's word must be taken against his. There would be every justification, on the other hand, if one's reports were incorrigible. And indeed it is hard to see how in these special cases they could fail to be so. If verbal mistakes are excluded, it is hard to see what could be meant by saying that someone honestly believed that he was feeling a twinge, or thinking about a philosophical problem, or day-dreaming about being rich, or trying to draw a ship, and yet was really doing nothing of the sort. What would such a situation be like? Admittedly, the range of what I am calling a verbal mistake is fairly wide. It covers not only the use of the wrong word, but also misidentification, referring to what one has in mind by a name or description which does not apply to it. I might for example honestly believe that I was thinking of Beau Brummell when I was really thinking of Beau Nash. And if this kind of mistake is not to count, the claim to infallibility is very much softened. Yet something of importance remains. Even if I refer to him wrongly, it is still true, in this example, that I am thinking of a man of such and such a sort; and about this at least, it may be said, it is impossible that I should be mistaken.

This is a question that has been much debated, and I cannot here go over it again in detail. It does seem to me, however, that there is much to be said on the other side. In particular, apart from the very special cases where the statement expresses a necessary condition for its being believed by whoever it may be, as if I were to say, for example, that I believe that I am capable of forming beliefs, I feel very reluctant to admit that the truth of any statement can simply follow from the fact that someone believes it. I am inclined to say that it must always be logically possible that the belief should be false. But then it may be argued that it is just these cases, where the statement refers to our present thoughts or feelings, that furnish the exceptions. I do not see how this argument is to be settled except by devising counter-examples. If someone wishes to maintain that these statements are not incorrigible, he must light upon a set of circumstances in which such a sentence as 'he thinks that he is thinking about a philosophical problem but he really is not' could plausibly be taken to express something true, and this not simply in the sense that the problem which he is thinking about should not be classified as *philosophical*. I think that this would be very difficult but I am not prepared to say dogmatically that it is impossible.

I am content to leave this question open because I am going to argue that my thesis does not depend upon it. The position which I wish to take is that one may be the best authority with regard to one's present thoughts and feelings, even though one's reports of them are not infallible. An obvious analogy would be that of a judge whose decisions are not subject to review by any higher court. There is a sense in which his decisions may be bad, so that he is to this extent fallible; but since his ruling settles the question at issue his authority is supreme. In one very important way, however, this analogy does not suit our purpose. For the point about the judge is that he is not issuing reports : when he delivers a verdict he is not making a statement which can be either true or false. Whereas, in the cases we are now considering, it is part of my thesis that when people make pronouncements about their thoughts and feelings, they are expressing statements, which they know to be true.

Surprisingly, I think a closer parallel may be found in the observation of physical events. The notion of an eye-witness is not precise. It leaves open the question how good a view one must have of the scene which one can be said to witness, whether one sees it with the naked eye or with the help of some instrument, what sort of instrument this may be. For instance, I think it would commonly be said that a person was an eye-witness of a scene that he had viewed through a telescope or seen reflected in a mirror, but not of one that he viewed only on a cinema or television screen ; but it is to some extent an arbitrary matter where one draws the line. In any case it must surely be admitted that not even the best-placed eye-witnesses are infallible. One proof of this is that their reports may disagree. All the same, they are collectively the best authorities with regard to the events which come within their view. Suppose, for example, that we were able to find a group of clairvoyants who claimed to know what was happening at a great distance from them. Suppose that their reports were always in agreement and that when checked against the testimony of observers who were present at the scenes which they described, they were consistently found to be right. We might very well come, in certain circumstances, to prefer the evidence of these clairvoyants to that of some individual eye-witness. But if a reasonable number of eye-witnesses agreed in their reports, then I think we should be bound to take their word against that of the clairvoyants, however reliable the clairvoyants had so far proved to be. The only possible exception would be the case in which the eye-witnesses' reports contradicted some well-established natural law; and this is only an apparent exception since the law itself would have been established on the basis of first-hand testimony. The reason why I think we should be bound to give the eye-witnesses preference is that it is only through its agreement with their evidence that the testimony of the clairvoyants could come to merit any credence at all. If they triumph over one set of eye-witnesses it is only because they are supported by another. In short, it enters into the logic of statements about perceptible physical events that the eye-witnesses have the final say in deciding whether they are true or false.

If this is correct, it provides us with a satisfactory model for the logic of the statements that a person may make about his present thoughts or feelings. He may not be infallible, but still his word is sovereign. If he is not infallible, others may be right when he is wrong. Even so their testimony is subordinate to his in the same way and for the same reason as the testimony of the clairvoyants is subordinate to that of the eye-witnesses. If his reports are corrigible it must be that he himself is ready to correct them, not after an interval of time in which a lapse of memory would rob him of his authority, but as it were in the same breath. We might allow that others were right against him if they pressed upon him a correction which he was immediately willing to accept. This is not sufficient, he might be wrongly overborne by them, but something of this sort is necessary. The logic of these statements that a person makes about himself is such that if others were to contradict him we should not be entitled to say that they were right so long as he honestly maintained his stand against them.

IV

To allow that a person's access to his own thoughts and feelings is, in this sense, privileged is not to maintain that it is exclusive. He may be the final authority on the subject of what he thinks or feels, but that does not imply that the opinions of others on this subject have no standing at all. The question how we are justified in ascribing certain thoughts and feelings to others on the basis of their physical demeanour, and of what they say and do, presents a stubborn philosophical problem. I am not sure that it has yet been satisfactorily answered, but I do not think that this obliges us to say that we can never have any good reason for the beliefs that we hold concerning other people's states of mind, any more than the lack of a satisfactory theory of perception would oblige us to say that we had no good reason for the beliefs that we hold concerning physical objects. In particular instances, we can justify such beliefs by adducing our evidence. And this is not conditional upon our being able to give a general proof that evidence of this type is reliable.

A feature which lends plausibility to the sceptical position concerning our knowledge of other minds is, once again, the construing of privileged access as the privilege of entering a private theatre. A person's thoughts and feelings are held to be private to him, in the sense of being his private property. They are objects which manifest themselves directly to him, and at best only indirectly to others. The question is then raised how these others can have any right to their belief in the existence of objects with which *ex hypothesi* they could never be acquainted.

But from the fact that a person is, in the sense and to the degree that we have explained, the best witness regarding what he thinks or feels, it does not follow that he is acquainted with any private objects, or indeed with any objects at all. For this is not a case in which we are committed to an existential inference. We can maintain that someone thinks or feels something without being bound to draw the conclusion that there *is* something which he thinks or feels. And if we do draw this conclusion, if we decide that it is convenient to speak of thoughts and feelings as objects, we are not bound to hold that they are private property. The privilege that I enjoy with respect to knowledge of my thoughts and feelings does depend upon my having them; but not necessarily upon my being the only one to have them. It is not incompatible with their being shared by somebody else.

But is it conceivable that anyone else should share them? This is a question that we are free to answer as we please. We do often talk as if they could be shared. We talk of a feeling spreading from one person to another, of people having memories or beliefs in common, of their having the same sensation, of their entertaining the same wishes or hopes; we use such expressions as 'the same thought struck them both'. But, some philosopher will protest, what we really mean in such cases is that they were struck by similar thoughts, by thoughts of the same kind, that when one person has a feeling another comes to have a feeling like it. We cannot mean that these thoughts and feelings are numerically the same; in other words, that there is in these cases only one thought or feeling which any number of different people can literally share. But why can we not mean this? What should prevent us? All that our philosopher is doing is to lay down a criterion of identity. He insists that if we treat thoughts and feelings as objects that can be counted, we are to count 'the same thought' in two different people's minds as two and not as one. This is a perfectly feasible suggestion, but, at least so far as thoughts are concerned, I cannot find any strong reason why we should adopt it; or indeed, why we should not.

We might have a motive for resisting it if the ruling that thoughts and feelings could be literally shared were a means to the solution of the other minds problem. But the most it could do in this way would be to weaken the hold upon us of the image of the private theatre. It would not help to vindicate our claims to know what was going on in other people's minds. For the fact, if it be made a fact, that if you are thinking what I am thinking, there exists a thought which we have in common, does not enable me to infer that you actually are thinking this at all. And if I do know what your thoughts are, and find that they coincide with mine, it can hardly matter to me whether or not I am entitled to say that they are literally the same. It is to be remarked also that if we do make thoughts public, in this special sense of making them common, they would still not be common in the way that physical objects are. For in the case of physical objects it is not just a matter of our being entitled to say that an object which is perceived by one person is literally the same as that which is perceived by another ; the important point is that if they are perceptible, then it is a necessary condition of their existence that they be perceptible, at least in theory, by more than one person. If I think that I am perceiving a physical object and become convinced that others, who would be in a position to perceive it if it existed, do not do so, then I have reason to doubt whether it exists. But this does not apply to thoughts. In certain circumstances I may expect others to have the same thoughts as I do : but the existence of a thought which I am thinking in no way depends upon another's sharing it.

In so far as feelings are spatially located, there is a special reason for denying that they can be shared. For the fact that they are spatially located may make us inclined to regard them as particular existents : and we are reluctant to allow that a particular can exist discontinuously in time, or that it can be in different places at once. But if feelings are to be treated as objects, they will be objects of a peculiar kind, and we are free to apply special criteria of identity to them. As I have argued elsewhere,[1] it might even suit us to go further and make them public in a fuller sense. If it were an empirical fact that people in a given neighbourhood habitually felt the same, or, if you prefer it, similar, feelings on the same occasions, we might come to think of such a feeling as an object, analogous to a physical sound, which pervaded the region and existed independently of any given person's feeling it, perhaps even independently of its being felt at all. What we now describe as a person's locating this feeling in some part of his body would then be regarded as his feeling it from a special point of view. Further, the fact that someone had the experience of feeling it would not be a sufficient proof that the feeling existed, nor therefore that he really did feel it. If others, who would be expected to share the feeling, did not do so, this would be an indication that the feeling did not exist, and consequently that the man who claimed to feel it really did not but only thought he did. In these circumstances, a return to our present way of speech would be a move in the direction of phenomenalism.

I think that the reverse process would also be possible. Instead of socializing what we now tend to regard as private property, we could as it were enclose the common land; we could deny any object the power of being accessible to more persons than one. This would be in line with the phenomenalist view that physical objects can be constructed out of private sense-data, but it would not commit us to it. All that would be needed would be to restrict our rules of identity so that it became impossible for the same thing to be perceived by different people. What we should then obtain would be a set of private 'worlds', where the things

[1] *Vide* 'Can there be a Private Language?', p. 36 *supra*.

which appeared in one world co-existed in a large measure with those that appeared in another. One could refer to the things in another person's world, but not by the same names as he did, unless it were understood that these names were systematically ambiguous: the same would apply of course to references to the persons themselves. It is clear that such a language would be intolerably inconvenient, but I do not think that the idea of it is logically vicious.[1]

The moral which I draw from these speculations is that, so far as the problem of solipsism is concerned, it does not matter whether the objects with which we suppose ourselves to be acquainted are private, in the sense of being 'owned' by only one person, or public, in the sense of being available to many. If we surround ourselves with private sense-data, we are obviously landed with the problem of showing how they can supply us with a reason for attributing experiences to others or for assuming the existence of a common world. But equally, though less obviously, a similar problem arises if we claim to be directly aware of physical objects. Admittedly, if we really do perceive the physical objects that we think we do, it will follow that they are capable, at least in theory, of being perceived by others. But this means that unless we have reason to believe that other people could perceive them, we are not justified in believing that we perceive them ourselves, since to say that we really do perceive them is to imply that they exist and so, in this case, to imply that they are public. Thus the problem of perception depends upon the problem of other minds. But the problem of other minds depends in its turn upon the problem of perception. For unless we knew that what

[1] Having tried to construct a language of this kind, I have come to doubt whether it is feasible. I am now inclined to think that in any language which allows reference to individuals there must be criteria of identity which make it possible for different speakers to refer to the same individual. This would not prevent the language from containing private sectors, but it would mean that my idea that these private sectors could be made to absorb the public sectors was not tenable.

appeared to be other human bodies really were so, the question of their being inhabited by other conscious persons would not arise.

V

In the course of this discussion I have distinguished four different criteria of privacy. One, which I only fleetingly considered, would make things private to a given person if their existence could be detected by him but not conceivably by anybody else. I maintain that nothing, whether it be mental or physical, is private in this sense. A weaker criterion of the same type would make things private to a given person if there is at least one way in which he can detect their existence but others cannot: it is not implied in this case that others cannot detect it in any way at all. If the possibility of co-consciousness is excluded, all mental states and processes at the conscious level are private in this sense: but so also are many bodily states and processes, unless we admit the possibility of our locating our kinaesthetic sensations in bodies other than our own. And if we take the doubtful step of distinguishing thoughts and feelings, as objects, from the processes of thinking and feeling them, we cannot say that the privacy of these mental activities extends, in this sense, to their accusatives, unless we also hold that thoughts and feelings cannot be literally shared.

Thirdly, a person might be said to have private access to those things concerning which his authority could not be overridden. This would not extend to anything physical, but neither would it cover a great deal that is ordinarily classified as mental. Perhaps we might say that only the thoughts and feelings to which it did apply were *strictly* mental. If we allow that one's present thoughts and feelings can be shared, one may not be the only final authority with regard to their existence, since others may have them too, though this will remain a point on which one cannot be overridden: one will in any case be the only final authority with regard to the fact that one is having them. Finally, the attribution of privacy may be made to turn on the question whether something is public or private property, in the sense that it is or is not capable of being shared. This is the criterion to which philosophers have perhaps paid most attention, without as a rule distinguishing it at all clearly from the others. It is not applied unambiguously, since physical objects are held to be sharable on the ground that different people can *perceive* the same physical object, while feelings are held to be unsharable on the different ground that two people cannot *have* the same feeling. Even if these rules of identity be accepted, this criterion does not in general distinguish between the mental and the physical, since if it is true that you cannot have my feelings, it is equally true that you cannot sleep my sleep, or smile my smile or speak with my voice. How ambiguously this criterion works is shown by the fact that it also makes these things public, since my sleeping, my voice, and my smile are all perceptible by others. I have included it not for its merits but because it is so often used.

A word remains to be said about the logical relations of these criteria. If anything were private according to the first criterion, in the order in which I have just listed them, it would be private according to the other three; but in no case does the converse hold. The fourth criterion may be thought to be a muddled version of the second but it operates differently. To say of something that its existence is detectable by a given person in at least one way in which it is not detectable by others neither implies nor excludes the possibility of its being something that he can be said to share. I maintain also that the third criterion is logically independent of the second and fourth. Plainly from the fact that something is exclusively mine, it does not follow, as was shown by the example of a smile, that I have privileged access to it ; and I have also tried to show that from the fact that I do have privileged access to my present thoughts and feelings, in the sense that my testimony concerning them cannot be overridden, it does not follow that they are exclusively mine. Again it is obvious that having a private method of detecting the existence of something is not sufficient to make one a final authority concerning it : neither, in my view, is it necessary. For I have argued that this authority is not destroyed even by the admission of co-consciousness. Why indeed such a privilege should exist in the cases where it does is a question to which I have not found an answer. We may just have to take it as a fact for which no further reason can be given.

4

THE CONCEPT OF A PERSON

THE problems which I intend to discuss are excessively familiar to students of philosophy. They are concerned with persons in the broad sense in which every individual human being can be counted as a person. It is characteristic of persons in this sense that besides having various physical properties, including that of occupying a continuous series of spatial positions throughout a given period of time, they are also credited with various forms of consciousness. I shall not here try to offer any definition of consciousness. All I can say is that I am speaking of it in the ordinary sense in which, to be thinking about a problem, or remembering some event, or seeing or hearing something, or deciding to do something, or feeling some emotion, such as jealousy or fear, entails being conscious. I am not at this stage committing myself to any view about the way in which this notion of consciousness should be analysed.

The first question which arises is how these manifestations of consciousness are related to the physical attributes which also belong to persons. The answer which I think would still be most acceptable to common sense, at least when it is made to consider the question in these terms, is that the relation is contingent, not logical, but only factual. In philosophy this view is mainly associated with Descartes ; if he did not originate it, he put it forward in the clearest and most uncompromising way. The view is that a person is a combination of two separate entities, a body and a mind or soul. Only the mind is conscious ; the physical properties which a person has are properties of his body. The two entities are separate in the sense that there is no logical connection between them. It is conceivable that either should exist without the other; that is, there is no contradiction in supposing that a person's mind exists in some other body, or apart from any body at all, and equally none in supposing that a person's body is animated by some other mind, or not by any mind at all. This does not, however, exclude the possibility of there being causal connections between them; so that even if they are separable in principle, there may still be grounds for holding that they are inseparable in fact. Descartes himself prejudged this question by defining the mind as a substance, which implied, in his usage, that its existence was causally as well as logically independent of the existence of the body. But this view that the mind is a substance is not entailed by the view that mind and body are logically distinct. It would be compatible with this sort of dualism to reject the notion of mental substance altogether and conceive of the mind, in Humean fashion, as a series of experiences.

Whatever may be the attractions of this dualistic view for common sense, the tendency of philosophers has been to try to replace it by some form of monism. Thus Berkeley, who held that physical objects were collections of sensible qualities which were dependent for their existence upon being perceived, and Hume, who saw no grounds for holding that anything existed but sensory impressions and the ideas which copied them, may both be regarded, in their different ways, as having tried to effect the reduction of body to mind. In more recent versions of this type of theory, such as those developed by William James and Bertrand Russell, the sense-data and images, which are taken as fundamental, are held to constitute a kind of neutral stuff, itself neither mental nor physical, out of which both mind and matter are to be constructed. Conversely, it was held by Hobbes, in opposition to Descartes, that there was no need to postulate the existence of minds in addition to bodies ; conscious states and activities could be attributed to the body itself. And modern philosophers, like Ryle and Carnap, have argued that it is a mistake to think of conscious states and processes as ghostly inhabitants of a private mental stage ; statements about people's mental life are reducible to statements about their physical constitution, or their actual and potential behaviour.

With all of these theories, except perhaps the last, there is a corresponding problem of personal identity. On any dualistic view an account is required of the way in which the mind is lodged in the body. Could there be more than one mind in a single body ? Could the same mind dwell in more than one body, at the same or at different times ? If the relation is one to one, how are its terms paired off ? How is it decided which mind goes with which body ? The most plausible answer is that they are causally connected in some special way, but it is not easy to see how this connection is to be defined. If the mind is regarded as a substance, the question arises how such a substance could ever be identified. If it is regarded as a collection of experiences, there is the problem, to which Hume himself confessed that he could see no answer, of showing how the collection is united. What is it that makes a given experience a member of one such collection rather than another ? With any view of this type, there is also the problem of identifying the experiences themselves. In the ordinary way, we identify experiences in terms of the persons whose experiences they are ; but clearly this will lead to a vicious circle if persons themselves are to be analysed in terms of their experiences.

An argument in favour of the physicalistic type of monism is that these difficulties are avoided. At least there is then no special problem of personal identity. The criteria for the identity of persons will be the same as those that determine the identity of their bodies; and these will conform to the general conditions which govern the identity of all physical objects of a solid macroscopic kind. It is primarily a matter of spatio-temporal continuity. Moreover, if persons can be equated with their bodies, there will no longer be any need to specify how minds and bodies are correlated. Once it is shown how states of consciousness can be ascribed to bodies, this problem will have been solved. But whether this can be shown is itself very much an open question. It is obvious that any view of this type encounters very serious difficulties; and it is not at all so clear that they can be satisfactorily met.

What is common to all these theories is the view that the concept of a person is derivative, in the sense that it is capable of being analysed into simpler elements; they differ only about the character of these elements and the way in which they are combined. But this premiss itself has recently been challenged. In his book on *Individuals*, Mr. P. F. Strawson has attempted to prove that the concept of a person is a primitive concept; and what he means by this is just that it is not analysable in any of the ways that we have outlined. Not everything that we want to say about persons can be construed as a statement about the physical objects which are their bodies; still less, when we refer to persons, are we referring to mental substances, or to collections of experiences. Neither, in Mr. Strawson's view, can it be maintained that persons are compound; that they are the product of two separate entities, or sets of entities, one the subject of physical characteristics and the other the subject of consciousness. He holds, on the contrary, that the subject to which we attribute the properties which imply the presence of consciousness is literally identical with that to which we also attribute physical properties. And if we ask what this subject is, the only correct answer is just that it is a person.

Mr. Strawson's main reason for rejecting dualism is, in his own words, that 'the concept of the pure individual consciousness — the pure ego — is a concept that cannot exist; or, at least, cannot exist as a primary concept in terms of which the concept of a person can be explained or analysed. It can exist only, if at all, as a secondary, non-primitive concept, which itself is to be explained, analysed in terms of the concept of a person.' [1] It might be thought that this would not affect the dualist who rejects the notion of the pure ego, and thinks of the conscious subject as a collection of experiences, but in fact the reasons which Mr. Strawson has for denying that there can be a primary concept of the pure ego apply equally to any idea of a non-physical subject of consciousness, whatever its composition may be thought to be.

His argument runs as follows. The first premiss is 'That it is a necessary condition of one's ascribing states of consciousness, experiences, to oneself, in the way that one does, that one should also ascribe them, or be prepared to ascribe them, to others who are not oneself'.[2] Now this is understood to imply that one ascribes experiences to others in exactly the same sense as one ascribes them to oneself. It excludes the view, which has been held by some philosophers, that the statements which a person makes about the experiences of others are to be analysed quite differently from the corresponding statements that he makes about his own, that whereas in his own case he is to be understood as speaking literally, what he says about the experiences of others can only be construed as a reference to their behaviour. But when one talks about the experiences of another person one cannot be attributing them to a pure consciousness; neither is it possible to regard the

[1] *Individuals*, p. 102. [2] *Ibid.* p. 99.

subject of one's statement simply as a collection of experiences. The reason for this is that in the case of another person neither the pure consciousness nor the collection of experiences would be things that one could have any means of identifying. But if our attributions of experiences to others cannot be understood in this way, neither can our attributions of experiences to ourselves : this follows from the principle that the same analysis must be applied to both.

An important consequence of this argument, if it is sound, is that we must give up the argument from analogy on which many philosophers have relied as a justification for believing in the existence of other minds. It is tempting to think that one can come by the idea of one's own experiences through introspection, observe that in one's own case experiences of certain kinds are characteristically associated with certain forms of behaviour, and so, when one observes other people behaving in similar ways, infer that they are having similar experiences. Even if one does not acquire the belief that there are other minds in this fashion, it may still be the ground for holding that the belief is rational. This reasoning has, indeed, met with various objections. Assuming that it is logically impossible for anyone directly to observe what goes on in another person's mind, some philosophers have maintained that this is not a valid argument from analogy ; for they hold that no inductive argument can give us any reason to believe in the existence of something which could not even in principle be observed. Others who think that this difficulty can be overcome find fault with the argument because its basis is so weak. As Wittgenstein put it, 'how can I generalize from the *one* case so irresponsibly ?' [1] The novelty of Mr. Strawson's attack lies in his refusal even to allow the argument to start. If my knowing how to ascribe experiences to others is a

[1] *Philosophical Investigations*, i. 293.

necessary condition of my being able to ascribe them to myself, then, Mr. Strawson suggests, the argument begins by presupposing what it is intended to justify.

Moreover, even if, without consideration of others, I could initially distinguish what are in fact my experiences from the body with which they are associated, and this body from other bodies, this still would not give me any ground, in Mr. Strawson's view, for supposing that any of these other bodies were 'owned' by subjects who also had experiences. I should discover empirically that certain feelings occurred when this body was acted on by certain stimuli, and that they did not occur when other bodies were so treated. But all that could ever be in question would be the presence or absence of experiences of my own. And even this goes too far, if it only makes sense for me to talk of my experiences in contradistinction to those of other people. To some extent this argument was anticipated by G. E. Moore, who maintained in his essay on 'The Nature and Reality of Objects of Perception' [1] that if one assumes with Berkeley that the objects of perception exist only so long as one is perceiving them, then no reasoning by analogy could give one any ground at all for ascribing experiences to other people ; the most that it could possibly authorize would be a belief in the existence of unconscious experiences of one's own. But for Moore this was just an argument against idealism ; he thought that if the objects of perception were allowed to be physical bodies which existed independently of our perceiving them, then we could rely upon analogy as a ground for believing that some of these bodies were inhabited by minds like our own. Mr. Strawson, on the other hand, holds that even if we grant this premiss about the objects of perception, there is still no basis for the argument from analogy.

[1] *Proceedings of the Aristotelian Society*, 1905/6. Reprinted in *Philosophical Studies*.

It might be thought that this line of reasoning would result in the elimination of anything but the body as a possible subject of consciousness, but Mr. Strawson does not take this view. He does not in fact discuss the thesis of physicalism, according to which statements about experiences are transformable into statements about physical occurrences, but instead goes on to examine a hybrid theory which he calls the 'no-ownership' doctrine of the self. This is the theory that the only sense in which experiences can significantly be said to have an owner is that they are causally dependent upon the state of some particular body. It is perhaps misleading to call this a 'no-ownership' theory, since in the sense which it allows to ownership, it does not imply that any experiences are unowned. Mr. Strawson's reason for so calling it is not so much that this sense of ownership is Pickwickian as that it does not yield a guarantee that experiences are private property. For he holds that it must on this theory be regarded as a contingent fact that the experiences which a person owns are causally linked to his body and not to some other body instead.

Mr. Strawson's objection to this theory is that it is incoherent. The proposition which it tries to state is that, with respect to any given person, all his experiences are dependent upon the state of his body; and this proposition is supposed to be contingent. But how are his experiences to be identified? In accordance with what principle are my experiences classified as mine? If the answer is that they are just those experiences which are causally dependent, in the requisite way, upon the state of this body, then the proposition that all my experiences are causally dependent upon the state of this body becomes analytic; it is just a way of saying that all the experiences which are causally dependent upon the state of this body are causally dependent upon the state of this body. But what the theory requires is that this proposition be contingent. And since it admits no other way of identifying a person's experiences, the consequence is that it defeats itself.

It is also true of physicalist theories that they admit no other way of identifying a person's experiences than by identifying his body. It might, therefore, be thought that they too were exposed to Mr. Strawson's argument, especially as it seems to be a contingent proposition that some particular body is the body of such and such a person. But here the physicalist has an effective answer. He can argue that the reason why this proposition is contingent is just that it presupposes that the body in question has been independently identified, either ostensively or by some other form of description. If we have identified a person, it follows, on his view, that we have identified that person's body ; but the converse need not hold. Neither is there any further problem for the physicalist about the identification of experiences, since he maintains that statements about a person's experiences are logically equivalent to statements about the condition or movements of his body. As we shall see, there are serious objections to any view of this kind ; but on this score at least, it is not incoherent. We may, therefore, conclude that Mr. Strawson's argument is not fatal to theories of this type. Whether it is fatal even to the 'no-ownership' theory is one of the questions that we shall have to consider later on.

Physicalist theories are based on a consideration of the way in which we ascribe experiences to other people. Since our only ground for this proceeding is our observation of their physical condition and behaviour, it is assumed that this is all that we can be referring to. Then, on the assumption that we must mean the same by the ascription of experiences to ourselves as we do by ascribing them to others, it is inferred that even when we speak about our own experiences we are referring to our physical condition or behaviour. To dualists, on the other hand, it is evident that when we speak about our own experiences we are not referring to the physical manifestations by which other people may be made aware of them. Our knowledge of our own experiences is of an entirely different character. So again assuming that when we speak about the experiences of others we must mean the same as we do when speaking about our own, they infer that the physical events on which we base our attributions of experiences to others are signs of these experiences and not to be identified with them. They hold that we have direct knowledge of our own experiences; but that such knowledge as we can have of the experiences of others is only inferred from their physical manifestations. And then they are faced with the problem how these inferences can be justified.

In maintaining that the concept of a person is logically primitive, Mr. Strawson hopes to secure the advantages, and at the same time avoid the difficulties, of both these lines of approach. He admits that the basis on which we ascribe experiences to others is different from that on which we ascribe them to ourselves, but he denies that, in the case of other people, we are reduced to making an inductive inference. There is not merely a factual connection between certain physical events and the experiences which they are understood to manifest. It is true that when we ascribe experiences to others we do not simply mean that they are in such and such a physical condition or that they are behaving, or disposed to behave, in such and such ways. These are just the criteria by which we determine that they are having the experience in question. But the point is that these criteria are 'logically adequate'. In our own case, we do not rely on these criteria. Our knowledge of our own experiences is not obtained by observation. But this does not mean that the sense in which we ascribe experiences to ourselves is in any way different from that in which we ascribe them to others. On the contrary, it is a necessary feature of predicates which imply that the subject to which they are attributed is conscious, 'it is essential to the character of these predicates, that they have both first and third person ascriptive uses, that they are both self-ascribable otherwise than on the basis of observation of the behaviour of the subject of them, and other-ascribable on the basis of behaviour-criteria'.[1] If we did not understand the use of predicates of this kind, we should not possess the concept of a person. For persons are essentially the subjects to which such predicates are attributed.

But how, to echo Kant, are such predicates possible? Or, as Mr. Strawson puts it, 'What is it in the natural facts that makes it intelligible that we should have this concept (of a person)?'[2] He does not attempt to answer this question in any detail, but he does suggest that if we are looking for an answer we should begin by directing our attention to predicates which are concerned with human action. He thinks that it is easier to understand how we can see each other, and ourselves, as persons, 'if we think first of the fact that we act, and act on each other, and act in accordance with a common human nature'. His reason for thinking this is that a study of the ways in which we do things should rid us of the belief 'that the only things we can know about without observation and inference, or both, are private experiences'. In cases of intentional action we also have knowledge, not based on observation and inference, about the present and future movements of our bodies. Not only that, but predicates which refer to forms of action do so as a rule 'while not indicating at all precisely any very definite sensation or experience'. The result of this is that although we ascribe such predicates to others on the basis of observation and do not in general ascribe them on this basis to ourselves, we find it much easier in their case than in the cases where there is a reference to some distinctive

[1] *Op. cit.* p. 108. [2] *Ibid.* p. 111.

experience to recognize that what is attributed on these different bases is nevertheless the same.

The suggestion that persons are to be distinguished in the first instance by their capacity for action has also been put forward by Professor Hampshire in his book on *Thought and Action*. 'The deepest mistake', he says, 'in empiricist theories of perception, descending from Berkeley and Hume, has been the representation of human beings as passive observers receiving impressions from "outside" of the mind where the "outside" includes their own bodies. In fact, I find myself from the beginning able to act upon objects around me. . . . I not only perceive my body, I also control it; I not only perceive external objects, I also manipulate them. To doubt the existence of my body would necessarily be to doubt my ability to move. . . . I find my power of movement limited by the resistance of objects around me. This felt resistance to my will defines for me, in conjunction with my perceptions, my own situation as an object among other objects.'[1] And not only is this in fact so: according to Professor Hampshire, it could not conceivably be otherwise. It is only because persons are themselves physical objects with a situation in space and time and with a power of movement which brings them into contact with other physical objects, including other persons with whom they can communicate, that they can even form the idea of an objective world.

Professor Hampshire also thinks that the concept of human action provides the key to the problem of personal identity. 'We have no reason,' he says, 'to seek for some criterion of personal identity that is distinct from the identity of our bodies as persisting physical objects. We find our intelligence and our will working, and expressing themselves in action, at a particular place and a particular time, and just these movements, or this voluntary stillness,

[1] pp. 47-8.

are unmistakably mine, if they are my actions, animated by my intentions. . . . I can only be said to have lost a sense of my own identity if I have lost all sense of where I am and what I am doing.' [1]

It appears that the action here envisaged is always at least partly physical ; so that it follows, in Professor Hampshire's view, that the notion of a disembodied person, and, therefore, the notion of personal survival in a disembodied state, is self-contradictory or meaningless. Mr. Strawson does not go quite so far. As we have seen, he thinks that there could not be an underived concept of a pure individual consciousness, but he sees no reason why such a concept should not have what he calls 'a logically secondary existence'. One can, therefore, intelligibly think of oneself as surviving one's bodily death. For one can imagine oneself continuing to have experiences of various kinds, without having any power to make physical changes in the world, and without having any perception of a body which is related to these experiences in the way that one's living body is related to one's present experiences. I suppose it might be necessary to add the further condition that one's experiences should not in any way suggest that other people perceived such a body either. If these conditions were fulfilled, then one could legitimately think of oneself as surviving in a disembodied state. It is not suggested that this could actually happen, in the sense that it is causally possible for there to be experiences which are independent of a body, but only that the idea is intelligible. Having made this concession, Mr. Strawson goes on to remark that there are two essential features of this form of existence which may somewhat diminish its appeal. The first is that one would be entirely solitary ; if there were other creatures in the same condition one would have no means of knowing it. The second is that one could retain one's sense of one's

[1] *Thought and Action*, p. 75.

own identity only in so far as one preserved the memory of one's embodied existence ; this might be eked out by taking a vicarious interest in the state of the world which one had left. In short one would exist, as it were on sufferance, as a former person. From this point of view the idea of there being persons, even of such an attenuated sort, who were not at any time embodied is not intelligible.

II

I have made a detailed summary of Mr. Strawson's theory because it gives an account of persons which, if it were acceptable, would remove many of the difficulties of the mind-body problem. It seems to me, however, that the theory has serious difficulties of its own. The cardinal point is the attempt to stop short of physicalism on the one hand, and dispense with the argument from analogy on the other, by maintaining that our observations of the physical condition and behaviour of other persons, on the basis of which we attribute experiences to them, are logically adequate for this purpose. But what exactly is meant here by saying that a criterion is logically adequate ? Not that the evidence entails the conclusion, for in that case we should not stop short of physicalism ; if a statement about a person's experiences is to follow logically from a statement about physical events, it also must be construed as a statement about physical events. Not that the evidence provides sufficient empirical support for the conclusion, for then the reasoning is inductive ; we are back with the argument from analogy. What is envisaged is something between the two, but what can this be ? What other possibility remains ?

That there can be a relation between statements which is not deductive and yet is in some sense logical is a view which Mr. Strawson is not alone in holding. It is maintained also by the followers of Wittgenstein, especially in connection with this problem, but they too fail to make it sufficiently clear what the relation is supposed to be. What Wittgenstein himself appears to have held is that it is only in so far as our so-called inner experiences have characteristic outward expressions that the statements which we make about them can have any meaning for us; and that so far as this goes it makes no difference whether one is referring to one's own experiences or to those of other people; it is in this sense that he denied the possibility of a private language. I do not think that he was right on this point, as I have argued elsewhere,[1] but even if he were right, even if it is only through their having physical manifestations that our experiences are communicable, even to ourselves, the relation between the statements which refer to these experiences and those which refer to their outward expressions remains obscure. We are not allowed to say that the experiences are identical with their outward expressions; and yet we are not allowed to say that they are logically distinct. This would seem to indicate that there is a relation of one-way entailment; but the entailment cannot run from the manifestations of the experiences to the experiences themselves, for the manifestations may be deceptive; and if it goes in the reverse direction, then in talking about our experiences we must be talking about their outward expressions and something else besides. But then the question arises what is this something else besides; and to this we are not given any answer.

But may not the reason why we get no answer be that the question itself is wrongly framed? If we begin by assuming a dichotomy between experiences on the one side and physical states or processes on the other, we shall surely end in the unhappy position of having to find some inductive ground for bridging the gap between them. But is this not just the assumption that Wittgenstein was trying to

[1] *Vide* 'Can there be a Private Language?'

discredit? His followers will claim that our notion of a 'pure experience' is utterly obscure to them. We talk of the experience of feeling pain, but do we really understand what it would mean to be in pain without having at least the tendency to display some physical reaction? Can we significantly divorce our thoughts and our emotions from their characteristic expressions in action or in speech? And when it comes to the way in which one observes the behaviour of another person, it is surely quite wrong to treat this as an ordinary instance of the observation of physical events. Human behaviour does not present itself to us as a physical process from which we have to make a dubious inference to the thoughts and feelings and purposes which lie 'behind' it. It is itself expressive of these thoughts and feelings and purposes; and this is how we actually see it. From the outset we observe it *as* human behaviour with all that this implies.

I do not question the facts on which this argument is based. No doubt we attach a significance to human behaviour which we do not attach to the movements of inanimate things; there is, indeed, a sense in which one can simply observe what another person is thinking or feeling. But however natural this process may be, it is still a process of interpretation; there is a distinction to be drawn between the sign and what it signifies. However intimate the relation between our 'inner' states and their 'outward' expressions, it is surely a relation between distinguishable terms. Indeed this is already implied by saying that the outward expression is a criterion for the existence of the inner state. But then we are entitled to ask what sort of criterion it is and what can be meant by the claim that it is logically adequate.

Mr. Strawson himself has tried to illustrate what he means by logical adequacy by appealing to another example. 'If', he says, 'one is playing a game of cards, the distinctive markings of a certain card constitute a logically adequate criterion for calling it, say, the Queen of Hearts; but in calling it this, in the context of the game, one is ascribing to it properties over and above the possession of these markings. The predicate gets its meaning from the whole structure of the game.' [1] In the same way, he suggests, the physical criteria which are held to be logically adequate for the ascription to persons other than oneself of predicates which imply the presence of consciousness do not exhaust the meaning of these predicates. The predicates get their full meaning from the structure of the language.

But what does this analogy come to? It is quite true that we recognize a card, such as the Queen of Hearts, by its markings; and it is also true that, in most contexts, when we identify a card as the Queen of Hearts we are saying not merely that it has a certain characteristic appearance, but also that it stands in certain relations to other cards, that it occupies a certain position in one of the series that makes up a suit. Even to say of it that it is a card implies that it is meant to figure in a game. This is one of the numerous cases in which the applicability of a term to a given object depends, in part at least, upon the object's function. All the same it is always a contingent fact that a thing with such and such a characteristic appearance fulfils the function that it does. If the observation that it has certain markings is an adequate criterion for a particular card's being the Queen of Hearts, the reason is that the rôle which is played by the Queen of Hearts in various card games is commonly bestowed on cards of that design. But this is an inductive generalization; there is no logical connection between the fact that a card looks as it does and the fact that if it is used in a game it is allotted certain powers, for example that of outranking other cards whose markings are in some respects like and in other respects

[1] *Op. cit.* p. 110.

unlike its own. That a card has the look of the Queen of Hearts does not itself guarantee that it would be suitable to play the rôle of the Queen of Hearts in any particular sort of game, or indeed that it is fitted for a part in any game at all. The correlation of its appearance with its function is a matter of convention; but it is an empirical fact that this convention holds.

This may, however, be mistaking the point. Perhaps the point is that, given the appropriate conventions, it is not a matter for empirical discovery that a card with such and such markings plays such and such a rôle. In the context of a game of bridge, to identify a card as the Queen of Hearts is to identify it as a card which outranks the Knave of Hearts and is outranked by the King. The reason why the appearance of the card is a logically adequate criterion for its function is that the connection between them is established by the conventions which allot to cards of various designs their respective powers in the game.

But if this is the point of the analogy, it does not achieve its end. For the connection between a mental occurrence and its bodily expression is just not on a par with that which is conventionally established between the appearance and function of a token in a game. To identify a piece in a game of chess as a bishop and to count anything other than a diagonal move with it as a move in the game would be a contradiction; the rules of chess being what they are, the identification of a piece can be construed as carrying with it the delimitation of its powers. On the other hand, there would be no contradiction in identifying a man's grimace as one which was characteristic of a man in pain, and yet denying that he felt any pain at all. The grimace and the feeling are logically separable in a way that, given the appropriate conventions, the appearance and function of a token in a game are not.

It has been suggested to me by Professor Alston that

the analogy may hold in a weaker form. So long as we confine our attention to particular instances, we shall not find anything more than an empirical connection between a mental occurrence and its bodily manifestation. It will always be logically possible in any given case that either should exist without the other. And if this is possible in any given case, it is natural to infer that it must be possible in all cases. The view suggested to me by Professor Alston, which he thinks may also have been held by Wittgenstein, is that this inference is incorrect. Though the liaison between the characteristic outward expression of an inner state and the inner state in question may fail in any particular instance, it is not logically possible that it should fail in all instances, or even in any high proportion of them. So the reason why behavioural criteria can be said to be logically adequate is that even though they are not infallible, their overall success is logically guaranteed.

The source of this guarantee is supposed to lie in the fact that it is only through their being associated with certain outward expressions that we are able to talk significantly about our inner experiences. As has already been noted, this is Wittgenstein's ground for denying the possibility of a private language. We are taught the use of a word like 'pain' in contexts in which the feeling for which it stands is outwardly manifested in some characteristic way; and the result is that this association is retained as part of the meaning which the word has for us. The association is not so close as to exclude the possibility of anyone's ever feeling pain without displaying it, or of anyone's ever displaying signs of pain, without actually feeling it, but it is close enough to make it a logical certainty that such cases are the exception and not the rule.

One of the attractions of this theory is that it bars the sceptical approach to the problem of one's knowledge of other minds. For if we have the *a priori* assurance that the passage from outward manifestation to inner state is generally secure, we need no further justification for trusting it in any given instance ; the onus then falls upon the sceptic to show that in these special circumstances it is not to be relied on. The question is, however, whether we are entitled to this assurance ; and here I am still disposed to think that the sceptic can maintain his ground. For even if one grants the premiss that we should not in practice be able to acquire an understanding of words which refer to inner states or processes, unless these inner states were outwardly detectable, it does not seem to follow that once our understanding of these words has been acquired, we cannot divorce them from their original associations. Indeed, it is admitted that we can do so in particular instances ; and it is not clear what should prevent us from doing so in all. If the suggestion is that we should then be landed in a contradiction, I can only remark that I do not yet see where the contradiction lies.

Whatever difficulties there may be in supposing that our mental states could in general be dissociated from their characteristic physical manifestations, the admission that they can be so dissociated even in a few particular instances is fatal to the strict theory of physicalism. For if to speak about a so-called mental event were always logically equivalent to speaking about its physical manifestations, it would not be possible even in a single instance that one should exist without the other. Physicalism of this type again has the merit of removing any difficulty about one's knowledge of other minds ; but it achieves this by too desperate a measure. The decisive objection to it was put most succinctly by Ogden and Richards in their *Meaning of Meaning* : one cannot apply it to oneself except at the cost of feigning anaesthesia. Not only do we not have to observe our own behaviour, or take account of our physical condition, in order to know what experiences we are having, but in many cases at least the occurrence of the experience appears to be logically consistent with the absence of its customary outward expression, or indeed of any outward expression at all. The exceptions are those cases where the words which we use to refer to the experience already associate it with some pattern of behaviour: this applies especially to words which stand for emotions, perhaps also to statements of intention. But even here it would seem that if we thought it useful, we could cut away the references to behaviour, and thereby obtain statements which were understood to refer to the experience alone. Even if it were true, as Wittgenstein seems to have thought, that our ability to talk significantly about our 'inner' experiences depends upon their having characteristic outward expressions, it still would not follow that these outward expressions could not be deceptive; not just in the sense that they failed to cohere with other physical manifestations, but in the sense that the person in question simply did not have the experience which they led us to attribute to him.

It has been suggested that even if statements about experiences are not logically equivalent to statements of a purely physicalistic character, it may still be the case that experiences are identical with physical events.[1] To speak of the brightness of the Morning Star is not logically equivalent to speaking of the brightness of the Evening Star; the sense of these two expressions is not the same; nevertheless the fact is that the Evening Star and the Morning Star are identical. So also lightning is in fact a discharge of electricity, though the terms are not logically equivalent. In the same way, it is argued that even though the reports which we make of our experiences do not entail any descriptions of the conditions of our brains, it does not follow that the two are not to be identified. It may be that

[1] See, for example, J. J. C. Smart, 'Sensations and Brain Processes', *Philosophical Review*, lxviii (1959).

all that actually takes place in this connection is a physical process in the brain; and that when it is one's own body which is in question one is able to apprehend this physical process in the form of an experience.

The difficulty here is to see what can be meant by saying that our experiences are not merely caused by physical occurrences which take place in our brains, but are literally identical with them. How could this claim be tested? What kind of experiment would establish that they were or were not identical? In the case of the Morning and the Evening Star we have a criterion of identity; there is empirical evidence that a star which is observed to shine at one period of the day is spatio-temporally continuous with one which is observed to shine at a different period; but this criterion is not applicable here. The case of lightning is more promising; for part of our reason for identifying the flash of lightning with an electrical discharge is that the electrical discharge produces it; even so, what is more important is that they occur at the same time and place. But although there are philosophers who have taken this view, it does seem rather strange to hold that our experiences are literally located in our brains. This is not, as in the other case, a spatial coincidence which can be empirically discovered; it is rather that if one makes the assumption that experiences must be somewhere in physical space, the brain seems the obvious place in which to put them. But of course the dualist's answer to this would be that they are not in physical space at all.

The most that can be empirically established is that our experiences are causally dependent upon the condition of our brains. To go beyond this and maintain that what appears to us as a correlation of the mental with the physical is really an identity, is simply to take a decision not to regard the mental correlates as entities in their own right. But even if this decision were accepted, it would not dispose of all our problems; for the identification of experiences with events in the brain is based on the acceptance of psycho-physical laws. And how do we know that these laws themselves are valid? A possible answer is that I can find out the connection in my own case, whether or not I choose to regard myself as 'owning' the experiences with which my body is associated; and that I can then infer that what has been found to hold for this body holds for other bodies also. But this brings us back once more to the argument from analogy.

III

An essential feature of the argument from analogy is that the justification, as distinct from the cause, of my ascribing experiences to others must issue from the premiss that I have experiences myself. The assumption is that I can come to think of myself as having both a body and a mind without having to raise the question whether or not I am unique in this respect; then, knowing myself to be a person in this sense, I can go on to consider what grounds I have for believing that others are so too. But this is just the assumption that Mr. Strawson wishes to deny. He maintains, as we have seen, that it is a necessary condition of one's ascribing states of consciousness to oneself that one should also ascribe them, or be prepared to ascribe them, to others who are not oneself; and from this he infers that any attempt to justify the belief that there are other persons by relying on the premiss that one knows oneself to be a person would be circular; the premiss would already assume what the argument is supposed to prove.

I shall now try to show that this inference is not correct. It is, indeed, a mark of a general concept, such as the concept of being a person, that no limitation is placed upon the number of individuals to which it can apply. It is, therefore, true that I could not think of myself as satisfying the conditions of being a person unless I admitted the possibility that others satisfied them too. But all that this excludes is the view, which has indeed been held by some philosophers, that it is meaningless to ascribe states of consciousness to anything but oneself; it is perfectly compatible with the view that one does not know, or even with the view that one cannot know, that such an ascription is ever true in fact. But if I can know that I am a conscious subject without knowing that there are any others, there need be no circularity in an argument which proceeds from the premiss that I have experiences and arrives at the conclusion that others have them also.

To this it may be objected that when it is said that I must be prepared to ascribe states of consciousness to others in order to be able to ascribe them to myself, what is meant is not just that I must be willing to regard the existence of other conscious beings as something which is abstractly possible, but rather that I must be disposed to treat it as established by certain observations which I actually make. In other words, I must already believe that I can be justified in ascribing experiences to others before I can significantly ascribe them to myself, and in that case an attempt to base this justification on my knowledge of my own experiences will be circular.

But the answer to this is that there is a difference between my believing that I am justified in accepting a given proposition and my really being so; and not only that, but a belief in a proposition may be justified without the proposition's being true. So even if I could not think of myself as a person unless I also thought that I had reasons to think the same of others, I could still consistently raise the question whether these reasons really did the work that was required of them; and even if I were able to decide that they were good reasons, I still should not be bound to hold that they were conclusive. It seems to me, therefore, that Mr. Strawson's argument needs a stronger premiss than the one that he states. It must hold it to be a necessary condition of one's ascribing states of consciousness to oneself not merely that one should ascribe them, or be prepared to ascribe them, to others, but that one should be sure of doing so successfully. It must, in other words, exclude the possibility of one's being invariably mistaken.

This premiss would establish Mr. Strawson's case if it were true. My objection to it is that it is false. I do not mean by this that one is invariably mistaken in ascribing states of consciousness to others: if this were put forward as a general proposition implying that everyone was so mistaken, it would be self-contradictory; and I certainly do not in fact believe that I am the only conscious subject in the world. What I mean is that if there were someone who was invariably mistaken in ascribing states of consciousness to others, whether because there were no other persons in the world or merely because he never encountered any, this would not necessarily prevent him from being able to ascribe them to himself. Since this degree of solitude has never been attained by anyone who has acquired the use of language, I cannot prove my point by citing any actual case. The only way I can substantiate it is by constructing a rather artificial example.

Imagine a child who, for reasons which need not trouble us, is kept from having any contact, at least throughout his formative years, with any other human being. He is fed by mechanical means, and confined to a nursery which contains, in addition to the usual furniture, a number of automata. These automata, some of which roughly imitate the appearance of human bodies, are so constructed that they respond to his actions in certain limited ways; cry out, for example, when he hits them, or retaliate by striking out at him; they can be made to nod or shake their heads in answer to his questions, and also to utter certain simple sentences; these utterances may be triggered off by visual or auditory signals. For his instruction in the use of language, and in other forms of behaviour, the child depends upon a voice which addresses him through a loud speaker. If it be objected that even though the child never sees the owner of the voice, it still introduces a human element, we can suppose that the sounds which the child hears are not spoken by any person, but transmitted, perhaps from written messages, by a machine. The voice teaches the child the names of the various types of objects in the room; it formulates sentences for him to imitate, which are sometimes also responded to by the automata. It teaches him his own name, the use of pronouns and demonstratives, and the use of words which describe his 'inner' states. In very much the same way as children normally do learn these things, he learns to say when he is hungry or satisfied, happy or in pain; he is coached, as other children are, to distinguish what he sees from what he imagines, or from what he remembers; and among his memories to distinguish those that are memories of dreams. Part of the method by which this is achieved is a stressing of the similarity between himself and the automata: the voice always speaks of them as though they too were conscious, and he finds that the attribution of consciousness to them, but not to the 'inanimate' objects in the room, corresponds to differences in their behaviour. In this way he learns how to apply the concept of a person: and he satisfies the condition of being ready to apply it to other things besides himself.

I said that this was an artificial example, but it is not excessively fanciful. The idea of such an experiment may be morally repugnant, but it would not be very hard to stage, and I see no reason to suppose that it could not lead to the result which I have described. But if this is so, the consequences are important. The example shows not only that one might be able to ascribe experiences to oneself, while being invariably mistaken in ascribing them to others, but also that the criteria which are taken to be logically adequate for ascribing experiences to others may determine no more than that some locution is correct, that in such and such conditions this is the proper thing to say ; it does not necessarily follow that what is said is true. Nor can this conclusion be escaped by saying that the child in my example would not possess our concept of a person, that the automata which he had been taught to regard as conscious subjects really would be persons in his sense of the term. There is no warrant for assuming that his concept of a person could not be the same as ours. He applies it to himself on the basis of his experiences and he applies it to the automata on the basis of their behaviour, which if they were very skilfully constructed, might not appear very different, within their limited field of operation, from that of human beings. It is not that he has a different concept of what it is to be conscious, or that he applies the concept incorrectly, but that he just happens to be in a situation where the things which he has every reason for thinking to be conscious are really not so. If he were an infant philosopher, he might begin to wonder whether his companions really did have experiences in the way that he did and infer that they did from their resemblance to himself. Or perhaps if he were struck by some stereotyped quality in their behaviour he would rightly conclude that they did not. Whichever conclusion he came to, his scepticism would not be senseless. How could it be if it were actually justified ?

The reason for saying that a doubt of this kind would be senseless, even in this artificial instance, is that it could never be laid to rest. There is nothing in this child's world, as we have described it, which would allow him to find out that his companions were, or were not, automata. If he were released from his nursery and allowed to mix with other human beings, he would have a standard of comparison. He would be able to observe how differently these human beings spoke and acted from the things which he had been brought up to regard as persons ; if he discovered how the automata were constructed, he would have a further reason for placing them in a different category from himself. But would this mean more than that he was requiring a stronger basis for his argument from analogy ? And might he not still doubt whether it was strong enough ? But then what would make it strong enough ? If no behavioural criteria are logically sufficient, there must always be room for doubt. But what is the significance of a doubt which could never be allayed ?

I do not know the answer to this question. The difficulty is not just that the argument from analogy, at least in the form in which it is usually presented, does not seem very powerful ; it is rather that any inductive argument allows for its conclusion to be false. So if my belief that other beings are conscious can be defended only as an inference from their behaviour, it is at least possible that I am the only person in the world. The short answer to this is that I know that I am not ; but this still leaves the problem how I can have the right to be so sure. If physicalism were true, this problem would give no trouble, but I do not see how the obvious objections to physicalism are to be overcome. I am, therefore, inclined to agree with Mr. Strawson that we ought to try to find a middle way. For the reasons which I have given, I do not think that he has yet succeeded : among other things, his notion of logical adequacy is rather too nebulous to bear the weight which he puts upon it. Nevertheless I think that the development of this notion, along the lines suggested by Professor Alston, may at least open up the road in which the solution of this problem lies.

Though I am by no means fully satisfied with the argument from analogy, I think it can be defended against the objection that the only experiences which it can give us any reason to believe in are experiences of one's own. This objection rests on the premiss that if the behaviour of others did not provide me with a logically adequate criterion for ascribing experiences to them, the very idea of their having experiences could have no meaning for me. The only facts in my possession would be that when my body was stimulated in certain ways, certain experiences occurred, and that when bodies similar to mine were stimulated in similar ways no such experiences occurred. But if this were all I had to go on, then, it is suggested, I could not even form the hypothesis of there being experiences which were enjoyed by persons other than myself.

This objection has force when it is backed by the assumption that my successfully ascribing experiences to others is a pre-condition of my being able to ascribe them to myself; but when this assumption is discarded, all that remains for the objection to rely on is a strict interpretation of the verification principle. Its conclusion will follow from the ruling that I cannot attach sense to any statement which I could never be in a position to verify directly. But this in itself appears to me now to be an objection against maintaining the verification principle in such a stringent form. If no more is required than that the statement be indirectly testable, then the argument from analogy will at least not be excluded at the outset. Whether its conclusion satisfies this condition of significance will in fact depend upon the question whether it is a legitimate form of inductive argument. There is indeed a special difficulty for those who think that one cannot conceive of physical objects except as logical constructions out of one's own private sense-data; for it may well be asked how I could possibly suppose that a logical construction out of my sense-data was endowed with a private world of its own. On the other hand, if I am entitled to assume that what I perceive, in some cases at least, are public objects which exist independently of myself, there seems to be no good reason why I should not be able to form the hypothesis that certain of these physical bodies have experiences connected with them in the way that experiences have been found by me to be connected with particular states of my own body. The objection that I must in that case already be conceiving of the physical bodies as the bodies of other persons does not seem to hold; the identification of such a body as a particular physical object will, as I hope to show, itself be sufficient for the numerical identification of the experiences which are causally dependent on it; further than that, the experiences themselves need be identified only in a qualitative fashion, as experiences of a certain kind.

If we are able to dispense with the notion of a subject, other than the body, to which both states of consciousness and physical properties are attributed, there will be no reason why we should especially direct our attention to predicates which are concerned with human action. The importance which was attached to these predicates was that they were supposed to provide us with an instance in which we had knowledge not based on observation and inference of something other than our own experiences. Thus our immediate knowledge of our own bodily movements would supply a precedent for taking our knowledge of the experiences of other persons to be non-inferential. But, if, as I have tried to show, our knowledge of the experiences of others is inferential, the need for this precedent will not arise. In any case, it seems to me very doubtful whether the precedent itself is valid. It is indeed true that we are made aware of our bodily movements by kinaesthetic sensation, and it is also true that we usually do what we intend to do, especially when the intention is one that can be immediately carried out. Nevertheless our kinaesthetic sensations can be delusive; they are not sufficient conditions of the physical movements with which we associate them; neither is one's consciousness of an intention a guarantee that it will be fulfilled. In both instances the exceptions are rare enough for us to overlook the distinction between the sign and what it signifies; we speak of feeling a movement or of doing things intentionally, as though the sensation were inseparable from the movement, and the intention from the action which fulfils it; but the distinction is there none the less.

Neither does it seem that the analysis of predicates which are concerned with human action will provide us with the answer to the problem of self-identity. Professor Hampshire may well be right in claiming that even in our infancy we are not simply the passive recipients of sensory impressions; it may be true that one comes to think of oneself as an object among other objects through feeling the resistance which these other objects oppose to one's will. But this fact, if it be a fact, about the way in which a person acquires the idea of his own identity does not tell us in what this identity consists.

IV

If the thesis of physicalism is to be rejected, it does not follow that we are forced back into the position of Descartes. It is possible to hold that states of consciousness are distinct both from their physical causes and from their physical manifestations, without being obliged to hold that there is a mental substance to which they are ascribable. Indeed, if this is what Hume was seeking when he tried to distinguish himself from his perceptions, it is not merely a contingent fact that he was unable to find it; there is no possible way in which such a substance could be identified.

It might seem, however, that we were then committed to Hume's own position. If experiences can be logically distinguished from physical events, then it might appear to follow that one can at least conceive of their existing on their own. Having rejected the notion of a mental substance, we shall have to look upon the self as 'a bundle of perceptions', in Hume's terminology; and it will be a contingent fact that separate bundles are associated with particular bodies. If we take the short step from Hume to John Stuart Mill and regard these bodies themselves as 'permanent possibilities of sensation', it will be a contingent fact that some particular 'perception' is both an element of a collection which constitutes a certain body and an element of a collection which constitutes an individual self.

But the answer to this is that all that we have so far allowed is that a statement which ascribes an experience to some person need not be equivalent to any statement which refers to that person's physical condition or behaviour. And from this it does not follow that it is even logically possible for states of consciousness to exist independently of any physical body. The reason why it does not follow is that it may not make sense to talk of states of consciousness except as the experiences of some conscious subject; and that it may well be that this conscious subject can not be identified except by reference to his body.

In favour of this view, it may be argued that the alternative of equating the conscious subject with the series of his experiences leaves us without any explanation of the nature of personal identity. Not only is it not clear how the individual experiences are to be identified, but there appears to be no principle according to which they can be grouped together; there is no answer to the question what makes two experiences, which are separated in time, the experiences of the same self. The most promising suggestion is that the bundles are tied together by means of memory; but this meets with serious difficulties. In the first place, it is exposed to the charge of circularity; for it is plausible to argue that remembering an experience already implies thinking of it as an experience of one's own: and even if this charge can be met, it is clear on other grounds that memory alone will not suffice. For not every experience can be remembered; otherwise each piece of remembering, which is itself an experience, would have to be remembered, and each remembering of a remembering and so *ad infinitum*: how then is it to be determined that two memory experiences which occur at different times are members of the same bundle? The only answer which suggests itself is that one of them accompanies an experience of which the other is directly or indirectly a memory: the relation may be said to be indirect when the second memory is a memory of some experience accompanying a memory which is either directly, or at one or more such removes, a memory of the experience in question. But what is this relation of accompanying? When dealing with this question, in my *Problem of Knowledge*, I said that it might be taken to be 'the relation that holds between two items of experience if and only if they are parts of the same total experience at any given moment'. But this does involve us in a circle, for 'what is meant here by a total experience is just the experience of one and the same person'. 'We can', I said, 'hold that the relation between its parts is *sui generis*, but then we can also hold that the relation between the successive experiences of the same person is *sui generis*; and in that case we do not need to bring in memory at all.'[1] In *The Problem of Knowledge* I did indeed fall back upon a solution of this kind: I spoke of a 'relation of which, perhaps, nothing more illuminating can be said

[1] p. 222.

than that it is the relation that holds between experiences when they are constituents of the same consciousness'.[1] But to be driven to postulating an unanalysable relation is, in this as in other instances, simply to abandon the problem, not to solve it.

One objection to making personal identity depend upon the identity of the body is that it rules out even the logical possibility of a person's existing in a disembodied state. On any view, the evidence that states of consciousness are causally dependent upon physical processes is strong enough to make it extremely improbable that any person ever does succeed in doing this; but the idea of its happening might at least appear to be intelligible. Surely one can imagine oneself continuing to have experiences which are very like the experiences which one has at present, except that they include none of the perceptions which establish the existence of one's own body; and if one can imagine that this could happen to oneself, one should also be able to imagine that it could happen to others. This is a legitimate form of argument, but in the present instance it may be deceptive. For if this picture of oneself in a future disembodied state is intelligible in its own right, why should it have to contain any link with one's present form of existence? Is it not also imaginable that one should lose all memory of one's embodied self? And could we not go even further? If it is conceivable that one should exist at some time without having any experiences which were indicative of one's having a body, why should it not be conceivable that this should be so at all times? Could it not be imagined that the whole of one's existence was passed in a disembodied state? The objection to these flights of fancy is that there would then be no means by which one could be identified. But does this not equally apply to the idea of a person's surviving the destruction of his body? The experiences

[1] p. 226.

which might then ensue may themselves be imaginable; but it would seem that in crediting them with an owner we are making a tacit reference to the body which is supposed to have been forsaken. Mr. Strawson's idea appears to be that one could retain one's identity through having memories of one's former life. But here he seems to have forgotten that something is needed to secure one's continued existence as a person; and for this we have seen that memory will not suffice.

I do not present these arguments as being in any way conclusive. I am, however, inclined to think that personal identity depends upon the identity of the body, and that a person's ownership of states of consciousness consists in their standing in a special causal relation to the body by which he is identified. I am not maintaining, of course, that this is how one actually becomes aware of one's own experiences, but only that the fact that they are one's own, or rather the fact that they are the experiences of the person that one is, depends upon their being connected with this particular body. This amounts in effect to adopting what Mr. Strawson calls 'the no-ownership doctrine of the self'. We must, therefore, try to rebut his charge that this theory is internally incoherent.

His argument, as we have seen, is that the theory requires it to be a contingent proposition that all my experiences are causally dependent upon the state of my body; but if my experiences are identified as mine only in virtue of their dependence on this body, then the proposition that all my experiences are causally dependent on the state of my body must be analytic; and so the theory is committed to a contradiction. I think, however, that these propositions can be reformulated in a way which shows that the contradiction does not really arise. The contingent proposition is that if my body is in such and such a state, then an experience of such and such a kind results ; the analytic proposition is that if an experience is causally dependent in this way on the state of my body, then the experience is mine. But now it is obvious that these propositions are distinct ; so that there is no inconsistency in holding that one is contingent and the other not. There would indeed be a vicious circle if the experiences had first to be identified as mine before it was discovered that they were dependent on my body, but this is not the case. The position is that a person can be identified by his body ; this body can be identified by its physical properties and spatio-temporal location ; as a contingent fact there are certain experiences which are causally connected with it ; and these particular experiences can then be identified as the experiences of the person whose body it is. There is nothing inconsistent in this.

What may have misled Mr. Strawson is the picture of a heap of experiences which have to be assigned to their respective owners. For this makes it natural to ask which of these experiences are dependent upon a given body, and to believe that one is raising a question of fact ; it will then seem to be an objection to our theory that it only allows the trivial answer that the experiences which are dependent on this body are those which are dependent on this body. But it is the picture that is at fault ; and the question to which it leads is illegitimate. We can not ask *which* experiences are dependent upon a particular body, and are, therefore, to be assigned to such and such a person, because this is to assume improperly that the experiences have been independently identified. The question which we can ask is *what* experiences are dependent upon a particular body, if this is just a way of asking what experiences the person who is identified by the body is having at the relevant time. It is analytic that if the experiences are connected with his body, they are his experiences ; but of course it is not analytic that experiences of one sort rather than another are at any given time connected with his body. Neither does our theory require that it should be.

Our difficulties, however, are not yet at an end. Merely to say that a person's experiences are causally dependent on the state of his body is to speak too vaguely. The nature of the causal relation which is to do the work of assigning experiences to persons needs to be precisely specified. If we are to do justice to the assumptions that are ordinarily made about the way in which experiences are distributed, this relation must operate in such a way that any individual experience is linked to one and only one human body. The problem is to find a causal relation which not only fulfils this task but is also such that its existence can plausibly be taken to follow from every statement in which a person is credited with some experience.

A simple answer would be to regard the relation as being that of causal sufficiency. An experience would then be said to be mine if and only if some state of my body were causally sufficient for its occurrence independently of the state of any other body ; this would exclude the experiences of other people on the assumption that I cannot act upon another person except by producing some physical change in him which is then itself sufficient for the occurrence of his experience. But apart from its needing this questionable assumption, the objection to this answer is that it relies on a causal relation, the existence of which we are hardly entitled just to take for granted. It is by no means universally agreed that all our experiences are physically determined, in so strong a sense as this would imply ; it has even been maintained, in the interests of free-will, that there are experiences which have no sufficient conditions at all. Now this may very well be wrong ; there is certainly no means of showing that any experience lacks a sufficient condition, and it may in fact be true of every experience that its sufficient condition consists in some state of its owner's body. But the point is that even if this hypothesis is true, it can significantly be questioned. It is not at all plausible to hold that its truth is logically implied by every statement in which a person is credited with some experience. To say that the experience is not physically determined may be false, but it does not appear to be self-contradictory.

I think, therefore, that the most that we can hope to maintain is that an experience belongs to a given person in virtue of the fact that some state of that person's body is a necessary condition of its occurrence. The justification for this would be first that experiences are individuated only by reference to the persons who have them, and secondly that persons are identified only by reference to their bodies. If these premisses are admitted, it follows that no experience of mine would have occurred unless my body had existed ; more particularly, it follows that the existence of my body will be implied by any statement in which an experience is attributed to me. But this does not settle the argument. For even if it were granted that an experience could not be mine unless it stood in this relation of causal dependence to my body, one might still maintain that something more than this was required to identify the experience as mine.

A strong argument in favour of this view is that if the relation of dependence is to be merely one of causal necessity, then every one of my experiences is dependent upon the existence of bodies other than my own. This follows simply from the fact that I must have had ancestors : since the existence of their bodies is a necessary causal condition of the existence of my body, it is also a necessary causal condition of the existence of my experience. Moreover, apart from this general condition which applies indifferently to all my experiences, a great many of my experiences owe their special character in part to the behaviour of other persons. It is very often the case that I should not be having the particular experience that I am having unless some other persons had spoken or acted in some particular way, or been in some particular state; and in all such instances the existence of these person's bodies will also be a necessary condition for the occurrence of my experience. It would appear, therefore, that while the relation of causal sufficiency is too strong for our purposes, the relation of causal necessity is too weak. It does not fulfil the task of assigning each experience to one and only one body.

The only way that I can see of overcoming this difficulty is to make a distinction between mediate and immediate necessity. Let us say that the existence of an event x is mediately necessary for the existence of another event y if, and only if, there is some event z, such that x is a necessary condition for the existence of z and z is a necessary condition for the existence of y; and let us say that the existence of x is immediately necessary for the existence of y if, and only if, it is necessary for the existence of y, but not mediately so. Then we may claim that the causal relation which links a person's experience to his and only his body is that of immediate necessity. What makes a given experience mine is the fact that the existence of some state of my body is an immediately necessary condition of the occurrence of the experience and that no state of any other body is so.

Let us now see whether this criterion gives an adequate result. If our reasoning has been correct, the first of its requirements presents no difficulty. Not only is the existence of my body a necessary condition for the existence of any of my experiences, but it also seems clear that it is immediately necessary. There is no other factor that intervenes between my body and this set of experiences which are dependent on it: indeed it is hard even to imagine in this case what such an intervening factor could be. The question is whether there is any difficulty about the second requirement. Does it safeguard us from having to assign experiences to what would ordinarily be regarded as the wrong owners ?

With some misgiving, for reasons which we shall come to, I am prepared to maintain that it does. The fact that the physical existence of my ancestors is also a necessary condition of my having any experiences now presents no problem. For clearly this is a case of mediate necessity. The existence of my own body is an intervening factor. It is also an intervening factor in at least the overwhelming majority of cases in which the character of my experiences depends upon the state or behaviour of another person. For in the normal course of things the only way in which another person can act upon me is by affecting my perceptions. If I am to be in any way influenced by him I must observe him, or observe some effect of what he has done. But in that case the existence or state of his body can at best be a mediately necessary condition of my having the experience which depends upon it. It is mediated by the occurrence of my perception, and so by a bodily state of my own.

We could leave the matter there were it not that we must allow at least for the possibility of para-normal experiences. Thus, there are alleged to be cases in which one person acquires information about the mental or physical condition of another without having to rely upon any form of sense perception. Now one may be sceptical about the authenticity of these reported cases of telepathy, though some of them at least appear to be very well attested; one may accept them as authentic, but still believe that they can somehow be explained in physical terms. This would be in line with the assumption that it is impossible to act upon another person except by causing him to undergo some physical change. Nevertheless, however little we may like the idea of accepting telepathy at its face value, that is, as a form of communication between persons which does not operate by physical means, I do not think that we are entitled to exclude it *a priori*. It may be a far-fetched notion, but it does not appear to be self-contradictory. But if we allow this, then the adequacy of our criterion for assigning experiences to persons is put in question. For suppose that someone communicates a thought to me in this telepathic fashion. In that case, his bodily state will be a necessary condition for his having the thought which he communicates ; it will, therefore, also be a necessary condition of my having the experience which results. But *ex hypothesi* the state of my own body is not in this instance an intervening factor. It is of course itself a necessary condition of my having the experience, but an independent one. It might, therefore, be thought that according to our criterion we should be obliged in a case of this kind to deny me the ownership of the experience.

This would, however, be a mistake. For what is required of our criterion is that no experience of mine shall have for an immediately necessary condition the state of any other body but my own. And this requirement is satisfied even in the case which we have just been envisaging. If we allow telepathy of this kind to be possible, then we are indeed allowing that the state of another person's mind may be an immediately necessary condition of my having some experience ; but the state of his body will still be only mediately necessary. It will give rise to my thought only through the medium of his. There is, therefore, still an intervening factor : not, as in the normal case, some state of my own body, but the other person's experience.

The only type of para-normal case which we could not so easily accommodate would be that in which my experience was dependent on the action of another person, without my being in telepathic communication with him and without my perceiving his action or any of its physical effects.

Thus in an experiment on extra-sensory perception, in which one of the experimenters selects a card, and the subject, sitting in another room, is required to guess what it is, it may be discovered that the subject scores significantly better when the experimenter touches the back of the card with his finger, even though the subject does not know what the experimenter is doing, and the experimenter himself does not know what the card is. If this were to happen, there would be a ground for saying that the experimenter's bodily movement was an immediately necessary condition of the subject's thinking as he did. But then we should be faced with the impossible consequence that, according to our criterion, the subject's thought was not ascribable to any single owner.

This example is troublesome, but not, I think, necessarily fatal to our theory. One way of meeting it would be to construe our criterion in such a way that the only type of bodily state which came within its scope would be an internal state. Such overt performances as the movement of a finger would not qualify. So certain experiences would be mine in virtue of the fact that such things as the condition of my brain and nerves were immediately necessary for their occurrence, and that they did not stand in precisely this relation to any other body but my own. Another defence would be simply to refuse to admit our paranormal case as a counter-example. It is not possible, one might argue, that the experimenter should affect the subject's thought under these conditions simply by moving his hand. This type of action at a distance is unintelligible. There must be some intervening mechanism, even though we do not know what it is. But the trouble with this defence is that it already assumes that the subject's thought has been assigned to him. Without this assumption, the complaint about action at a distance would have no basis as it stands. We could, however, attempt to modify it in such a way as to avoid this objection. We should have to maintain, as a general principle, that in a case where an experience would be manifested in a given body, if it were manifested at all, it was impossible that it should be causally dependent upon a different body, without the operation of some intervening factor. But how are we to decide which is the body in which the experience would be manifested ? If we are reduced to identifying it as the body of the person who has the experience, then clearly we are back in our circle ; and it does not seem certain that it could always be identified by other means. In view of these difficulties it seems preferable to adopt the course that I first suggested : that is, to try to deal with the awkward para-normal example by narrowing our interpretation of what is to count for our purposes as a bodily state.

A more far-reaching objection to this whole procedure is that we are introducing a recondite, if not dubious, theory into the analysis of statements which function at a much simpler level. The use of statements which ascribe experiences to persons is an everyday occurrence : one of the first things that a child learns is to employ and understand them. Can we seriously maintain that these statements incorporate such a sophisticated and unfamiliar notion as that of an immediately necessary condition ?

The answer to this objection is that it is beside the point. In attempting to analyse statements about persons, we are not proposing to discover what those who make such statements commonly have in mind. Our aim is rather to redescribe the facts to which the statements refer in such a way that their nature becomes clarified ; and for this purpose there is no reason why we should not resort to technical terms. In the same way, it is not a fatal objection to a causal theory of perception that a child may learn to talk of the physical objects which he perceives before he has acquired the notion of cause, neither is it fatal to a phenomenalist theory that comparatively few people understand what is meant by a sense-datum. The only relevant question is whether these theories are adequate to the facts: that is, whether they correctly represent the truth-conditions of the statements which they serve to analyse. In the present instance, the way to refute our theory would be to find an example in which it clearly made sense to speak of a person's having some experience, even though the experience was not uniquely dependent on his body in the way that the theory requires. So long as no counter-example is forthcoming which the theory can not be adapted to meet, we may regard it as provisionally acceptable. In a field in which so many theories have had to be discarded, I should not wish to claim more for it than that.

In claiming even so much, I am assuming that it has at least been shown that the theory is free of any vicious circularity. But this may still be questioned. The reason why it may be questioned is that the theory presupposes the existence of psycho-physical laws. Admittedly they are fairly modest laws: we are not assuming that every experience is physically determined; the physical factor is taken only to be necessary, not sufficient. Even so, it may be argued, these laws have had to be empirically discovered. And how could we ever have set about discovering them unless the experiences, which were found to be correlated with certain physical states, had themselves been independently identified? But this means that the charge of circularity returns in full force. How is it finally to be met?

The only way that I can see of meeting it is to draw a distinction between the general proposition that every experience is causally dependent, in the required sense, upon a body and the more specific propositions which describe the different forms that this dependence takes. The general proposition must be held to be necessary, on the ground that causal dependence upon a body is an essential part of what we mean by an experience. On the other hand, the more specific propositions are contingent. The precise nature of the psycho-physical laws which correlate experiences of various types with certain sorts of physical conditions remains a matter for empirical discovery.

In taking the more general proposition to be necessary, I am not implying that in order to know that I am having some experience, I have first to find out that it is dependent on my body. I do not need to find this out, any more than I need to find out that this body is my own. The identification of the body, which carries with it the numerical identification of the experience, is a problem for other people, not for oneself. The reason for this is that in referring to myself at all I am presupposing my ownership of this body; in claiming an experience as mine, I imply that it is dependent on this body and not on any other. This does not mean, of course, that my body could not have been qualitatively different; we are concerned here only with numerical identity. It is not a necessary fact that my body has the physical attributes that it does, but given that this is the body by which I am identified, it is a necessary fact that *this* body is *mine*.

But now a further question arises. If my argument is correct, it is essential that a person be identified at any given time by reference to some body. But is it essential that he be identified at all times by reference to the same body? It would seem natural and convenient to hold that it is, but the consequence of this would be that certain hypotheses which have been thought to be significant, even if highly improbable, would be ruled out *a priori*. We should, for example, be making it logically impossible that a person should be reincarnated, or that two persons should exchange bodies with one another. Yet however fanciful a story like Anstey's *Vice Versa* may be, it is not ordinarily thought to be self-contradictory.

What makes such fantasies appear legitimate is that there are subsidiary criteria of personal identity which may at least be conceived as running counter to the main criterion of physical continuity. These are the criteria of memory and continuity of character. Thus, in Anstey's story, the ground for saying that Mr. Bultitude has been translated into the body of his schoolboy son is that, from a certain moment onwards, the person who is identified by the schoolboy's body displays the mental characteristics which previously belonged not to the son but to the father, and that it is the father's and not the son's experiences that he ostensibly remembers. In such a case, we could insist on saying that the persons who were respectively identified by the two bodies remained the same as before but that they had mysteriously acquired each other's character and memories; it does, however, seem a more natural way of telling the story to say that the two persons have exchanged bodies. On the other hand, even if someone could convince us that he ostensibly remembered the experiences of a person who is long since dead, and even if this were backed by an apparent continuity of character, I think that we should prefer to say that he had somehow picked up the dead man's memories and dispositions rather than that he was the same person in another body; the idea of a person's leading a discontinuous existence in time as well as in space is just that much more fantastic. Nevertheless, I think that it would be open to us to admit the logical possibility of reincarnation merely by laying down the rule that if a person who is physically identified as living at a later time does have the ostensible memories and character of a person who is physically identified as living at an earlier time, they are to be counted as one person and not two. For given that this condition is satisfied, the question of their numerical identity is a matter for decision and not a question of fact.

But even if the subsidiary criteria of personal identity could in these strange cases be allowed to override the primary physical criterion, they are still parasitical upon it. It is only because the different bodies provide us with subjects of reference that we can entertain these queer hypotheses at all. What we should in fact be doing in these cases would be to revert to a Humean theory in which a person's identity is made to depend upon relations between experiences, irrespective of the body with which they are associated. But we have seen that a theory of this kind is not tenable unless the experiences themselves can be identified; and I have argued that the only way in which they can be identified is through their association with a body, the body being that which supplies an immediately necessary condition of their occurrence. It may well be thought a defect in my position that it requires the existence of these psycho-physical relations to be assumed *a priori*. But if this is a defect it is one that I see no way to remedy.

5

NAMES AND DESCRIPTIONS

IN the ordinary way, we do not talk of the meaning of a proper name. If I say 'Napoleon died at St. Helena' and someone fails to understand me because he does not know what the word 'died' means, he may be said to be ignorant of the English language. But if it is my reference to Napoleon or St. Helena that he fails to understand, he is thought to display ignorance, not of English, but of history or geography. We say that he does not know who Napoleon was, or that he does not know that St. Helena is an island, not that he does not know what the words 'Napoleon' or 'St. Helena' mean. Indeed, in the sense in which a dictionary may give a list of English words, these are not counted as words at all. It would not be thought a defect in an English dictionary that it did not contain them. On the other hand, it also seems incorrect to say, with John Stuart Mill, that proper names have no meaning, that they are 'simply marks'. For they help to determine the meaning of the sentences into which they enter. If in the sentence 'Napoleon died at St. Helena' I substitute the name 'Wellington' for 'Napoleon', or 'Elba' for 'St. Helena', I obtain a sentence with a different meaning. But if we admit that a change of name can produce a change of meaning, it seems odd to insist on saying that the names themselves have none.

What Mill meant, of course, was that proper names have no connotation: 'they denote the individuals who are called by them; but they do not indicate or imply any attribute as belonging to these individuals'.[1] We shall see later on that it is doubtful whether the use of proper names is purely denotative. But even if it were, this would not be a sufficient ground for denying meaning to them. For denotation has itself been taken to be a mode of meaning; indeed it has been held by nominalists to be the primary mode. Thus it has been suggested that the meaning of predicates is to be identified with their extension, and this amounts to saying that they are compendious proper names. This suggestion is not in fact acceptable. It is open to the objection that it makes all true statements analytic and to other objections as well. But the fact that our use of proper names has been so often taken as the standard case of meaning, the fact also that demonstratives like the words 'he' or 'this' or 'here', the use of which is also supposed to be purely denotative, are commonly said to have meaning, should make us try to find some better way of marking the difference between proper names and expressions of other types than by saying that they are not meaningful. I propose, therefore, to make light of ordinary usage in this instance, and allow myself to speak of the meaning of proper names.

What then is their meaning? This sounds a silly question. How could one answer it except by saying that as a rule different names have different meanings? If you will tell me what proper names you have in mind, then I will try to tell you what they severally mean. Nevertheless the question has been thought capable of being answered in general terms. It has been widely held that the meaning of a proper name is to be identified with the object which it denotes.

One reason for this is that normally names acquire their meaning only by being, as it were, affixed to the objects which they are then said to denote. We shall see in a

[1] *A System of Logic*, ch. ii, sec. 5.

moment that this is not in fact true of all proper names, but it is the standard case. Thus we speak of the 'bearer' of a name as though the name were a mark, like a street sign, which is physically carried by the thing, or person, named. Pointing to the bearer is then regarded as the essential way of teaching people to use the name. In many cases this is not possible ; we have to rely upon description, but this is thought to be an inferior substitute for the direct method. The fact that the meaning of common nouns like 'table' or adjectives like 'red' is also taught ostensively may be an explanation for the desire to assimilate words of these types to proper names, in their case also to identify meaning with extension. How great is the power of this theory is shown by the prevalence of primitive word magic. It is because the meaning of a name is identified with its bearer that knowledge of the name is supposed to yield power over the person who bears it, and an abuse of the name to be an injury to the person. It is for this reason that in many forms of religion the name of the deity is kept secret, that blasphemy, which is a disrespectful use of the deity's name, is thought to be a sin, that writing a man's name may be part of the process of laying a spell on him, that children are given the names of virtues or graces in the hope that they will grow up to possess them. The Bible is full of examples of this way of thinking ; for instance the sentence from Revelations, which is quoted by Ogden and Richards in their *Meaning of Meaning* : 'There were killed in the earthquake names of men seven thousand'.[1] Ogden and Richards remark that this is analogous to the practice of calling factory workers 'hands'. The name of a person is regarded as his most important feature.

But, whatever may be the motives for holding it, the theory is not defensible. For if the meaning of a name were identical with its bearer, then it would seem that everything

[1] p. 27.

that is true of the bearer must somehow be contained in the use of the name. On this view, when I say that 'Napoleon died at St. Helena,' I am implying also that he was born in Corsica, that he won the Battle of Austerlitz and lost the Battle of Waterloo, and all the rest of the infinite number of things that could truly be said about him. The result here again is that every true statement, in which an individual is mentioned by name, becomes analytic and every false statement contradictory. It remains contingent that Napoleon existed: but given that he existed, to say, for example, that he died at St. Helena would be analytic, because the assertion of this fact would already be implied by the use of the name, and the false statement that he did not die at St. Helena would be self-contradictory, for the same reason. Moreover, many true statements about Napoleon will also contain references to other persons, for example, the Duke of Wellington, or Talleyrand, and so will have to imply everything that is true about them as well. And since every person is in some way related to every other, if it be only spatio-temporally, then, on the assumption that they can all be named, any true statement about anybody who is named in it will imply the whole of human history; from which it will follow also that they are all equivalent. This view, or something very like it, was indeed held by Leibniz, but that does not save it from absurdity.

At this point it may be objected that the identification of the meaning of a name with its bearer does not imply that the use of a name commits us to asserting every fact about the person, or object, named but only to the assertion of those facts which are essential to its being the thing or person that it is. But the trouble with this is that there are no such facts. As we shall see later on, it can plausibly be argued that it is a necessary condition for understanding the use of a name that one should know some identifying fact about its bearer; but there is never any one fact, or any special set of facts, which is essential for this purpose. The most, therefore, that could be maintained in this way would be that the use of a name in a given context committed us to the assertion of whatever facts were taken as identifying the bearer on that occasion. But this leads to an inconsistency. For since the choice of identifying facts will vary, the use of the name will have different implications on different occasions, and to this extent the meaning of the name will be different. But if it is to be identified with the bearer it must remain the same.

In fact there are not many philosophers nowadays who would wish to identify the meaning of a name with its bearer. They have been taught by Wittgenstein that it is a mistake to suppose that the meaning of a proper name, or indeed of any linguistic expression, is a special type of object: instead of looking for meanings, in this sense, we should ask how the expression is used. There is, however, a consequence of this discredited view which is still very widely accepted. A proper name may not be thought to mean what it denotes; but it is still held that it must denote something in order to be meaningful. Thus Miss Anscombe, in her commentary on Wittgenstein's *Tractatus*, maintains that 'a genuine proper name must have a bearer'.[1] 'If', she says, 'a proper name has in fact no bearer in the use that is being made of it, then nothing has been ascribed to any object by sentences in which it occurs; and so nothing has been said, truly or falsely.'[2] In other words, proper names are used to refer to individuals, and they are meaningful only if the reference succeeds.

Now it is true that a proper name can have no use unless some attempt is made to denote something by it. If nothing would count as the bearer of the name, the sentences in which it figured in a referential rôle would indeed be

[1] *An Introduction to Wittgenstein's Tractatus*, p. 42. [2] *Ibid.* p. 41.

empty of content. It does not follow, however, that a sentence is being used to say nothing whenever it contains a proper name which attempts to denote an individual that does not in fact exist. On the contrary it seems quite clear to me that the sentence may be used to say exactly the same thing when the intended reference of the proper name fails as when it succeeds. For instance it has been maintained that Plato's Socrates is a literary invention, so that the person to whom we think we are referring when we use the name 'Socrates' did not in fact exist. I think this is a most unlikely theory, but that is not the point. The point is that if it were true it would not in the least entail that when people talked as they do about Socrates they were saying nothing. It is surely quite obvious that they would still be making meaningful statements; and, I should add, statements which had the same meaning whether the person they were supposed to be about existed or not. Of course, in this example, the existence or non-existence of Socrates would affect the truth-value of the statements which were supposed to be about him; but this is not to say that it would in any way affect their meaning. And this would apply, in my view, to all such uses of proper names. Whatever meaning the sentences into which they enter may have, it is consistent with it that the individuals to which they ostensibly refer should not in fact exist.

I wish to remark in passing that these cases are to be distinguished from those in which the individual referred to is understood to be fictitious. Names like 'Mr. Pickwick', as it occurs in Dickens's novel, are certainly meaningful, though there is a problem about their reference. It has been suggested that when we talk about a fictitious character, knowing it to be so, we are actually referring to the author, or to the work in which the character appears. But, apart from other obvious difficulties, this can hardly apply to the use of the name which is made by the author himself.

Even if our saying that Mr. Pickwick took a coach to Rochester were an elliptical way of saying that Dickens wrote a passage to this effect, or that it was so stated in the *Pickwick Papers*, this cannot have been what Dickens was saying; he was not writing about himself. Perhaps the correct answer is that these names have no reference. However, this is not a question that I wish to pursue here. The only point I want to make here is that the use of a name like 'Mr. Pickwick' differs from the normal use of a name like 'Socrates' in that it serves to make statements which make no claim upon fact. I mean by this that there is nothing that would count as showing that they were either true or false. If someone were to consult the waybills of the coach company in order to discover whether anyone answering to the description of Mr. Pickwick and his friends did travel to Rochester at the time in which Dickens set his story, he would be missing the point. Even if he discovered that this was so, he would not have proved that Mr. Pickwick really did travel to Rochester, but only that Dickens took his characters from life. It would be quite otherwise if 'Mr. Pickwick' were intended like 'Socrates' to be the name of an historical character. Thus the distinctive feature of the fictitious use of names is not that they have no reference, for this may also be true of names which are used historically, but that in what may be called their normal form the sentences in which they occur are not truth-claiming. It is only in the historical use of proper names that the question of the success or failure of the reference arises, as bearing on the truth of the statements which they help to express. And it is only with this use of proper names that I am concerned in this paper.

The mistake which Miss Anscombe has made, in the passage which I quoted, is that of pouring new wine into an old bottle. She assumes a fashionable theory of reference, according to which, in a case where a sentence would express a referential statement if the reference succeeded, it is a pre-condition of the truth or falsehood of the statement that the reference should succeed, that is, that the individual ostensibly named or described should really exist; and she combines this with loyalty to the law of excluded middle, that is, with the assumption that every statement is either true or false. The result is that when what purports to be a proper name, the name of a historical character, or place, or other object, has no denotation, she concludes that a speaker who assigns to it the rôle of designating the subject of a statement is not saying anything; that since what he affects to state is neither true nor false, he does not make any statement at all.

The same line, indeed, is taken by Mr. P. F. Strawson, who is the chief proponent of this theory of reference.[1] He distinguishes carefully between a sentence, the use of a sentence, and the statement which the sentence may be used to make; and he maintains that when a sentence is used in such a way that it purports to refer to something, it does not express a statement unless the object to which it ostensibly refers exists. His ground for this is that, in the case where the object in question does not exist, he does not think it proper to say that the sentence is being used to state anything which is either true or false. But, as I have already argued, this is not a sufficient ground for denying that the sentence is being used to make a statement. The right course, for those who wish to adopt this theory of reference, is rather to sacrifice the law of excluded middle. They cannot plausibly deny that a sentence of the form 'S is P', where 'S' is a proper name or a definite descriptive phrase, expresses the same statement whether 'S' denotes anything or not. They can, however, claim that it is only in the case where 'S' does denote something that the statement is either true or false; true if what is denoted by 'S'

[1] *Vide* 'On Referring', *Mind*, vol. lix, no. 235, July 1950.

does have the property designated by 'P' and false if it does not. In the case where 'S' does not denote anything the statement is neither true nor false; one might call it a non-starter. Thus the sentence 'Robin Hood was an outlaw', when used historically, expresses a statement, and the same statement, whether or not Robin Hood really existed; the statement is, however, a non-starter if Robin Hood did not exist.

I think that this is a tenable position. The law of excluded middle is not sacrosanct; it is open to us to admit the possibility that statements may be neither true nor false, if there is anything to be gained by this step. In the present instance, what we are supposed to gain is a more adequate theory of reference. I doubt, however, if this theory of reference is more adequate than one which preserves the law of excluded middle. So far as I can see, apart from some criticisms of Russell's theory of descriptions which do not directly bear on this issue, the only argument which Mr. Strawson and his followers have produced in favour of their theory is that it is in better accordance with the way in which the words 'true' and 'false' are used by most people. It is claimed that people are not in general willing to say that a statement of the form 'S is P' is false unless there is a designated individual S which lacks the property P. In the case where the individual in question does not exist, they would say that the question of truth and falsehood did not arise, which might be taken as a way of saying that the statement was neither true nor false. Now this may be so. It is a matter for sociological investigation which, so far as I know, has not yet been made. My conjecture is that opinion would be found to be fairly evenly divided, but that perhaps the balance would come down on Mr. Strawson's side. But even if it could be shown that the theory was favoured by ordinary usage, this would not be decisive. It might still be that the theory had inconvenient consequences which more than offset this rather slight advantage. And, in fact, I think that this is so.

One of these consequences is that a strain is placed on the relation between asserting a statement and asserting the statement to be true. There may be various opinions about the effect of prefixing a statement 'S' with the expression 'It is true that', but one would not ordinarily think that it could produce a change of truth-value. It seems obvious that whatever the truth-value of 'S' the truth-value of 'It is true that S' must be the same. But if we introduce a category of non-starters, it will be hard to avoid drawing the conclusion that 'S' and 'It is true that S' may have different truth-values: for in the case where 'S' is a non-starter, it would seem to follow that 'It is true that S' is false. This objection can be met by contending that if the question of the truth or falsehood of 'S' does not arise, the question of the truth or falsehood of 'It is true that S' does not arise either; if one is a non-starter, so is the other. But this view has the very awkward consequence that the statement that 'It is true that S' will not necessarily be equivalent even in truth-value to the statement that 'S' has the truth-value 'true': for if 'S' is a non-starter this latter statement must be false. Now if we retain the law of excluded middle these difficulties are avoided.

In justice to Mr. Strawson, it should be remarked that he escapes this objection by denying that the statements which I have called non-starters are statements at all. For if 'S' is not a statement, it can plausibly be argued that to predicate truth of 'S', in whatever fashion, is not to make a statement either. However, the view that a would-be referential statement ceases to be a statement if the reference fails is one that I have already given reasons for rejecting.

There is another objection to the admission of non-starters, which also holds against the view that they are not genuine statements. In many cases where a sentence has for its subject a referential expression which fails to denote anything, the sentence can be reformulated in such a way that it is given a subject which has a denotation. Thus, to take a familiar example from Russell's Theory of Descriptions,[1] the sentence 'The present King of France is bald' can be transformed into the sentence 'France at present has one and only one king and no king who is not bald'. Now it may be claimed that these two sentences do not express equivalent statements, perhaps just on the ground that the longer sentence is used to assert what the use of the shorter sentence presupposes, namely the existence of a present King of France. Even so, it seems to me that they are close enough in meaning to make it unsatisfactory to hold that whereas the sentence which has 'France' for its subject expresses a false statement, the other sentence either expresses no statement at all or else expresses a statement which is neither true nor false. If this has to be balanced against the slight affront to ordinary usage which might result from agreeing with Russell that sentences like 'The present King of France is bald' are to be construed as expressing false statements, I should have little hesitation in coming down on Russell's side.

But, whatever may be the case with definite descriptions, is there not something counterfeit about a proper name which does not denote? Might it not be said that the use of proper names in fiction is a mimicry of the use of genuine proper names? And should we not regard the failure of reference, in the historical use, as a degenerate case? The answer is that this can be done. We can introduce the notion of a genuine proper name and stipulate that a name is to be regarded as genuine only if it succeeds in its reference; that is, only if the individual to which it

[1] *Vide, Principia Mathematica* (2nd ed.), vol. i, pp. 30 ff., 66 ff., 193 ff., and *Introduction to Mathematical Philosophy*, ch. 16.

is intended to refer exists. But this procedure, though feasible, would be misleading. For one would expect the distinction between genuine and false proper names to be a semantic distinction ; one would expect it to turn upon the meaning of the names in question. But if the mark of a genuine name is to be just that it denotes, then the distinction will not be semantic but historical, in my extended sense of this term. There is a semantic distinction, at least prima facie, between terms which are used referentially, that is for the purpose of designating an individual, and terms which are used predicatively ; I say a prima facie distinction because we still have to consider how far the first class can be reduced to the second. But whether a term of the referential type succeeds in its reference, whether the individuals which are intended to be named by such appellations as 'King Arthur' or 'Socrates' or 'the present King of France' really exist or not is not at all a question of semantics but a question of historical fact. I think, therefore, that we should avoid talking in a way that muddles these questions up. To say that proper names are genuine only if they denote is to allow matters of fact to encroach on the territory of meaning. It would be as if we were to say that a predicate was genuine only if it had instances. But, semantically, 'being a centaur' is just as 'good' a predicate as 'being a lion'. It just happens to be the case, biologically, that there are lions and there are not centaurs.

Furthermore, in the case of proper names at least, it is not altogether clear what is to count as a successful reference. Plainly it is not enough that there should be some individual to whom, or to which, the name is commonly applied. It is not enough even that there should be just one individual who satisfies this condition. For the speaker might be using the name to apply to someone or to something else. It has to be the individual that the speaker means the name to apply to, the individual that he has in mind when he uses the name. But how is this to be determined? There is a story told of Warden Spooner that after preaching a sermon he returned to the pulpit and announced, 'Whenever in the course of my sermon I said "Aristotle" I meant "St. Paul"'. Such a case presents us with no great difficulty. It was a mere slip, or series of slips, of the tongue. Even if Dr. Spooner had been under the illusion, while he was giving his sermon, that St. Paul was called Aristotle, it might still have been clear that he was referring to St. Paul. This would be a strange mistake to make in this instance, but it is of a type which is quite common. It goes beyond a mere slip of the tongue in that it manifests the false belief that the individual of whom such and such things are true is called by a name by which it would in fact be incorrect to call him: incorrect in the sense that on the strength of the name alone one would be taken to be referring to someone else. But so long as a particular individual is clearly identified by the statements that are made, identified in the sense that they are true of him and him only, then we say that this is the individual that is being referred to, no matter what name is used. It would, however, be a great mistake to think that even this condition is always satisfied. If a schoolboy is asked to write an essay about Dickens and shows up an answer in which he gives a fairly accurate account of Scott's life and character and also discusses the Waverley novels, one can say that he has written about Scott and just been unlucky enough to think that he was called 'Dickens'. One might still say this if together with the Waverley novels he discussed the *Pickwick Papers*. But if he wrote of a Londoner who settled in Edinburgh, became a lawyer, enjoyed amateur theatricals, wrote *Pickwick Papers* and *Bleak House* and *Ivanhoe* and *Marmion*, went bankrupt through the failure of his publishers, and left his wife for an actress, all we could say would be that he had thoroughly mixed up Dickens and Scott, not that he really meant to refer to either one of them. In this instance, one might say that he had both of them in mind, but clearly it would be easy to construct examples in which, though everything that was said was true of someone, so many different individuals were involved that it could not properly be said that the speaker had any one of them in mind. In these cases no one is identified ; from our present point of view, however, they are less interesting than the intermediate cases in which it is not clear whether we are to say that someone has been identified but a lot of false statements have been made about him, or simply that the reference fails.

The source of these puzzles does not just lie in the fact that proper names have no determinate connotation. It is rather that there is nothing by which an individual is essentially identified, no set of properties the possession of which makes him the individual that he is. If there were, then the criterion for the individual's having been successfully identified would be just that these properties were ascribed to him ; we should probably then use proper names in such a way that they were understood to connote such properties. As things are, there is no sharp distinction between making false statements about someone who has been successfully identified, and failing to identify anyone at all. If enough of what is said applies to a single individual, and it is sufficiently distinctive of him, and it is not mixed up with too much falsehood, then he has been identified. If a proper name is used to refer to him, the reference is successful. But how much is enough, what is sufficiently distinctive, how far one can go wrong without failing to identify, are questions that have to be settled *ad hoc*. It is not possible to lay down any general rules.

The fact that proper names do not have any fixed connotation makes it technically wrong to say, as Russell does, that they are abbreviations for descriptions, if what is understood here by a description is some piece of information which individuates the bearer of the name. The statement that Sir William Hamilton was a Scotsman cannot be equivalent to the statement that the man who invented the Quantification of the Predicate was a Scotsman, even when it is put forward by someone who knows nothing else about him. For it is not a necessary truth that Sir William Hamilton invented the Quantification of the Predicate. This is not to say, however, that descriptions of this kind do not give us all we need, that we should sacrifice anything vital if we renounced the use of proper names. We should not be able to make exactly the same statements; but it might be argued that we could still do equal justice to the facts. This is an important question, which I shall try to answer later on.

It might be thought that one could eliminate proper names, and yet preserve the sense of the statements in which they occurred, by adopting Quine's device of introducing special *ad hoc* predicates which would be attributed to various individuals just in virtue of their being the individuals that they are.[1] Thus the statement 'Brutus killed Caesar' would be rewritten as 'The one and only thing that is Brutus killed the one and only thing that is Caesar', and this would be expanded in the way laid down by the theory of descriptions. This device would not yield more than a paraphrase if 'being Brutus' were itself a mere abbreviation for some set of predicates which do in fact serve to identify Brutus; for in that case 'Brutus' and 'the one and only thing that is Brutus' would clearly not be synonymous. But it might be held that 'being Brutus' could be introduced not as a conjunction of other more familiar predicates, but as a primitive predicate the use of

[1] *Vide* 'On What There Is', *Review of Metaphysics*, 1948. Reprinted in *From A Logical Point of View*. Also *Word and Object*, ch. ii.

which, in the most favourable circumstances, could be learned ostensively. Even so I do not think that this could be a way of obtaining synonymity. For if to say that Brutus is the one and only thing that is Brutus is just a way of saying that Brutus is Brutus, then 'being Brutus' is not a genuine predicate; but if it is a genuine predicate it must, unless there is some indication to the contrary, be general in its application: there must be no limit to the number of objects that could fall within its range. I say 'unless there is some indication to the contrary' because there are predicates like 'being the first man to land on the moon', 'being the tallest man in the room', which are explicitly restricted. They apply to only one thing, if they apply to anything at all. But they are only apparent exceptions to our rule, for it is essential that they contain a predicate like 'being a lander on the moon', or 'being taller than such and such other men', which is unrestricted. Consequently, it must be possible for more than one thing to be Brutus, or else to satisfy the unrestricted predicate that 'being Brutus' contains. But since it is not possible, as proper names of this sort are ordinarily used, for more than one thing to be denoted by the name, the equivalence has not been established.

In fact, I do not suppose that this conclusion would very much worry Quine. He would not claim that the use of his device preserved synonymity, the notion of which he in any case regards as suspect. He would claim only that his predicates could serve us just as well as the use of proper names. But since the same claim can be made for more conventional descriptions, the introduction of these highly artificial predicates appears to have no point.

There is, however, one point of interest that emerges from the suggestion that the use of such predicates could be learned ostensively. It is tempting to think that even though proper names are not synonymous with definite descriptions, they are dependent on them for their meaning. The suggestion is that it is a necessary condition of the significant use or understanding of a proper name that one should be able to furnish some description of the individual to which the name refers. Thus Mr. Strawson says in his book on *Individuals* that 'a name is worthless without a backing of descriptions which can be produced on demand to explain its application'.[1] No doubt it would be too much to require that these descriptions should always characterize the individual uniquely, though so long as they did not the use of the name might be charged with ambiguity; but if one were unable to give any description whatever of the individual in question, how could one be said to understand the name at all?

The answer to this is that in order to understand the use of a proper name one must know which individual it is intended to refer to; but this knowledge need not consist in the ability to furnish a verbal description of the individual in question. It may be enough that one picks out the right person, or object, when the occasion arises. A child who learns to call its brother by name does not have to be able to formulate true propositions about him before it can be said to use the name correctly. In this matter there is no difference between the understanding of proper names and the understanding of predicates which are learned ostensively.

Not all names, however, can be learned ostensively. In very many cases the names which one uses refer to individuals which one has not been in a position to observe; and then we do acquire the use of the name by learning to associate it with some description. This is indeed a practical rather than a logical necessity. It is after all a contingent fact that our understanding of the use of both names and predicates is not innate. The consideration of the ways

[1] p. 20.

in which words are learned is often a useful clue to the ways in which they function, but the two questions must be kept distinct. Even in practice the fact that one has acquired the understanding of a name by being told that its bearer satisfies a given description does not entail that one must have this, or indeed any other, description actually in mind when one uses or interprets the name correctly. It is not even logically necessary that one should be able to furnish a description, when asked to explain the reference of the name, so long as one could pick out the right individual if one were given the opportunity. On the other hand, this is a feat that one would hardly be capable of accomplishing in the case of an individual one had never in fact encountered, unless one were able to describe this individual in some way or other. I do not think, however, that this is a point of any great theoretical importance.

What is important is the fact that, whether or not one is able in the absence of an object to give a verbal description of the features by which one would distinguish it, it is its possession of these features that makes it recognizable. There is no possible way of inspecting an individual object without inspecting its properties. Thus one sense in which names may be said to need the backing of descriptions is that it is only because its bearer answers to description that a name can fulfil its function. To say that each individual object must satisfy a unique description would be to assume the identity of indiscernibles which has not been conclusively shown to be a logical necessity. But even if the identity of indiscernibles could conceivably fail to hold, it remains true that it is only their distinctive features, among which I include their spatio-temporal properties, that actually enable us to distinguish one object from another. This does not imply that the identifying description need actually be formulated, but only that it is theoretically available. Whether it follows that names are replaceable by descriptions is a question which we have still to consider.

Another point of interest is that it is only through their connection with descriptions that proper names can fail in their reference. A proper name fails in its reference if the individual to which it is intended to refer does not exist. But this comes about only if the description by which it would be individuated is not satisfied.

It was for this reason, I believe, that Russell came to take the view that ordinary proper names like 'London' or 'Socrates' were convertible into descriptions. He saw that such names could fail in their reference and therefore that their meaning did not depend upon their denotation. But then, instead of giving up the attempt to identify the meaning of a name with its bearer, he merely drew the conclusion that these were not genuine names. As Strawson has pointed out,[1] it was because Russell did equate the meaning, at least of referential expressions, with their denotation that he thought it necessary to explain how expressions like 'the present King of France', which had no denotation, could still be meaningful, and this was perhaps his main motive for developing his theory of definite descriptions. For the reasons which I have given, I think that this motive was mistaken ; but, of course, this does not necessarily invalidate the theory of descriptions itself.

Since Russell believed, correctly, that the analysis of definite descriptive phrases like 'the author of Waverley' or 'the present King of France' must be the same, whether they happened to succeed in their reference or not, he was led by his theory of meaning to conclude that the apparent reference of such descriptions, and consequently of the proper names which he thought were convertible into such descriptions, could not be their real reference. The objects to which all these expressions really referred were those that satisfied the functions which stood at the lowest level in his

[1] *Vide* 'On Referring'.

hierarchy ; the functions at which we finally arrive when all descriptive phrases have been unpacked into the appropriate predicates and all the predicates reduced to their most simple constituents. The individuals which satisfy these predicates will then be designated by what Russell calls 'logically proper names'. And what is required of a logically proper name is not just that it succeeds in denoting something, but rather that its having a denotation is a necessary condition of its being meaningful.

We may note that this is a point at which Russell's logic makes contact with his epistemology. For among indicative expressions, the only ones that could with any plausibility be taken for logically proper names are pure demonstratives : the objects for which they stand must therefore be observable, and they must also be such that the reference of the name is guaranteed against illusion. Now the only objects which satisfy these conditions, except perhaps for one's self, are sense-data ; and in fact it is to sense-data that Russell makes his logically proper names refer. A further point of interest is that for Russell the objects of acquaintance also included universals ; and though I do not think that he anywhere says that he regards predicates as logically proper names, it would be consistent for him to do so. For if we take predicates as denoting not their extensions, the objects which are characterized by the properties for which they stand, but these properties themselves, then they are bound to have denotations if they have meaning ; to say that they are meaningful will entail that there are properties for which they stand. But whether it is correct to regard predicates as the names of properties is another question.

Setting predicates aside, does our language provide us with any examples of logically proper names ? The obvious candidates are demonstratives like 'this' 'I' 'here' 'now', but if the condition of their being logically proper names is that they must have a denotation on each occasion of their use, it is doubtful if they satisfy it. The difficulty is that they can all be used to sustain illusions of one sort or another. For example, the tailors in the Hans Andersen story of the Emperor's clothes would have been using the word 'this' in the ordinary way if they had said, 'This is a particularly fine coat', but since the coat did not exist and nobody believed that he saw it, the demonstrative would not in fact have referred to anything; not to any physical object and not even to any sense-data. The demonstrative 'I' is in a stronger position since the fact that someone uses it correctly entails that its reference succeeds. It can, however, be put into the mouth of a fictitious person, whether or not the fiction is avowed. Similarly the word 'here' can be used to refer to an imaginary place, and I think, though this is more disputable, that there are cases in which one could say that the word 'now' was being used to refer to an imaginary time. We could indeed ensure that all these demonstratives were logically proper names by requiring no more of a logically proper name than that it should succeed in denoting something on every genuine occasion of its use, and then interpreting the word 'genuine' in such a way as to exclude the use of these words in dreams or in fiction or even for the purpose of pretence. There would, however, be little point in this procedure. The meaning of demonstratives is given not by their denotation but by their function. In a given context, they serve to call attention to the identity of the speaker, or to his spatio-temporal position, or to some object in his immediate environment. These devices would not be useful unless they commonly succeeded but we do not have to insist on their being infallible. The fact that they can also serve to mislead, or that their use can, as it were, be parodied does not raise any serious problems.

It is not difficult, however, to see why Russell felt the

need for logically proper names, even apart from his identifying meaning with denotation. For if one pursues the technique of his theory of descriptions to its theoretical limit, one must come in the end to names which have no connotations, simply because if there is any connotation it is transformed into a predicate and assigned to the body of the function. And from this it might very well be thought to follow that the ultimate replacements for the signs which stand for variables in the lowest level functions must be logically proper names, because their rôle is purely demonstrative. For what does '$f\alpha$' add to '$(Ex) fx$' ? *Ex hypothesi* the name 'α' has no descriptive content; for whatever content it had would turn into a predicative expression, 'f'. It therefore cannot fail to identify in the obvious way, by purporting to describe what in fact does not exist. Its function is simply to point to something, and if it fails to do this it has no meaning. It is like a gesture and may in practice have the ambiguity that gestures have; but it cannot fail to indicate something, any more than a gesture can fail.

There are two questions at issue here. The first, which we have already dealt with to some extent in our discussion of the use of ordinary demonstratives, is whether gesticulatory expressions are logically bound to have a reference. The second and more interesting question is whether there is any logical need for such expressions at all. Why should not the Russellian analysis be allowed to terminate in statements of the form '$(Ex) fx$' ?

Why not indeed? The proposal is that we should replace ordinary proper names by descriptions and that we should then dispense with purely demonstrative expressions. As a result we should obtain a language in which only general statements could be made. We could say that there was something, and, if we were bolder, only one thing that had the property f, but if we wanted to go further and say *what* it was that had the property *f* all we could do would be to say that it was a thing or the thing that had *g*, thereby obtaining the statement 'There is just one thing that has *f* and *g*' and so on. All our attempts to pin down the subject would merely serve to enlarge the predicate. In other words, things would be identified only through their properties. What are the objections to this ?

Let us first be clear what question is at issue. It is not suggested that all the sentences which are formulated in a language which contains singular terms and other demonstrative expressions can be translated without alteration of meaning into one which does not contain them. We have already seen that the replacement of proper names by descriptions does not preserve synonymity, and the same would apply to the replacement of spatio-temporal indicators, including tenses, by spatio-temporal predicates. The statement that I am writing these lines here and now is at best only paraphrased by a statement to the effect that a person answering to a certain description also has the property of being the writer of such and such a series of words at a place and time which stand in such and such relations to other places and times, these other places and times being themselves identified by descriptions of the things which occupy them. The question is whether such paraphrases are adequate in the sense that they can be made to provide at least as much information as the statements which they paraphrase. They are bound to be more prolix, since everything that the use of demonstrative expressions leaves to be picked up from the context has to be made explicit. The question is whether there is anything that cannot be made explicit by this means. To put it another way, is the narrative function that demonstrative expressions fulfil merely a function of economy ?

The obvious answer to this is that the primary function of demonstratives is not to diminish prolixity but to locate the individuals to which we intend to refer. How then will this work be done if we eliminate singular terms ? When we try to test the statements which we make in our non-referential language how shall we know where to look ? We can be given spatio-temporal directions, but only in an indefinite form. We may be told that there is an *x* which has the property *f*, and a *y* which has the property *g*, and that *x* is so many spatial units away from *y* in a direction fixed by their spatial relations to other unnamed individuals at a time which is so many temporal units earlier or later than such and such an event which occurred in the history of another individual z, which again is identified only by description. Unless we have the good fortune to light upon one or more of these individuals, we are left with a set of wandering adjectives, as Bradley put it, which we cannot fasten on to reality.

But is this so very different from the position in which we actually find ourselves ? We rely very largely for our orientation on the use of place-names and of dates, but their reference is not self-explanatory. We have to be able to identify the places and times which they denote. But we identify places by identifying the things which occupy them, or the things which occupy other places to which we can specify their relation, and we identify times by identifying the events which occur at them, or more commonly by specifying their relation to other times which are identified by events which function as landmarks in a temporal system ; and these objects and events are recognizable by their distinctive properties. But in that case, if we can give an unique description of these objects and events, it should serve us just as well as if we named them. It is true that in a non-referential language we lack the services of tenses and of words like 'here' and 'now' by means of which we indicate our own position and so can proceed to locate other things by their relation to ourselves. But if we can describe landmarks by reference to which we can fix the spatio-temporal position of anything we please, including ourselves, the lack of this egocentric method of orientation would hardly seem to be a serious deficiency.

An advantage which is claimed for singular terms is that they guarantee uniqueness of reference in a way that descriptions cannot. This guarantee is logical rather than practical. In practice the use of a description often allows less opportunity for misunderstanding than the use of a proper name, just because of its greater explicitness : demonstratives give more security, but even their use can be misinterpreted. I am not thinking here of the trivial point that any symbol at all is liable to misconstruction, but rather of the fact that knowledge of the rules which govern the use of demonstratives like 'this' and 'here' may not be enough in some contexts to remove all uncertainty about their intended reference. Still, these practical difficulties are not insuperable, and once they are overcome there remains no logical risk of ambiguity, either in the case of demonstratives or in that of proper names. For it is a presupposition of the correct use of these singular terms that if they refer to anything at all they refer to it uniquely. There cannot be more than one Julius Caesar. Of course any number of people can be called 'Julius Caesar' but that is another matter. What I say about Julius Caesar cannot be falsified by the fact that it fails to apply to anyone else who is called by the same name. If someone takes my statement to refer to one of these other persons, he has just misunderstood me. On the other hand, if I individuate only by description, so that part of what I assert is that there is just one thing that has a certain property, my statement will be falsified if there is more than one ; if I have chosen the description carefully, the practical danger of this may be very small ; but it will always remain a logical possibility.

But why is this thought to be objectionable? The reason seems to be that while we want our statements to be open to falsification, we do not want them to be falsified in what might be called the wrong way. A statement would be falsified in the right way only if we in fact picked out the right individual, the individual to which its author intended the statement to refer, and found that this individual lacked the further property which the statement ascribed to it. But if we are employing a non-referential language, any individual which satisfies our identifying description is the right individual. In practice, the misunderstandings which could result from this would not be more serious than those which result from different individuals having the same name: they could generally be cleared up by a little further explanation. But it may be thought that there is a theoretical point at issue. How much does it matter theoretically that we can never be sure that any description is uniquely satisfied?

The answer is that if our requirement is just that our statements be falsifiable, or even that they be falsifiable in what I have called the right way, it does not matter at all. For suppose that we are asserting that there is just one individual which has the property *f*, and that this individual which has the property *f* also has the property *g*: and suppose that we come across an individual which has the property *f* but lacks the property *g*. Then there is no question but that our assertion is false. For either this *is* the only thing that has *f*, in which case our assertion is falsified by its not also having *g*, or it is not the only thing which has *f*, in which case our assertion is falsified on this ground alone. We do not have to bother with the question whether we have hit upon the right individual: for if we have found a single case of *f* unconjoined with *g*, we know then it cannot be true of any individual that it alone has *f* and also has *g*.

If there is a difficulty with regard to testing statements of this form, it relates rather to the possibility of their being verified. For here it does matter that we can never be sure that there are no other things which have the identifying property besides the one which we have found. We might attempt to palliate this by saying that it is not to be expected that verification should be conclusive; but the objection, for what it is worth, is not just that the statements which we can express in our non-referential language cannot be conclusively verified, but rather that they cannot be so strongly verified as the referential statements which they are supposed to paraphrase. In both cases we have to satisfy ourselves, subject always to the possibility of error, that a designated individual exists and that it has such and such a property. But whereas, in the case of a referential language, this is all that we have to do, in the other case it is not. We have still to establish that our identifying description does apply uniquely; and this is something of which, short of inspecting the whole universe, we cannot make absolutely sure.

In view of this, it might seem to be advantageous to avoid making the claim that our identifying descriptions are uniquely satisfied. We should in fact choose descriptions which we believed to apply to only one individual, but we should not explicitly assert that this was so. Our basic statements would be of the simple form: '$(Ex) fx . gx$'. Now clearly there is no special problem about verifying statements of this kind. All that we have to do is to find some individual which has both f and g. But our gain would be set off by a more than equal loss; for not only would the question about finding the 'right' individual be revived but these statements would not be falsifiable; we should have to inspect the whole universe in order to establish that there was nothing which had both f and g. It might be suggested that we could meet this difficulty by falling back upon some social convention, which would allow us under certain specified conditions to count such statements as being at least provisionally falsified. But if we are going to have to introduce a convention of this sort, we should do better to retain the uniqueness clause and let the convention govern the acceptance of statements rather than their rejection. Thus the ruling might be that a statement of the form '$(Ex) fx . (y) fy \supset y = x : gx$' should count as being provisionally verified if there were found to be just one thing, either in the neighbourhood of the speaker or in a specified relation to some other identified individual which had the property f, and the thing which satisfied these conditions also had the property g. That a convention of this kind would be quite innocuous is shown by the fact that if the uniqueness clause is violated, if we come across more than one individual which has the property f, we have only to select some property the possession of which differentiates one of these individuals from the other, and modify our identifying description so that, to the best of our knowledge, it uniquely fits the individual which we wish to single out. And this procedure can be repeated whenever the occasion for it arises.

But do we not then face the objection that our theory commits us to the identity of indiscernibles? The answer is that it does not commit us to maintaining anything more than that there is no way of discovering that two individuals are different except by discovering that they have different properties. We do not have to accept the stronger principle that there cannot *be* two different individuals each of which satisfies exactly the same list of purely indefinite descriptions, unless we also adopt Russell's definition of identity from which this conclusion follows. And this definition can be rejected as Wittgenstein rejected it in the *Tractatus* on the ground that 'even if this proposition [that two objects have all their properties in common] is never true it is nevertheless significant'.[1] If we take this view we are indeed left with no criterion of identity; we have to treat merely numerical differences as a primitive notion. But so far as this goes, one is no better off if one brings in logically proper names. The only difference that it would make is that instead of merely being able to entertain the hypothesis that there are two things which satisfy all the same descriptions, one would have the means of severally naming these things in the impossible event of one's ever finding them. In neither case would there be any possibility of specifying how they differed. Whether in these circumstances it would not be preferable to admit the identity of indiscernibles is a question into which I shall not enter here.

An objection of a different order to this whole enterprise is that it is not at all clear what purpose it fulfils. It can hardly be claimed that there is any practical advantage in employing a language without singular terms. Neither, on theoretical grounds, do we need anything so drastic as a means of coping with the fact that a referential expression may fail in its denotation. But in that case what philosophical interest is being served?

I think that the answer to this is that if a programme of this sort can be successfully carried out, it vindicates the belief that what can be shown can also be said. To speak a little more precisely, it proves that it is possible to free the interpretation of all narrative statements from any dependence upon their context of utterance; everything that we are ordinarily required to pick up from these contexts can be made explicit. This concords with the assumption that all that should really be necessary for understanding whatever a given language has the resources to communicate, at least in the way of factual information, is the knowledge of the rules which govern it: the identities and the spatio-temporal positions of the persons who employ it need not

[1] *Tractatus Logico-Philosophicus*, 5. 5302.

come into the picture: the language can be so reconstructed that the same sentence can correctly be employed to make the same statement by any speaker at any place at any time. If this is true, it follows that the demonstrative function which is performed by the use of tenses or pronouns or words like 'here' and 'now', or occasionally by proper names, is not indispensable. As I have already said, these are economical devices; but what they serve to indicate could in theory be spelled out.

I accept this thesis. The only drawback which we have found it to involve is that the claim that a given description is uniquely satisfied cannot be conclusively established; so that in deciding when to accept a statement which includes a uniqueness clause, we shall have to rely upon conventions which fall outside the rules of the language itself. We have seen, however, that these conventions are innocuous, since there is a corrective procedure which comes into operation if ever they lead us to a false result. The part that they play is not an infringement of the thesis that the statements which are expressible in any contextual language can be adequately paraphrased in an abstract language, the mark of an abstract language being that nothing more is needed for the understanding of it than a knowledge of its semantic rules. For these conventions relate only to the acceptability of statements, not to their interpretation.

No doubt the main reason why it is thought that an abstract language cannot be an adequate substitute for a contextual language is to be found in the belief that a language without demonstrative expressions would offer us no anchor in reality. But the answer to this is that we already have an anchor if our language is such that its rules allow us to correlate its predicates with types of empirical situations. Moreover it should not be overlooked that the anchor which the use of demonstratives affords us is a shifting anchor. For the reference of words like 'here' and 'now' varies from person to person, and from moment to moment. Consequently, if all referential statements have ultimately to be reduced to statements which indicate the spatio-temporal position of the speaker, it will usually not be possible for the same referential statement to be expressed by different speakers, or by the same speaker at different times. In practice this will not be a great handicap to communication: it will not be hard to supply the extra premisses which will secure identity of reference. But it does mean that the guarantee of uniqueness of reference, which the use of demonstratives is intended to secure for us, is less straightforward than it is often taken to be.

This difficulty is avoided in the cases where we rely for our spatio-temporal orientation upon public landmarks; but this gain may be thought to be offset by a theoretical loss in security. We can designate the landmarks by proper names, but, as we have seen, the use of a proper name does not absolutely guarantee the existence of the object or event which it purports to denote. It does presuppose that if its reference succeeds, it succeeds uniquely, but this presupposition is effective only on the condition that the descriptions which give backing to the name do genuinely individuate. But then the name offers no better security than the descriptions. It is useless unless the object which it designates is recognizably unique; and all that can make an object recognizably unique is the possession of some unique feature which a description can pick out. In either case we have to admit at least the logical possibility that the object so described is duplicated, as well as the possibility that it does not exist.

In view of this it would seem that if we really feel the want of an absolute guarantee of uniqueness, the best procedure might be simply to forge one. Having identified various things, or events, as standing in various spatio-temporal relations to one another, we can then give the whole system a fictitious point of origin. The uniqueness of the things which we have identified is then guaranteed by the fact that if anything else is found to answer to the same description it is just denied the postulated relation to the point of origin. The name or description by which the point of origin is itself referred to is not taken seriously. That is to say, nothing will be allowed to count as a failure in its reference or as a misplaced success. If we find that something does answer to the description, but that it stands in the wrong relation to the other identified events, we shall simply allow it to take its place in the system, without ceasing to regard the point of origin as unique.

We can, indeed, find an illustration of this in our actual system of dating. It is now generally agreed that if a person answering sufficiently to the description of Jesus Christ existed at all, he was born in the year 4 B.C. On the face of it, this hypothesis is self-contradictory, but we do not so regard it ; neither do we infer from it that it is, for instance, false that the Battle of Waterloo was fought in the year A.D. 1815 since it was in fact fought not in the 1815th but in the 1819th year of the series which started in the year in which Christ was born. The reason for this is that once we have got the system working, the relation of its constituents to the alleged common point of origin is not treated as a question of fact, but as a matter of convention. What remains as a question of fact is the relation of the constituents to one another.

It can be seen that if we have conventions of this kind, we can dispense with the conventions which are needed in an abstract language to decide when any statement is to count as being sufficiently established. In fact the two sets of conventions operate in very similar fashions. Neither would be workable unless the world presented us with a number of objects and events which are as it were conspicuous for their idiosyncrasy. In the one case, we allow ourselves to take it for granted that their salient features are not duplicated ; in the other, we make sure of this with the help of an appropriate fiction. I shall not here attempt to weigh the relative merits of these two procedures. The question with which we have chiefly been concerned is not whether an abstract language can match a referential language in convenience, but whether it can equally satisfy our criterion of adequacy ; and I think the answer is that it can.

It is to be noted finally that our Russellian language, though abstract, is not wholly adjectival. I believe that an underlying motive for getting rid of singular terms is a desire to dispense with the category of substance. To show that all the work of singular terms could be done by predicates would be a way of vindicating Berkeley's thesis that things are bundles of qualities. We have not, however, gone so far as this. Though we have developed a language in which no particular individual can be the subject of any statement, it would not be true to say that individuals are not mentioned in it at all. They are mentioned indefinitely by means of the quantified variables. These individuals are exactly like Lockean substances, since the work which the variables perform is first that of making it possible for us to entertain the idea of purely numerical diversity, and so to avoid committing ourselves to the identity of indiscernibles, and secondly, and more importantly, that of tying predicates together. Now it seems likely that this second task could be accomplished by some combinatorial relation between predicates, so that, if one were prepared to assume the identity of indiscernibles, it should be possible to develop an adequate language of a purely adjectival character. Some steps have indeed been taken towards this end, but so far as I know, no satisfactory theory of this kind has yet been worked out in detail. Until this has been accomplished, or else shown to be impossible, the tenability of the thesis that things are nothing more than bundles of qualities remains an open question.

6
TRUTH

AT first sight there is nothing very puzzling about the concept of truth. It is not clear why there should be any need to look further than the straightforward account which Aristotle gave of it; 'To say of what is that it is not, or of what is not that it is, is false, while to say of what is that it is, or of what is not that it is not, is true.'[1] In modern dress, this has developed into Tarski's formula: '"*p*" is true in L if and only if *p*',[2] which is exemplified in such unexciting statements as that the sentence 'snow is white' is true in English if and only if snow is white. There are indeed objections to making truth a predicate of sentences, as opposed to the statements or propositions which the sentences express; the most serious being that sentences which contain pronouns, or demonstratives, or proper nouns, or tensed verbs, are used to make different statements on different occasions, so that a sentence like 'I have a headache' will be both true and false according as it refers to different persons or to different times. It follows that, if we wish to predicate truth of sentences without falling into inconsistency, we have to free our language from dependence upon context, to replace proper names and pronouns by descriptions and to employ spatio-temporal

[1] *Metaphysics*, p. 7, 27.

[2] *Vide* A. Tarski, 'The Concept of Truth in Formalized Languages', in *Logic, Semantics, Metamathematics*, and 'The Semantic Conception of Truth', in *Philosophy and Phenomenological Research*, vol. iv, 1944, and also in *Readings in Philosophical Analysis* (ed. Feigl and Sellars).

co-ordinates to do the work which is done by tenses or by demonstratives like 'here' and 'now'. It is, however, a disputed question how far this is feasible.[1]

If I do not pursue this question here, it is not that I do not think it interesting and important in itself, but only that it does not have a vital bearing upon the definition of truth. For it is obvious that in any case in which we are able to define truth as a predicate of sentences, we can also define it as a predicate of statements. We have only to rule that a statement is to be accounted true when it can be expressed by a sentence which satisfies our definition. Even in the case of a sentence of which the interpretation varies according to the context, it may still be possible to define its truth or falsehood with respect to the use that is being made of it on any particular occasion; and we can then extend the definition, in the same simple fashion, to the corresponding statement. Of course this still leaves us with the problem of making clear what it is for a sentence to express a statement, but for those who regard truth as a predicate of statements or of propositions, this problem will arise in any case.

A point which concerns us more at this stage is that Tarski's formula is not itself a definition of truth but only a schema. His actual definition of truth, in terms of the satisfaction of sentential functions, applies as it stands only to the set of sentences which he chooses as an example: that is, to the sentences which constitute what he calls the language of the class-calculus. But, subject to certain provisos, the method can be extended to sentences of other formal systems. There are, however, technical reasons for concluding that a general definition of truth along these lines is not obtainable. Nevertheless there is a sense in which the schema achieves as much as can be expected. If we apply it to any given sentence, then provided that we

[1] *Vide* 'Names and Descriptions'.

know what statement the sentence is being used to make, the formula will tell us what we mean by saying that the sentence is true.

If this is all there is to it, it may even be suggested that the concept of truth is not only not problematic, but not of any special interest. There are, indeed, philosophers who have taken this view. They maintain that the words 'true' and 'false' and their cognates play no essential rôle in our language: that we use them to say nothing that we could not say equally well without using them at all.[1] This position is made plausible by concentrating on examples in which the assertion that a given statement is true explicitly contains the statement itself. Thus it is always possible to preface any assertion that one makes with the expression 'it is true that', but in the way of information at least nothing seems thereby to be gained. If I assert, for example, that it is true that London is the capital of England, I appear to give no more information than I should give by simply asserting that London is the capital of England. Similarly, to assert it to be false that cows are carnivorous appears to be exactly the same thing as asserting that cows are not carnivorous. So if one generalizes from instances of this kind, one may come to the conclusion that the statement that it is true that p is merely an expanded version of the statement that p, and the statement that it is false that p a version of the statement that not p. And then one may undercut the question whether truth and falsehood are predicates of sentences or statements by taking this to show that they are not predicates at all.

It must be remarked, however, that it is not entirely fair to take this as the standard example of the way in which we use the words 'true' and 'false'. There are indeed

[1] *E.g.* F. P. Ramsey, 'Facts and Propositions', *Supplementary Proceedings of the Aristotelian Society*, vol. vii, 1927. Reprinted in *The Foundations of Mathematics*.

occasions on which the expression 'it is true that' is employed as a stylistic or rhetorical device; most frequently it has a concessive use; we say 'it is true that *p*' to mark our acknowledgement of a fact, the fact stated by '*p*', which might be adduced as an objection to what we have been saying. But it is much more common for us to use the words 'true' or 'false' and their cognates not as a preface to some assertion which we are in the course of making, but rather as a means of expressing our agreement or disagreement with an assertion that someone else has made. We say 'Yes, that is true' or 'No, that is not true' in reply to something that has been said to us; or else we couple the expressions 'is true' or 'is false' with some description of a statement, to make such sentences as 'What he told you is false', or 'What you said is true'. When they are employed in this way the words 'true' and 'false' are not eliminable, or at least not in any straightforward manner, and they do appear to function as predicates. For while it may plausibly be said that to preface a statement with the expression 'it is true that' is not to talk about the statement, or about the sentence which expresses it, but merely to state it in a different fashion, surely this does not apply to the cases where the word 'true' is used as a comment upon a statement which has already been made. When I utter such a sentence as 'What you said was true', there may be a sense in which I am reasserting your statement. But it would seem perverse to deny that I am anyhow talking about it, that it is the subject of which I am predicating truth.

I have just said that there may be a sense in which one is reasserting a statement of which one predicates truth, but it can well be argued that this need not be so. Thus if I know someone to be honest and reliable, I may enjoin others to believe him, not because I independently agree with some statement that he has made, but simply on the grounds of his general veracity. Without even knowing what it was that he said, I still may be willing to assume that what he said was true. But it seems rather odd to say that I am thereby reasserting a statement which I am not even capable of identifying, and still odder to say that I am restating it.

All the same one must not make too much of this point. What I am doing in such a case is to give a blank cheque, as it were, to the person in whom I am reposing confidence. Though my ascription of truth to his statements is not a restatement of them, it commits me to a share of the responsibility for them. It is the same responsibility as I should be assuming if I said to someone, in a context where I believe that I can exclude the possibility of my having been honestly mistaken : 'I forget what I told you, but I know that I would not lie to you : so whatever I said, I am sure that it was true'. Here again, I am not repeating my statement, but there surely is a sense in which I am reaffirming it. What happens in this case is that one makes what could technically be called a variable assertion. The use of the expression 'is true' in conjunction with a descriptive phrase is a way of according one's assent to any statement which satisfies the description. But to make a variable assertion is in a sense to assert the values of the variable. If a statement satisfies the description with which I conjoin the predicate 'true' or 'false', then I am implicitly asserting, or denying it, as the case may be, even though I may not know what the statement is.

I conclude from this that though it is strictly incorrect to refuse to accord the words 'true' and 'false' the status of predicates, yet those who have taken this line are basically in the right. For even when they do function as predicates, the rôle which these terms essentially fulfil is that of assertion or negation signs. The material content of a statement *s* which implicitly or explicitly ascribes truth to a statement p, may differ from the material content of p inasmuch as it may refer to p in a way in which p does not refer to itself; but the information which we gain from s by way of this reference to p, adds nothing to what we gain from p alone. Whatever criticisms may be made of Tarski's formula, this is one point which it brings out clearly.

What is not so clear is why there is thought to be such a problem about truth. If the question were only what is meant by truth, in the sense in which we have so far interpreted it, then, as we have seen, the answer is extremely simple. But just because it is so simple, we may suspect that we are mistaking the problem. If this is all there were to it, it is hard to see how anybody, even a philosopher, could ever have supposed that the question 'What is Truth?' presented any serious difficulty. Yet philosophers have been puzzled about truth: they have put forward conflicting theories about it. All the same they must have known well enough how the word 'true' was actually used. Such information as that it is true that London is the capital of England if and only if London is the capital of England could hardly be expected to come upon them as a revelation, nor yet as something which they would wish to dispute. They would complain only that it did not provide an answer to the questions that concerned them. But what then are these questions?

I think that what these philosophers were seeking was not a definition of truth, in the sense of an explanation of our use of the word 'true', but rather a criterion of validity. The question which they raised was not, What do we mean by truth? but, What is it that makes a statement true? This second question is indeed ambiguous. It might be construed as an inquiry into causes. How does it come about that such and such a statement is true? How does it come to be true that I am now in Oxford? Because I have business there, and caught a train from London, and so on. It might be construed as a request for truth conditions. What does the truth of the statement that I am now in Oxford consist in ? In my being in Oxford and whatever this logically entails. Or thirdly, it may be, or at any rate has been, construed in a more general way as an enquiry into the relations that must obtain between a statement, or sentence, or judgement, or whatever else truth is ascribed to, and something in the world, something other than the statement itself, in order for it to be true. How is the statement that I am now in Oxford made true by what is going on in the world ? Because it is a fact that I am now in Oxford. But perhaps this calls for further elucidation.

Now clearly we are not concerned here with the causal question. We are not concerned to find the scientific explanation why this or that statement is true. For one thing, this would only remove the problem to another stage. For the truth of the statements which enter into the explanation will itself have to be accounted for. It is more nearly right to say that we are looking for truth-conditions and would be entirely right if what we wanted was a definition of truth which would be adequate, in Tarski's sense. For what Tarski's definition of truth with respect to the language of the class-calculus depends on is his being able to summarize the conditions under which any sentence of the language is true. Since the only statements which can be made in the language are statements to the effect that one class is included in another, and statements which are truth functions of these, one can find a general formula which contains an exhaustive specification of the conditions under which any sentential function of this language will be satisfied. In the case of a natural language, these favourable circumstances do not obtain. It is very doubtful if its molecular sentences are all truth-functional, witness the problem of subjunctive conditionals, and its atomic sentences are not all of the same pattern. So instead of summarizing the truth-conditions, we fall back on enumeration. This accounts for the production of such a trivial seeming statement as that the sentence 'snow is white' is true in English if and only if snow is white.

But even if the truth-conditions of the statements expressible in a natural language could be summarized, this still would not give our philosophers what they need. For what this would enable us to do would be to give a general description of the kinds of statement that can be made in the language in question, and then go on to say that what would make them true is that this, or that, or the other set of conditions is satisfied. But the philosophical problem is supposed to be that of explaining what it means to say that *any* set of conditions is satisfied. The question which is put to us is, What makes anything so ? where the answer sought is not a causal one, which would in any case be empty at this level of generality, but something about criteria of validity. It is to this quite general problem that the various theories of truth, the correspondence theory, the coherence theory, the pragmatic theory, are taken to provide the solution.

But now we may well ask : Is this a genuine problem at all ? Can we significantly ask for a general criterion of truth ? Surely what makes a statement true must depend upon what the statement is. One can describe how one would set about verifying any given statement, but one cannot describe how one would set about verifying statements in general for the very good reason that they are not all verified in the same way. So that if any one insists on putting the general question, the most that we can do for him is to give him, in one guise or another, the cruelly uninformative answer that what makes a statement true is what makes a statement true.

I feel the force of this objection, but I do not think that our efforts to generalize need be quite so futile as it makes out. It is indeed correct to say that any two different statements have different criteria for their truth; but it does not follow from this that these criteria cannot be informatively classified, and classified in a quite general way. Thus if we admit the distinction between *a priori* and empirical statements, it is quite plausible to say that what makes an *a priori* statement true is either that it exemplifies a rule of usage, or that it is tautologous, in the sense of tautology which is defined by the truth tables, or that it follows, in accordance with certain specifiable rules of deduction, from axioms which themselves can be treated as implicit definitions. The existence of Gödelian sentences does introduce a complication here. We now know that in any formal system which is rich enough to express arithmetic, there are true statements which are not provable within the system. But it is not obvious that even these statements cannot be accommodated within some general formula of this kind.

For the purpose of this inquiry, however, I intend to pass over the special problems which arise in connection with the validity of formal statements and deal only with the case of empirical statements, where the position is different but no less complex. And here I think we must begin by making a distinction between those empirical statements which can be directly tested and those that can be tested only indirectly. This is not indeed an altogether clear-cut distinction. It is to some extent a matter of convention what statements are to be regarded as directly testable. It depends partly on the resources of the language which we are employing. In a given language L, however, in which we are able to express a statement *s*, it is often the case that we are also able to express statements, *t*, *u*, *v*, which are more directly testable than *s*. And here what I mean by saying that *t*, *u*, *v*, are more directly testable than *s*, or that *s* is less directly testable than *t*, *u*, *v*, is that while it is not possible to verify *s*, without verifying *t*, *u*, *v*, it is possible to verify *t* or *u* or *v* without verifying *s*. A straightforward example of this would be the case of statements about nations and statements about persons. It is not possible to verify any statements about the French nation without verifying some statements about individual Frenchmen, but the converse does not hold. Another example of a different sort would be that of universal statements and singular statements. A universal statement may be deduced from some theory, but the theory itself can in the end be verified only through the making of some observation at some specific place and time, that is through the verification of a singular statement. On the other hand the verification of the singular statement does not depend upon the verification of the theory, though it may not be independent of some other theory. I doubt if one can ever come to statements which are in no degree theory-laden, but I do not think that this invalidates the relative distinction that I am now trying to make. If this is so and it is possible to define the concept of relatively direct testability with respect to the statements which are expressible in a given language, one can then go on to define direct testability in terms of it. We can say that a statement *s* is directly testable with respect to a given language L if there is no statement expressible in L than which it is less directly testable.

Let us call the statements which are directly testable in this sense basic statements. It does not matter, for our present purpose, what these basic statements are taken to be. Clearly they must fall into the category of what some philosophers have called observation-statements, but we need not at this stage resolve the difficult question whether these statements are to be construed as statements about physical objects or statements about sense-data. The important point, so far as we are concerned, is that these basic statements, whatever they may be, supply the truth-conditions for all the other empirical statements which are expressible in the language in question. It will not in general be found to be the case that these higher level statements are logically equivalent to any combination of the basic statements ; but it is necessarily the case, according to our definition, that they are verifiable only in so far as basic statements are derivable from them. With regard to many such higher level statements, for example those that constitute some abstract scientific theory, it is not very easy to show what is their observable content. But if we are able to specify their observable content, then we have also specified what would make them true.

But what of the basic statements themselves ? By definition they are not verified through the verification of any other statements, at any rate not through the verification of statements of any other type. They are verified, if at all, by being directly confronted with the relevant facts. But this raises two problems. What is the nature of this confrontation ? And what is it that statements are confronted with ? Facts, but what are facts ?

Let us try to deal with the second question first. One suggestion which we must dispose of, if we are to proceed any further along this road, is that facts are simply to be equated with true statements. There is indeed a common and proper usage of the word 'fact' in which this is so. The expression 'it is a fact that' may be employed as an alternative to 'it is true that' in the rôle of an assertion sign. In this usage of the term we have to admit as many forms of fact as there are forms of statement : not only affirmative categorical facts, but negative facts, hypothetical facts, disjunctive facts, and so on. But this is not obviously objectionable, nor out of accord with ordinary usage. We do constantly talk of its being a fact that something or other is not the case, and while we may be a little less ready to talk of conditional facts, it is not unknown for us to do so. A historian might claim, without absurdity, that it was a fact that if Hannibal had besieged Rome after the Battle of Cannae he would have taken it.

However, if this were the only usage of the term, it would not serve us here. For in that case to say that a true statement corresponded to a fact, would merely be a rather misleading way of saying that a true statement was true. What we require is the different, perhaps less common, sense of fact, in which a fact is not identified with a true statement, but rather distinguished from it as that which makes it true. We want to be able to characterize facts, not as linguistic entities of any kind, but somehow as objective states of affairs. Our task is to show that this usage is legitimate and to try to make it clear.

One feature of it is that we no longer have a one to one correspondence between true statements and facts. For we now want to say that different true statements may be made true by one and the same fact. Thus the following statements, 'Some Greek philosopher died from drinking hemlock', 'The master of Plato died from taking poison', 'Socrates died from drinking hemlock', 'Socrates did not die a natural death', 'Either Socrates died from drinking hemlock or Plato was the father of Aristotle', and many similar ones that we could add to the list, are all different. Some are entailed by others though in no two cases is there a relation of mutual entailment: some are logically independent. Yet they are all made true by the same fact: namely the fact which consists in a particular man dying in just the fashion in which he did at a particular time and place. The diversity comes about because there are ever so many ways of describing or referring to the various features of the situation. The descriptions may be more or less definite, *e.g.* 'someone' as opposed to 'Socrates', and they may be only synthetically connected, *e.g.* 'the master of Plato' and 'the husband of Xanthippe', with the result that the statements into which they enter have different contents. Nevertheless, it is held, there is only one state of affairs that they all refer to, one single fact or set of facts, that makes them all true.

But how are these facts to be characterized? How are we to distinguish among true statements between those which do, as it were, delimit facts and those which do not? Thus the statement that in the room where I now am some Englishman is writing an essay on a philosophical topic reports a fact in the sense that it is true, but it does not delimit a fact, because the fact which makes it true is not just that some Englishman is writing an essay, but that *I* am, and not just that any sort of philosophical essay is being written, but precisely *this* one. And here it would seem that what prevents the statement which I have just cited from delimiting the appropriate fact is that it is so indefinite, that it is consistent with so many possible states of affairs: in other words it is insufficiently specific.

This is the reason, I believe, why so many philosophers have been reluctant to admit the possibility of negative or disjunctive facts. Thus the statements 'London is not the capital of France' and 'London is the capital of either England or Denmark' are both true, but it is argued that there is no fact which consists in London's not being the capital of France, neither is there a fact which consists in London's being the capital of either England or Denmark: there is only the fact that London is the capital of England. The refusal to countenance negative facts sometimes, indeed, appears to be a mere prejudice, inasmuch as the distinction between affirmative and negative statements is not sharp; in some instances it is only a matter of the way in which a statement is formulated, in others it is chiefly a matter of emphasis. It is, however, generally the case that the statements which we regard as negative are less specific than those that we take to be affirmative. Thus the information given by saying that London is not the capital of France is less precise, in the sense that it leaves more possibilities open, than the information given by saying that London is the capital of England. In the case of disjunctive statements this is quite obvious. Since all that is needed for a disjunctive statement to be true is that one of the disjuncts be true, it follows that if it is true that p it must also be true that p or q, no matter what proposition q is. But merely to say that one or other of a pair of disjuncts is true is less specific, it leaves more possibilities open, than ascribing truth just to one of them.

The ground for our reluctance to admit general or conditional facts is not so much that general or conditional statements are unspecific as that they are not directly testable. It is, however, also true that general statements are unspecific in the sense that they do not pin-point their instances. To say that all ravens are black is not to identify any particular object as a raven.

Unfortunately, this concept of specificity is not at all easy to define. The obvious first step is to say that p is more specific than q, if p entails q but q does not entail p. Thus the statement that I am writing an essay entails, but is not entailed by, the statement that someone is writing an essay; the statement that my shoes are black entails, but is not entailed by, the statement that my shoes are not brown; the statement that London is the capital of England entails, but is not entailed by, the statement that London is the capital of England or Denmark. So in each case we say that the first mentioned statement is the more specific.

This is all right so far as it goes. It is, however, clear that it provides us only with a limited concept of relative specificity. It does not permit us to compare statements which are logically independent of one another. Still there may be ways in which this restriction can be removed. For example, we may begin by saying that a statement is absolutely specific with respect to a given language L if there is no statement expressible in L by which it is entailed and which it does not entail. Then if we were able to make a catalogue of all the absolutely specific statements which were expressible in L, we might be able to construct a hierarchy on this basis in such a way that we could determine the relative specificity even of statements which were logically independent of one another, by comparing their relation to the statements of the lowest level. We should have to allow that a statement which was absolutely specific with respect to one language might not be so with respect to another, but I do not think that this is a serious objection. In theory at least, a language can always be added to ; and if the language in which we are speaking is, by comparison with some other language, deficient in its power to express specific statements, we could always make this deficiency good.

The real difficulty in this line of approach stems from the fact that we can always make a statement more specific by conjoining another one with it. For while p does not in general entail p and q, it is always the case that p and q entails p. But this would mean that we should be left with only one fact, namely that which was stated by the conjunction of all true mutually independent statements. Even if we eliminated from this list all those that are not directly testable, the conclusion could still not be accepted. The only way that I can see to avoid it is to add to our definition of specificity the saving clause that p is not a component of q. But then we must have some means of determining when one statement is a component of another. What we need, in other words, is a rule for deciding what are simple statements, and this may not be very easy to devise.

In spite of such technical difficulties, I hope that I have succeeded in throwing enough light on the usage of 'fact' with which we are here concerned. The first step is to delimit a class of statements which satisfy the following three conditions: first, that they are directly testable; secondly, that they are simple in the sense that they are not compounded of other statements; and, thirdly, that they are absolutely specific with regard to the language in which they are expressed. Then facts are to be identified with the states of affairs which form the objective contents of the true statements of this class.

But now it may seem that we are turning in a circle. We set out to explain the truth of statements in terms of their relation to facts, but we have ended by explaining what facts are in terms of the truth of a certain class of statements. This important sense of 'fact', in which facts were not just to be identified with true propositions, amounts to no more, it may be said, than limiting the type of true proposition with which they are to be identified. We have shown how the validity of some statements depends on that of others, but, so the criticism runs, we have not begun to show how any statements can be compared with facts.

It is the belief that the circle is unbreakable, that we can attach no sense to the claim that statements are compared with facts, unless it is a disguised way of saying that they are compared with one another, that leads to the coherence theory of truth. And one very good reason for supposing that the circle is not unbreakable is that the coherence theory of truth can easily be shown to be untenable.

When I speak of the coherence theory of truth, I am not referring to a theory which, in England at least, most frequently goes by that name, that is, to the theory adopted by such neo-Hegelians as F. H. Bradley and H. H. Joachim.[1] For this is not a theory of truth at all, but a theory of meaning. The premiss from which it springs

[1] See especially H. H. Joachim, *The Nature of Truth.*

is that it is impossible to identify and so to refer to any object unless it can be specified completely; but to specify an object completely must include the description of all the relations that it bears to other objects. So, since every object is in some way related to every other, to specify any object is to specify them all. But this leads to the conclusion that there is only one statement which can significantly be made, the one that tells the truth, the whole truth and nothing but the truth. The statements that we actually make, assuming, that is, that we ever succeed in referring to anything, must all be shorthand for this one true statement, and, therefore, are all equivalent to one another, an unfortunate consequence which appears to have escaped the notice of the proponents of this theory. Alternatively, if they are not shorthand for the one big statement, they all fail in their reference and are, therefore, false or meaningless. The line which is taken by the advocates of this theory is that the statements, or judgements to use their terminology, which we actually make are at best partially true, but this is merely disingenuous. Apart from the difficulty of attaching any sense to the expressions 'partially true' or 'partially false' (unless we are dealing with a conjunction of statements, some of which are true and others false), the argument just does not allow for any discrimination, any difference of degree among statements with respect to truth and falsehood. On this view either they are all true and all say the same thing (*i.e.* everything), or they are all about nothing and so are all completely false, if not meaningless. All this comes from the initial step of supposing that you cannot refer to anything without completely specifying it: a mistake which is incorporated in the so-called dogma of internal relations. What is hard to understand is that so many idealist philosophers should have seriously taken this premiss to be true.

This curious theory is to be distinguished from what

may be called a proper coherence theory of truth ; such a theory, for example, as was put forward by some of the Viennese positivists in the nineteen-thirties.[1] They did not deny that it was possible to make statements which were logically independent of one another ; they were not led astray by any fidelity to internal relations. But because they had persuaded themselves that it was metaphysical, and so meaningless, to talk of comparing statements with facts, they thought that truth must consist in some relation which statements bear to one another. But if one rules out any reference to fact, the only relations which statements can bear to one another are logical relations : relations of logical independence, entailment, or incompatibility. So the conclusion drawn was that for a statement to be true it was necessary and sufficient that it be a member of a self-consistent system. An attempt was made to put observation statements (or protocol statements as they were sometimes called) into a privileged position, but since these protocol statements were distinguished only by their form, and since the only criterion for their truth was their coherence with the other statements in the system, so that there was no reason to accept them if they did not fit in, this privilege came to nothing. The feeling that they ought to be privileged was a back-sliding : it came from tacitly regarding them as reports of fact.

It is easy to see that this theory is indefensible even on its own terms. One obvious and fatal objection to it is that there may be any number of systems of statements, each of which is internally consistent, but any two of which are incompatible with one another. Since they are mutually incompatible they cannot all be true. How then is it to be decided which is the true one ? When faced with this

[1] *E.g.* by R. Carnap, O. Neurath, and C. Hempel. *Vide* Carnap's and Neurath's articles on 'Protokollsätze' in *Erkenntnis*, vol. iii, and Hempel, 'On the logical Positivists' Theory of Truth', in *Analysis*, vol. ii.

difficulty Carnap, who held this theory for a time, replied that the true system was that which was accepted by the scientists of our culture circle. But it is plain that this answer does not meet the difficulty at all. For every one of the competing systems might consistently contain the *statement* that it alone was accepted by the scientists of our culture circle. What Carnap had in mind was that only one of these systems was accepted by the scientists in *fact*. But this is to break the bounds of the coherence theory. And if the reference to fact is permissible in this case, why not in others also ?

Since the coherence theory is false, the premiss from which it follows must be rejected. There is nothing improperly metaphysical in the idea of testing statements by reference to fact. Of course we cannot state a fact without stating it : there is no way of characterizing facts except by making true statements. But this does not mean that the statements have to be identified with the states of affairs which they describe. The circle is broken by observation and by action. I shall recur to this point later on.

It is interesting to note that Carnap's attempt to save the coherence theory was a deviation into pragmatism. For it is the cardinal feature of pragmatic theories of truth that true propositions are characterized as those that we accept. Sometimes this is conjoined with the theory that the propositions which we accept are those that suit our purpose ; it may also be strengthened by the proviso that not just any propositions that we happen to accept are true, but only those which we are warranted in accepting on the basis of scientific method. But the identification of truth with acceptance is the fundamental point.

A variant of pragmatism which is not often recognized as such is to be found in the equation of facts with propositions which have been ascertained to be true. This leads to the conclusion, which goes back to Aristotle, that statements about the future are neither true nor false. I mention this theory only in passing, as it is open to the objections which hold against pragmatist theories in general, apart from incurring some special difficulties of its own.

The strength of the pragmatist position is that the distinction between what is true and what one accepts as being true is a distinction that one cannot draw in one's own case. If you ask me to produce a list of true propositions, the best I can do is to give you a list of propositions which I *believe* to be true — propositions which I accept. But it does not follow from this that when I say that a proposition is true I *mean* only that I accept it. On the contrary I am bound to admit the possibility that what I believe is false. Neither can I simply mean that I am warranted in asserting it : for what gives me a warrant for asserting something is that I have evidence in favour of its *truth*. So although it is the case that to ask someone what is true always comes down in *practice* to asking him what he believes, this does not mean that we can dispense with the concept of objective truth. The rôle which it plays may be only formal, but it is still essential. The pragmatist theory itself presupposes it and cannot be coherently stated without it.

This might seem to leave the field clear for the correspondence theory of truth. But at least in its traditional form, the correspondence theory is itself confused. Its merit is that it separates facts from statements : its demerit is that it then tries to connect them by invoking a relation of correspondence which is conceived as a relation of resemblance or structural similarity. I shall now try to show that if the idea of mirroring is taken at all literally, it is a serious mistake to suppose that statements (or sentences, or beliefs, or judgements) are true because they *mirror* facts.

The model on which this theory is based is that of a

photograph or a map. For it is tempting to think that what makes a map or a photograph a true reproduction of the state of affairs which it portrays is a relation of similarity; similarity of structure in the case of the map, similarity of structure and also in some degree of content in the case of a photograph, or painting. And then one might go on to suppose, as Russell did in his Logical Atomism lectures [1] and Wittgenstein in the *Tractatus*, that sentences, or propositions, were also portraits and owed their truth, when they were true, to their fidelity. How even sentences could be regarded as portraits has never been made clear: it would seem that for all but the crudest type of ideographic language this could only be a metaphor; and surely it is just false that a language like English is implicitly ideographic. But we need not belabour this point since the theory does not even fit its paradigm cases. It is not true even of photographs or maps. For it is not just the structural similarity of a map say of Europe to Europe, the fact that the distance between the dots marked 'Berlin' and 'Vienna' on the map faithfully mimics according to scale the distance between Berlin and Vienna, and so forth, it is not just this that makes the map an accurate map of Europe, any more than it is *just* the likeness, however complete, of such and such a photograph to Princess Margaret that makes it a true photograph of Princess Margaret. So far as this goes, the map might be a map of China, the photograph a photograph of Mr. Macmillan. Another condition is needed, and it is this condition which is all important; there must be a convention according to which the map, or the painting, or the photograph, is interpreted as a sign of that and only that which it resembles, as stating as it were, truly or falsely, that there exists something which in this way corresponds to it. Without this convention all that we have is the existence of two objects which resemble

[1] Reprinted in *Logic and Knowledge*.

each other more or less closely, as closely maybe as the two sleeves of a coat: but there is no more a question of one's being true of the other than there is that my right sleeve is true of my left. The fact of physical likeness only becomes relevant when it is *selected* as a method of representation. It is indeed a natural choice to make, because we instinctively tend to associate like with like, but it is not the only possible, or even the most effective, method, as the development of non-ideographic languages shows. It is not for that matter even the only possible method of portraiture. The fact that a picture does not seem to us to resemble the thing which it is intended to depict does not in itself make it non-representational. It may just be that the style of representation is different from what we are accustomed to.

In short, the question whether and in what fashion a method of representation is pictorial is irrelevant to the question of truth: or rather, it is relevant only in the trivial sense that the answer to the question whether a given series of signs expresses a true statement depends in part on the way in which the signs are interpreted. If the symbolism is pictorial, it is the resemblance of the signs to some possible state of affairs that determines what they signify; but then what decides the question of their truth or falsehood is whether or not this state of affairs exists. To put it another way, we can regard a map or portrait as a sort of propositional function; if it is used to make a statement, it affirms that there is something to which it physically corresponds. Then what makes it true is simply that the function is satisfied, not that we employ this or that method of determining what the function is. The usual talk about correspondence confuses a question about the conventional character of the symbolism with the quite different question whether what is symbolized is so.

This confusion is to be found even in more sophisticated versions of the theory, such as that which has been put forward by J. L. Austin.[1] Having argued that 'if there is to be communication of the sort we achieve by language at all', there must among other things 'be two sets of conventions: *descriptive* conventions correlating the words (= sentences) with the *types* of situation, thing, event, etc., to be found in the world; *demonstrative* conventions correlating the words (=statements) with the *historic* situations, etc., to be found in the world', Austin contends that 'a statement is said to be true when the historic state of affairs to which it is correlated by the demonstrative conventions (the one to which it "refers") is of a type with which the sentence used in making it is correlated by the descriptive conventions'.[2] One obvious objection to this is that not all meaningful statements are explicitly referential; general and indefinite statements may well be expressed by sentences which contain no demonstrative signs at all. But this objection may be met by saying that the truth of such statements always depends upon the truth of other statements, and that in the case of these other, basic, statements Austin's two conditions are always fulfilled. Even this seems to me disputable, but I shall not pursue the matter here. For if Austin's remark is taken, perhaps unfairly, as an account of what is meant by calling something true it is open to a much more serious objection. It implies, as Mr. Strawson points out in his contribution to the same symposium,[3] that whenever one declares a statement to be true one is engaging in a semantic disquisition about the conditions of its being meaningful. Since Austin himself criticizes the semanticists for making truth a predicate of sentences, it is possible that he is not here intending to give a definition of truth but merely to describe the conditions

[1] J. L. Austin, 'Truth', *Supplementary Proceedings of the Aristotelian Society*, vol. xxiv, 1950. Reprinted in *Philosophical Papers*.

[2] *Op. cit.* p. 116.

[3] P. F. Strawson, 'Truth', *Supplementary Proceedings of the Aristotelian Society*, vol. xxiv, 1950.

under which a statement is true: and certainly for a statement to be made true in the way that it is, it is necessary that it should have the meaning that it has. But this is not to say that in calling it true, we are saying that it has this meaning, still less that we are talking about the semantic conditions which it has to satisfy in order to be meaningful. 'Certainly', to quote Strawson, 'we use the word "true" when the semantic conditions described by Austin are fulfilled: but we do not, in using the word, *state* that they are fulfilled.'[1] It may be that Austin himself would have agreed with this, but if we strip his 'definition' of its semantic accretions, what it comes down to is that a statement is true if what it states, or what the sentence which expresses it means, is so. This is indeed a truism, but it is hardly a vindication of the correspondence theory of truth.

I hope that it has now become clear where the correspondence theory has gone wrong. In its traditional form, it mistakes a cardinal feature of a certain type of symbolism for an essential feature of all symbolism, and then confuses a key to the interpretation of these symbols, a clue for deciding in this special type of case what it is that they state, with a criterion for deciding whether what they state is satisfied. In this way a defective theory of meaning is turned into a defective theory of truth.

But if the relation between statements and the facts which make them true is not the relation of correspondence, what sort of relation is it? The answer to this is that it is a mistake to look for a relation of this type at all. As I implied at the end of my discussion of the coherence theory of truth, there is nothing mysterious about our ability to compare statements with facts. If one understands a sentence, then one already knows how to compare it, or the statement which it expresses, with a fact. How do I compare the English sentence 'It is a fine day', or the

[1] *Op. cit.* pp. 144-5.

statement which I use it to make, with the facts or with reality, or whatever it is that one chooses to say that sentences, or statements, are compared with ? Well, I look out of the window, see that the sun is shining, and so accept the statement : or perhaps I see that it is raining and reject it. My understanding the sentence, my attaching the right meaning to it, the meaning that it conventionally has in English, just *is* among other things my being willing to accept or reject it in these various conditions. Of course, if I wish to state the conditions, to *say* what makes the statement true, then all I can do is to formulate another statement which is equivalent to it, or entailed by it, or a corroboration of it. But, as I said before, this does not mean that we are imprisoned in a ring of statements. We break the circle by using our senses, by actually making the observations as a result of which we accept one statement and reject another. Of course we use language to describe these observations. Facts do not figure in *discourse* except as true statements. But how could it be expected that they should ?

What I am suggesting, in short, is that this is not a theoretical problem. If someone does not know how to find out whether a given sentence is being used to make a true statement, we may try to explain it to him by means of sentences which he does know how to use. Or we may show him the appropriate state of affairs and hope that he catches on. The problem is a practical one and in practice often quite easily solved.

Of course there are theoretical problems in the neighbourhood. There is the problem of giving an analysis of what it is for a sentence to express a statement : there is the problem of specifying the conditions under which one statement confirms another and more particularly of determining the relation between theoretical statements and the basic statements of fact : there is the problem of the status of the basic statements themselves, which is allied to the philosophical problem of perception. Unless it is backed by a solution of at least the first and last of these problems, such an account as I have given of the concept of truth may not be thought to have achieved very much. All the same, it is a form of progress in philosophy to discover what are the proper questions to ask. Though my argument has followed a slightly different line from his, I hope that I have at least vindicated F. P. Ramsey's contention that there is no separate problem of truth.

7

TWO NOTES ON PROBABILITY

(i) *The Conception of Probability as a Logical Relation*

THERE is a fairly widespread view that, at least in one important sense of the term, probability is most properly attributed to statements: and that what is being asserted when it is said that a statement is probable, in this sense, is that it bears a certain relation to another statement, or set of statements, which may also be described as confirming, or supporting, or providing evidence for it. There are some, indeed, who maintain that this is the only sense in which it is correct to speak of probability; that what we 'really mean' when we assert anything to be probable is always that some statement bears the requisite relation to such and such a piece of evidence. Thus Keynes [1] assumes that every significant probability statement can be fitted into his formula '$a/h = p$', where a is the proposition which is said to be probable, h is the evidence on which it is probable, and p is the degree of probability that h confers on a, a quantity which may or may not be numerically measurable. And Kneale [2] takes it for granted that probability is relative to evidence: if this is often overlooked, it is because in talking about probability we seldom bother to specify the evidence on which we are relying: 'our probability statements are commonly elliptical'.[3] Other

[1] J. M. Keynes, *A Treatise on Probability.*
[2] W. Kneale, *Probability and Induction.*
[3] *Op. cit.* p. 10.

writers, like Carnap,[1] distinguish this sense of probability from one in which to speak of the probability of an event is to attribute a numerical frequency to the distribution of some property among events of a given class. Carnap himself allows that we have a use for this conception of probability in terms of observed frequencies, or of the limits towards which they are supposed to tend. He calls it probability$_2$ to differentiate it from the other, logical, conception of probability, which he calls probability$_1$. It is, however, on the basis of probability$_1$ that he develops his inductive logic.[2]

Not all the advocates of this conception of probability agree with Keynes in regarding probability as an unanalysable logical relation. Certainly Carnap does not suppose his probability$_1$ to be unanalysable. But he does recognize that, on this interpretation of them, probability statements come to resemble statements of formal logic in the sense that if they are true they are analytic. This might, indeed, be disputed by philosophers like Kneale who wish to hold on to the synthetic *a priori*, and so to confine analyticity within more narrow limits: but they would at least allow that statements of probability, in this sense, are not empirical. They are necessarily true, if they are true at all. For it is characteristic of any view of this type that the existence of a probability relation between statements is made to depend, not on any contingent matter of fact, but solely on the meaning of the statements concerned. And this is my ground for saying that the advocates of such views treat probability as a logical relation, whether they assent to this form of words or not.

Now it seems to me that there is a very simple objection to theories of this type, which has strangely escaped the

[1] R. Carnap, 'The Two Concepts of Probability', *Philosophy and Phenomenological Research*, vol. v, no. 4.

[2] Vide *The Logical Foundations of Probability*.

notice of their supporters and even of their critics. Let us suppose that a disciple of Keynes has decided to bet upon a horse-race and that he is considering the chances of a horse named 'Eclipse'. He is determined to be rational and so to bring his degree of belief in the horse's victory into exact accordance with the objective probabilities. He assembles the evidence: h_1 that Eclipse will be ridden by the champion jockey; h_2 that the going will be hard; h_3 that Eclipse is suited by the distance; h_4 that it went lame after its last race; h_5 that it has previously beaten the more fancied of its competitors; h_6 that it has recently dropped in the betting, and so forth. Assume that he evaluates all the relevant evidence that he can acquire, or, in other words, that, so far as his knowledge goes, he has not omitted any true proposition which, if it were conjoined with his other data, would make any difference to the resultant probability. So, taking a to be the proposition that Eclipse will win, he decides that the probability of a on $h_1 = p_1$, $a/h_2 = p_2$, $a/h_3 = p_3$, $a/h_1h_2 = p_x$, $a/h_{1\text{-}4} = p_y$, . . .; and finally that $a/h_{1\text{-}n}$, where $h_{1\text{-}n}$ represents the totality of the relevant evidence at his command, $= p_z$. How is he to place his bet?

To common sense the answer is obvious. If his degree of belief in the proposition that Eclipse will win is to be rational, it must correspond to the probability p_z. He must find a means of comparing this with the odds that he is offered and bet accordingly. But what reason can he have, on his principles, for accepting the common-sense answer? In what way is the probability p_z better than the other probabilities, $p_1, p_2, \ldots p_x, p_y$, which he has also estimated? If his estimates are correct, all these statements of probability are necessary truths. And in that case how can any one of them be superior to the others? What one wants to say is that the probability p_z, since it is the only one that is estimated on the basis of all the relevant evidence, provides the best appraisal of what is actually likely to happen. But what can this mean to Keynes ? An event will happen, or it will not. To say that it is likely to happen is, on his theory, only a misleading way of saying that the statement that it will happen is probable on the basis of certain other statements. But this leaves us free to choose these other statements in any way we like, provided only that we have sufficient warrant for accepting them. It may seem, indeed, that even this proviso sets a problem ; for to say that we have sufficient warrant for accepting a given statement must mean, for Keynes, that it follows from, or is made probable by, another statement, or set of statements, which we have sufficient warrant for accepting : and then one appears to be threatened with an infinite regress. Keynes meets this difficulty, however, by assuming that there are certain statements which we can know directly to be true : and it is on statements of this sort that all rational judgements of probability must finally depend. This assumption may be questioned ; but even if it be admitted, our original objection still holds. Once we have assembled some trustworthy data by these means, there can be no reason, on Keynes's system, why we should trouble to carry our investigations any further. The addition of more evidence may, indeed, yield a higher or lower probability for the statement in which we are interested. But unless we have made some logical mistake, this probability cannot be said to be more, or less, correct than the one that was yielded by the evidence with which we started. Neither can any sense be given to the claim that it is a better estimate of what is likely to happen.

Carnap has seen that there is a difficulty here, and he has tried to meet it by introducing what he calls 'the principle of total evidence'. 'Let $c(h, e)$', he says, 'be the degree of confirmation of the hypothesis h with respect to the evidence e. Let us suppose that we have a definition of the function c and, based upon this definition, a theorem

"$c(h, e) = q$", which states the value q of c for given h and e. A principle which seems generally recognized, although not always obeyed, says that if we wish to apply such a theorem of the theory of probability to a given knowledge situation, then we have to take as evidence e the *total evidence* available to the person in question at the time in question, that is to say, his total knowledge of the results of his observations.' [1]

But why *have* we to take as evidence the total evidence available to us, whatever that may mean? What sort of principle is this? It can hardly be a *moral* principle. So far as morality goes, we might equally well choose to rely on the evidence which yielded the highest degree of confirmation for the hypothesis in which we were interested, or on that which yielded the lowest, or on whatever evidence we found most pleasing. Unless we miscalculate, the result at which we arrive will in each case be a necessary truth; and there can surely be no moral reason for preferring any one of these necessary truths to any other. It might, however, be thought that there was a practical reason: and indeed one may suppose that Carnap intended his principle of total evidence to be pragmatic. The suggestion would seem to be that we should trust hypotheses to the degree to which they are confirmed; and that by taking all the available evidence into account, we diminish the risk of falling foul of the facts, that is, of over- or underestimating the likelihood of the actual occurrence of the event to which our hypothesis refers. Once again, this is in accordance with common sense: but how can it possibly be justified on Carnap's principles? The event will occur or it will not. To say that there is a probability, of a given degree, that it will occur is to say only that the hypothesis that it will occur is confirmed to that degree by such and

[1] R. Carnap, 'On the Application of Inductive Logic', *Philosophy and Phenomenological Research*, vol. viii, no. 1.

such evidence. If this proposition is true, it is necessarily true: but so are all the other true propositions which, on the basis of greater, or less, or partly, or wholly different evidence, assign to the hypothesis a different degree of confirmation. There is no sense, therefore, in which the proposition which brings in all the available evidence can be superior to any of the others as a measure of probability. And this being so, there can be no practical reason why we should take it as a guide.

So far as I can see, the only way in which Carnap might hope to meet this objection would be to make his principle of total evidence a part of the definition of probability_1. He might claim that what we must be understood to mean by saying that a hypothesis is probable, in this sense, to a certain degree is just that it is confirmed, to this degree, by the totality of the evidence which is available to us. But what is this totality? If it be only 'the total knowledge of the results of our observations', then the difficulty will not be met. For, to revert to my example of the horse-race, it may well be that the only information I have bothered to acquire, which is in any way relevant to the hypothesis that Eclipse will win, is that it is to be ridden by the champion jockey; and in that case I shall be justified in regarding the hypothesis as probable to the extent that this single piece of evidence confirms it, and betting accordingly. No doubt if I were to investigate further, as any sensible punter would, I should find evidence which would lead me to revise my estimate of Eclipse's chances. But why should I take the trouble? If what I mean by saying that it is probable to such and such a degree that Eclipse will win is that the hypothesis that it will win is confirmed to this degree by the totality of the relevant observations that I have actually made, then the fact that the probability might be different if I had extended my observations need not concern me. For, on this view, if I do not miscalculate, there is no sense in which this second estimate of probability could be any better than the first.

The answer to this might seem to be that the probability is to be defined by reference not to the results of all the relevant observations that one happens to have made, but to those of all the relevant observations that one could make if one chose. The totality of evidence that is available to me will not as a rule be limited to the evidence that I actually have. But then what are its limits ? What means is there of deciding which are the observations that it is possible for me to make ? Presumably, in the case of the horse-race, the condition of the horse's lungs is relevant. Is this within the range of evidence that is available to me ? Well, I could use X-rays to find it out. But what if I have not the skill ? Then, I can employ a radiologist to do it for me. But what if I cannot discover a radiologist who is willing ? What if he asks more money than I can afford to pay ? Then, perhaps, I can find some way of forcing him to do it : perhaps I can steal the money. But will this always be possible ? I do not see how there can be a general answer to such questions ; nor, therefore, how there can be a rule for determining what is the totality of the available evidence. But in default of such a rule, this definition of probability would seem to be both vague in principle, and of little practical use.

Furthermore, it makes judgements of probability at least partly subjective. If the stable guards its secrets well, the totality of the evidence that is available to me will fall short of the totality of the evidence that is available to the horse's trainer. Let us make the implausible assumption that both he and I are in fact possessed of all the relevant evidence that is respectively available to us, and that we correctly calculate the degree of confirmation of the hypothesis that Eclipse will win, arriving naturally at different results. Both results will be valid, but the one that is valid for him will not be valid for me. If I take over his estimate I shall fall into error, for I shall then be asserting that the hypothesis is confirmed to the degree he says by the totality of the evidence that is available to *me*, when it is not in fact confirmed to that degree by the totality of the evidence that is available to me, but only by the different totality of the evidence that is available to *him*. It follows also, on this view, that there is no such thing as *the* probability of a hypothesis: there are as many different probabilities as there are persons who have access to different quantities of evidence. This conclusion may or may not be objectionable in itself; but I think it would be regarded as disturbing at least by some of those who wish us to look upon probability as a logical relation.

It may be suggested that they can avoid this conclusion by assuming that everyone has access, in principle, to all the evidence that there is. Then to say that a statement is probable to such and such a degree will be to say that it is confirmed to that degree by the totality of true statements. There is no need to put in the proviso that these statements must all be relevant, since the inclusion of irrelevant truths will make no difference to the result. This does indeed yield an objective definition of probability, but it has the fatal disadvantage that the probability of every hypothesis becomes either 0 or 1. For the totality of true statements must include either the negation of the hypothesis in question, or the hypothesis itself.

To escape from this predicament, one would have to restrict the range of the available evidence in such a way that it excluded any statement, or set of statements, which entailed either the hypothesis or its negation. And then one might equate the probability of the hypothesis with the degree to which it was confirmed by the totality of true statements that satisfied this condition. One objection to this would be that in assessing probabilities we could never draw on any universal statement of law. For if the event, to which our hypothesis referred, were subject to causal laws, the relevant statements of law, when combined with the statements affirming the appropriate initial conditions, would always entail the hypothesis or its negation. We could indeed keep the statements of law if we excluded the singular statements which joined with them in producing the entailments; but this would be an absurd proceeding since it is only through establishing singular statements that we ever acquire any evidence at all. And just for this reason, it may be said, we can afford to forgo the universal statements of law; for they draw all their support from the singular statements which are derivable from them; and these we shall have. Moreover, statistical laws, with frequencies of less than a hundred per cent, will not be excluded, though it may well be argued that they too will be superfluous, if all true singular statements are to be comprised in the available evidence.

A more serious objection to this definition of probability is that it allows us to have very little confidence in any of the judgements of probability that we actually make. For it can very seldom be the case that we in fact know every true singular statement that is relevant to the hypothesis in which we are interested. But in so far as the evidence at our disposal falls short of the total evidence, we cannot infer that the hypotheses which it is supposed to confirm are at all likely to be true. For all that is meant by their being likely to be true is that they are confirmed, to whatever degree, by the total evidence; and this is not in our possession. What we want to say is that, even if we can never be sure of having all the requisite evidence, nevertheless by acquiring more evidence, and incorporating it into our calculations, we bring our estimates of probability nearer to the truth. And clearly this is the view that Carnap holds. But I am not at all sure that he, or anyone else who conceives of probability as a logical relation, is entitled to hold it. For, as we have already remarked, each necessary truth to the effect that a given hypothesis is confirmed by some collection of evidence to such and such a degree is in itself as good as every other: we can pick out a special set of these propositions and say that they alone are to be regarded, by definition, as statements of probability; but then it will follow that the others, which fall outside this privileged set, are not statements of probability at all; there will be no justification for treating them even as approximations to the measures of objective probability for which we are in search.

Perhaps this difficulty could be met by introducing the concept of second-order probabilities. They might then be defined in such a way that one could assign a probability to the hypothesis that a given statement of confirmation was a statement of probability: and this probability would be made to increase, as one added to the evidence on which the statement of confirmation was based.

It seems to me, however, that such devices do not, in the end, remove the fundamental weakness of the logical theory. It has been well remarked by Kneale that 'no analysis of the probability relation can be accepted as adequate, *i.e.* as explaining the ordinary usage of the word "probability", unless it enables us to understand why it is rational to take as a basis for action a proposition which stands in that relation to the evidence at our disposal'.[1] And, even if the other objections to it can be met, I maintain that the view which we have been considering fails this test. For, if we are presented only with a stock of necessary facts to the effect that certain statements, or groups of statements, bear logical relations to each other in virtue solely of their meaning, I do not see what reason there could be for differentiating between the items of this stock

[1] *Probability and Induction*, p. 20.

as bases for action. I am not clear even what could be meant, within the terms of this theory, by saying that one of them was a better basis for action than another. It is true that one may select a subclass of these necessary propositions and decide to *call* its members statements of probability; but in so doing one will beg the question. For the use of the word 'probability', in this connection, itself implies that it is most rational to act on the basis of the propositions which have thus been selected: and this has not been proved.

In conclusion, I do not wish to say that probability, in the sense which here concerns us, is in no way relative to evidence. It seems clear that an appeal to evidence is needed to justify the belief that such and such an event is more or less likely to happen; and also that it is rational in such cases to take all the evidence at our disposal into account, the ground for this being, I suppose, that experience has shown us that our forecasts are more often right when this is done than when it is not. It does not follow, however, that statements of probability, in this sense, are statements *about* the relations of hypotheses to their evidence; and I do not think that they are. Nor, in the sense in which probability is the guide of life, do I think that statements of probability can be logically true.

(ii) *On the Probability of Particular Events*

I have tried to show that a most serious objection to what is now usually called the logical theory of probability is that it cannot explain why our estimate of probability judgements should be in any way affected by the amount of evidence on which they are based.

The question which I now wish to consider is whether

a similar objection holds against the frequency theory. What is common to all versions of this theory is that statements of probability are construed as referring to the distribution of properties among the members of some class. The question whether a given event will occur can always be rephrased as a question whether some property is instantiated. Then, according to the frequency theory, to ask how likely it is that the event will occur is to ask what proportion of the members of some appropriately chosen class possess the relevant property. In one version of the theory, the reference class is represented as an infinite sequence of terms; it is assumed that at some point in the sequence the proportion of terms which have the property in question reaches a value from which it does not subsequently deviate by more than an arbitrarily small amount, and the probability that any given member of the sequence has the property is then identified with this limiting ratio. If the frequency of the property throughout the sequence does not attain such a limit, it is held that no judgement of probability with respect to it is applicable. In another version of the theory it is stipulated that the reference class be large but finite; the probability that any term has a given property is then identified with the ratio which the number of members having the property bears to the total membership of the class. A third version identifies the probable distribution of a property in a given reference class with the frequency with which it has actually been found to occur in a sufficiently large sample. The judgement of probability then becomes tantamount to the judgement that the recorded ratio will also obtain in other samples of comparable size.

I shall not here attempt to decide between these different versions of the frequency theory, or to consider further alternatives to them, as the difficulty which I wish to examine is common to them all. It is a very simple difficulty and it can be illustrated by a simple example. Suppose that I am seeking to determine the probability of my living to the age of 80 : according to the frequency theory, in any of its versions, the answer depends upon the proportion of octogenarians existing in some class to which I belong. But now the problem is that I belong to an enormous number of such classes, and that the choice of one or other of them as my class of reference will make a great difference to the result. The measure of my probable life-span will vary to a very great extent according as it is referred to the class of organisms in general, the class of all human beings, the class of male Europeans, the class of Englishmen, the class of professional philosophers, the class of university teachers born in England in the 20th century, the class of contemporary Englishmen who belong to such and such an income group, the class composed of the members of this income group who have attained the age of 50 in such and such a physical condition, and so on indefinitely. What reason can there be, within the terms of the frequency theory of probability, for basing the estimate of my chances of longevity on the ratio obtaining in any one of these classes rather than any other ?

It will be seen that this difficulty reproduces the objection which we found to the logical theory. In each case we have divergent judgements of probability with regard to the same occurrence, all of which may be correct on their respective bases, and no ground furnished by the theory for deciding between them. As interpreted by the frequency theory, judgements of probability are not logically true ; it will be a matter of empirical fact that the proportion of the members of a reference class which have a given property, or the limit to which this proportion tends, has the value that it does. But again each one of these empirical facts is as good as any other. No more than in the case of the logical theory are we given any ground for saying that one or other of them yields a better estimate of what is actually likely to happen.

It is, however, obvious that when we are dealing with particular cases the choice of a reference class is not a matter of indifference. If I am concerned with my chances of living to the age of 80, it would be highly irrational for me to assess them on the basis of the proportion of organisms that live to that age, or even on the basis of the life-spans of contemporary Englishmen. What I should do, if I had access to the relevant statistics, would be to refer the question to a much narrower class. I should take into consideration the character of my profession, the material conditions in which I lived, the longevity of my ancestors, my present state of health, the nature of my habits, the state of medical science in my community, and other factors of this type. Thus by conjoining the properties of being a man of sedentary occupation, enjoying the standard of living of a member of the professional classes in one of the more prosperous societies of the contemporary western world, being a heavy smoker and a moderate drinker, and coming from a not especially long-lived family, I might reasonably regard the set of persons who satisfied these conditions as forming an appropriate class of reference; and if I were then to narrow the class still further by asking what proportion of its members, say in the last quarter of a century, had died between the ages of 50 and 80, it might be held rational for me to estimate my chances accordingly. Of course no one would go about it in this way. The relevant statistics are too troublesome to obtain, and such factors as the rapid advance of medical science on the one hand, and the menace of atomic warfare on the other, make them rather unsafe to extrapolate. Insurance companies do not assess, and to obtain their profits do not need to assess, the individual case with this degree of precision. The example does, however, provide us with an illustration of the kind of procedure that has to be adopted if one is going to apply the frequency theory with any show of rationality to judging the likelihood of particular events.

From this we can extract a general principle which corresponds to the principle of total evidence in the logical theory. The rule is that in order to estimate the probability that a particular individual possesses a given property, we are to choose as our class of reference, among those to which the individual belongs, the narrowest class in which the property occurs with an extrapolable frequency. What constitutes an extrapolable frequency is a matter for scientific judgement. It will depend on the extension of the class, the type of property in question, the range over which its distribution has hitherto been found to be stable, and so forth. In the special case in which the individual belongs to a class the defining property of which is rationally believed to be connected by causal law with the property we are inquiring about, either as determining or excluding it, we need not bother to look for a narrower class; for if a property P1 causally determines or excludes a property P2, then any conjunction of properties which contains P1 must also determine or exclude P2. Equally there is no point in narrowing the class of reference in other cases where it makes no significant difference to the frequency of the property we are concerned with. Our principle is therefore subject to the rider that the injunction to choose the narrowest class of reference applies only so long as the alteration in the class of reference ensures a corresponding alteration in the extrapolable frequency.

Like the principle of total evidence, this principle of narrowing the reference class is one that it seems rational to accept; but again it does not seem that any grounds for accepting it can be supplied within the terms of the frequency theory. If all that we can mean by saying that a given event has such and such a likelihood of happening is that the relevant property is distributed with such and such a frequency throughout the members of some class of reference, then clearly there can be no sense in trying to compare the merits of alternative classes of reference in estimating the probability of the event. Except in the case where there is a difference of opinion about the distribution of a property within a given class, the discrepancy between ostensibly different estimates will be only apparent. If the different judgements of probability refer the question to different classes, they may all be equally right ; they are not competing with each other, they are saying different things. So far as the frequency theory goes, there can be no reason for preferring any one of these true judgements to any other. The principle of narrowing the reference class must also be entirely arbitrary.

On this point the parallel between the frequency theory and the logical theory is complete. The best that can be said for the frequency theory is that, unlike the logical theory, it does not seriously attempt to deal with the individual case. It makes a pretence of doing so, but the pretence is threadbare. Let us take another even simpler example. Suppose that we have a biassed coin and that we have reason to believe that the frequency with which it will come up heads in a sufficiently long series of tosses is two times out of three. We may then infer that our chance of getting heads with the next toss of the coin is two-thirds. But this inference, though valid, is completely trivial. For all that we are supposed to mean by saying that we have a two-thirds chance of getting heads with any single toss of the coin is just that it is one of a series of tosses in which heads comes up on the average two times out of three. In short, we are making an identical inference ; a statement about the distribution of a property among the members of a given class is deduced from itself. The individual instance does not come into it, except for the assertion that it is a member of the class.

This remains true when we ascend to probabilities of the second order. To continue with our example, it may be said that the greater the length of the run in which the two-thirds frequency of heads has been maintained, the greater is the probability that the probability of getting heads with the next toss is two-thirds. But again to speak in this way of the probable result of the next toss is only a misleading way of speaking of the probable distribution of heads throughout the whole sequence. What is being asserted is that the larger we make our sample, the greater is the probability that the frequency with which a given result occurs is the same as its frequency in the sequence as a whole. And this in its turn is merely a way of expressing the mathematical truism that if we divide a finite sequence, in which some property occurs with a certain frequency, into all the possible sub-sequences which collectively yield the same result, then the proportion of sub-sequences in which the property occurs with a markedly different frequency varies inversely with their length. Once again the individual case does not come into it.

A consequence of this is that the cases which are favourable to the frequency theory are those in which we do not care about the individual instance. A physicist will predict that under such and such conditions a certain proportion of a group of electrons will pass from one orbit to another; he does not claim to be able to predict which individual electrons will do so, nor is this question of any interest to him; from his point of view the resulting state of the system will be the same whichever they are. A geneticist can deduce from Mendel's laws of heredity that some characteristic will be transmitted in such and such a ratio to the third generation; so far as the validation of the theory goes, it is a matter of indifference which members of the family in that generation display the characteristic and which do not. A traffic manager tries to forecast what percentage of the population of a city will be travelling by train on a given day to such and such a set of other places. It does not affect his calculations whether it is Mr. Smith or Mr. Jones who chooses to spend the holiday at home. In all such cases the frequency theory gives us what we want.

But what of the cases in which we are interested in the individual instance? We do very often raise such questions as What are my chances of living to 80? Is the weather likely to be fine to-morrow? How much chance does the Labour Party have of winning this by-election? How probable is it that the favourite will win the next race? We seldom look for precise answers to questions of this kind, but we do expect such answers as that the event is very improbable, or that it is rather more probable than not. But what force do such answers have? What indeed do the questions mean? If, as I believe, in saying that a particular event is probable, we are not in cases of this kind talking either about any logical relations which statements bear to one another, or about the distribution of a property within some class of reference, what is it that we are saying? Is this a distinctive sense of probability?

I am inclined to answer that it is. It seems to me that when we talk about such things as the chances of its being fine to-morrow, or the chances of winning an election, we are not talking about chances at all, in the sense in which to talk about chances is to make a statistical statement of one sort or another. What we want to know is whether the event in question will or will not take place, and when we enquire into its likelihood, the question which we are really asking is how far we are justified in expecting it. To reply that it is more probable than not is not to say anything about the available evidence, nor yet to make a statistical prediction ; it is rather to concede to the questioner the right to have some confidence in the event. Roughly speaking, one is advising him to bet on it at equal odds.

But this only shifts the difficulty to another place. For the advice is not arbitrarily given, or if it is, it is worthless. We may not be talking about the available evidence, but at least we are talking in the light of it. We are implying that there is good reason to believe that the event in question will occur. And how is this claim to be analysed ?

In the most favourable case, the answer seems fairly clear. The best reason we can have for believing that the event will occur is that we can deduce it from the evidence at our disposal in conjunction with some causal law. Admittedly, we are then faced with the question how our belief in the causal law is itself to be justified ; we come in the end to the problem of induction. But whatever view we take of the problem of induction, it remains true that being able to derive it from some accepted causal law is the strongest justification for believing in the existence of any unobserved event.

Very often, however, this is not possible. The examples which we have been considering are all cases in which we are not in a position to rely on causal laws. Whether or not we believe that the state of to-morrow's weather, or the result of such and such a future by-election, is causally determined, the fact is that we do not have the knowledge which would permit us to make the causal inferences. The best that we can do is to find evidence which points in one direction or another. And these are the cases in which we talk of probability.

But what is it for the evidence to point in this or that direction ? What do we take this to imply ? In the most favourable case, again, I think it is a matter of our being able to rely on some generalization which is not far short of being a causal law. We cannot read off to-morrow's weather from to-day's weather chart, because the connection is not invariable. What we can say is that very much more often than not, under the prevailing conditions of atmospheric pressure and so forth, the weather, say, continues to be fine. And then the question that we have to ask is why this case should be one of the exceptions. If we can see no reason why it should be, we assume that what most commonly happens under the known conditions will happen in this instance also. If on the other hand we do find such a reason, it will have the effect of weakening the generalization on which we were going to rely ; and then we must look further in the hope of finding a stronger generalization to put in its place. Thus when the problem is put in this way, the principle of going by the total evidence ceases to be arbitrary.

Unfortunately, this is not the whole answer. There remain a great many instances in which the most conscientious survey of the evidence does not provide us with anything that even approximates to a causal law. In the case of the horse race, for example, not only are the relevant generalizations commonly rather weak, but their tendency may well be conflicting ; one horse will be preferred on account of its breeding, another because of the capabilities of its jockey, and so forth. In these circumstances the prudent bettor will try to weigh all the factors and will eventually conclude that the scale comes down most heavily on such and such a side. And if we ask him how he has come to this conclusion, we may press him to a point where the only answer he can give is just that this is how it strikes him. If he is right sufficiently often, we shall say that he has good judgement ; his conclusions will help to set the standard by which we estimate the likelihood of such events. In a sense, it would be wrong to say that he weighed the evidence any more correctly than the rest of us, for there is no objective standard of correctness by which this could be measured. In cases of this kind, the argument goes in the reverse direction. The reason why the most successful predictors are the best judges of probability is that it is in terms of their judgement that the probabilities themselves are assessed.

8

WHAT IS A LAW OF NATURE?

There is a sense in which we know well enough what is ordinarily meant by a law of nature. We can give examples. Thus it is, or is believed to be, a law of nature that the orbit of a planet around the sun is an ellipse, or that arsenic is poisonous, or that the intensity of a sensation is proportionate to the logarithm of the stimulus, or that there are 303,000,000,000,000,000,000,000 molecules in one gram of hydrogen. It is not a law of nature, though it is necessarily true, that the sum of the angles of a Euclidean triangle is 180 degrees, or that all the presidents of the third French Republic were male, though this is a legal fact in its way, or that all the cigarettes which I now have in my cigarette case are made of Virginian tobacco, though this again is true and, given my tastes, not wholly accidental. But while there are many such cases in which we find no difficulty in telling whether some proposition, which we take to be true, is or is not a law of nature, there are cases where we may be in doubt. For instance, I suppose that most people take the laws of nature to include the first law of thermodynamics, the proposition that in any closed physical system the sum of energy is constant: but there are those who maintain that this principle is a convention, that it is interpreted in such a way that there is no logical possibility of its being falsified, and for this reason they may deny that it is a law of nature at all. There are two questions at issue in a case of this sort: first, whether the principle under discussion is in fact a convention, and secondly whether its being a convention, if it is one, would disqualify it from being a law of nature. In the same way, there may be a dispute whether statistical generalizations are to count as laws of nature, as distinct from the dispute whether certain generalizations, which have been taken to be laws of nature, are in fact statistical. And even if we were always able to tell, in the case of any given proposition, whether or not it had the form of a law of nature, there would still remain the problem of making clear what this implied.

The use of the word 'law', as it occurs in the expression 'laws of nature', is now fairly sharply differentiated from its use in legal and moral contexts : we do not conceive of the laws of nature as imperatives. But this was not always so. For instance, Hobbes in his *Leviathan* lists fifteen 'laws of nature' of which two of the most important are that men 'seek peace, and follow it' and 'that men perform their covenants made' : but he does not think that these laws are necessarily respected. On the contrary, he holds that the state of nature is a state of war, and that covenants will not in fact be kept unless there is some power to enforce them. His laws of nature are like civil laws except that they are not the commands of any civil authority. In one place he speaks of them as 'dictates of Reason' and adds that men improperly call them by the name of laws : 'for they are but conclusions or theorems concerning what conduceth to the conservation and defence of themselves : whereas Law, properly, is the word of him, that by right hath command over others'. 'But yet,' he continues, 'if you consider the same Theorems, as delivered in the word of God, that by right commandeth all things ; then they are properly called Laws.' [1]

It might be thought that this usage of Hobbes was so far removed from our own that there was little point in mentioning it, except as a historical curiosity ; but I believe

[1] *Leviathan*, Part I, chapter xv.

that the difference is smaller than it appears to be. I think that our present use of the expression 'laws of nature' carries traces of the conception of Nature as subject to command. Whether these commands are conceived to be those of a personal deity or, as by the Greeks, of an impersonal fate, makes no difference here. The point, in either case, is that the sovereign is thought to be so powerful that its dictates are bound to be obeyed. It is not as in Hobbes's usage a question of moral duty or of prudence, where the subject has freedom to err. On the view which I am now considering, the commands which are issued to Nature are delivered with such authority that it is impossible that she should disobey them. I do not claim that this view is still prevalent; at least not that it is explicitly held. But it may well have contributed to the persistence of the feeling that there is some form of necessity attaching to the laws of nature, a necessity which, as we shall see, it is extremely difficult to pin down.

In case anyone is still inclined to think that the laws of nature can be identified with the commands of a superior being, it is worth pointing out that this analysis cannot be correct. It is already an objection to it that it burdens our science with all the uncertainty of our metaphysics, or our theology. If it should turn out that we had no good reason to believe in the existence of such a superior being, or no good reason to believe that he issued any commands, it would follow, on this analysis, that we should not be entitled to believe that there were any laws of nature. But the main argument against this view is independent of any doubt that one may have about the existence of a superior being. Even if we knew that such a one existed, and that he regulated nature, we still could not identify the laws of nature with his commands. For it is only by discovering what were the laws of nature that we could know what form these commands had taken. But this implies that we have some independent criteria for deciding what the laws of nature are. The assumption that they are imposed by a superior being is therefore idle, in the same way as the assumption of providence is idle. It is only if there are independent means of finding out what is going to happen that one is able to say what providence has in store. The same objection applies to the rather more fashionable view that moral laws are the commands of a superior being: but this does not concern us here.

There is, in any case, something strange about the notion of a command which it is impossible to disobey. We may be sure that some command will never in fact be disobeyed. But what is meant by saying that it cannot be? That the sanctions which sustain it are too strong? But might not one be so rash or so foolish as to defy them? I am inclined to say that it is in the nature of commands that it should be possible to disobey them. The necessity which is ascribed to these supposedly irresistible commands belongs in fact to something different: it belongs to the laws of logic. Not that the laws of logic cannot be disregarded; one can make mistakes in deductive reasoning, as in anything else. There is, however, a sense in which it is impossible for anything that happens to contravene the laws of logic. The restriction lies not upon the events themselves but on our method of describing them. If we break the rules according to which our method of description functions, we are not using it to describe anything. This might suggest that the events themselves really were disobeying the laws of logic, only we could not say so. But this would be an error. What is describable as an event obeys the laws of logic: and what is not describable as an event is not an event at all. The chains which logic puts upon nature are purely formal: being formal they weigh nothing, but for the same reason they are indissoluble.

From thinking of the laws of nature as the commands

of a superior being, it is therefore only a short step to crediting them with the necessity that belongs to the laws of logic. And this is in fact a view which many philosophers have held. They have taken it for granted that a proposition could express a law of nature only if it stated that events, or properties, of certain kinds were necessarily connected; and they have interpreted this necessary connection as being identical with, or closely analogous to, the necessity with which the conclusion follows from the premisses of a deductive argument; as being, in short, a logical relation. And this has enabled them to reach the strange conclusion that the laws of nature can, at least in principle, be established independently of experience: for if they are purely logical truths, they must be discoverable by reason alone.

The refutation of this view is very simple. It was decisively set out by Hume. 'To convince us', he says, 'that all the laws of nature and all the operations of bodies, without exception, are known only by experience, the following reflections may, perhaps, suffice. Were any object presented to us, and were we required to pronounce concerning the effect, which will result from it, without consulting past observation: after what manner, I beseech you, must the mind proceed in this operation? It must invent or imagine some event, which it ascribes to the object as its effect: and it is plain that this invention must be entirely arbitrary. The mind can never find the effect in the supposed cause, by the most accurate scrutiny and examination. For the effect is totally different from the cause, and consequently can never be discovered in it.' [1]

Hume's argument is, indeed, so simple that its purport has often been misunderstood. He is represented as maintaining that the inherence of an effect in its cause is something which is not discoverable in nature; that as a matter of fact our observations fail to reveal the existence of any

[1] *An Enquiry concerning Human Understanding*, iv. 1.25.

such relation: which would allow for the possibility that our observations might be at fault. But the point of Hume's argument is not that the relation of necessary connection which is supposed to conjoin distinct events is not in fact observable: it is that there could not be any such relation, not as a matter of fact but as a matter of logic. What Hume is pointing out is that if two events are distinct, they are distinct: from a statement which does no more than assert the existence of one of them it is impossible to deduce anything concerning the existence of the other. This is, indeed, a plain tautology. Its importance lies in the fact that Hume's opponents denied it. They wished to maintain both that the events which were coupled by the laws of nature were logically distinct from one another, and that they were united by a logical relation. But this is a manifest contradiction. Philosophers who hold this view are apt to express it in a form which leaves the contradiction latent: it was Hume's achievement to have brought it clearly to light.

In certain passages Hume makes his point by saying that the contradictory of any law of nature is at least conceivable; he intends thereby to show that the truth of the statement which expresses such a law is an empirical matter of fact and not an *a priori* certainty. But to this it has been objected that the fact that the contradictory of a proposition is conceivable is not a decisive proof that the proposition is not necessary. It may happen, in doing logic or pure mathematics, that one formulates a statement which one is unable either to prove or disprove. Surely in that case both the alternatives of its truth and falsehood are conceivable. Professor W. C. Kneale, who relies on this objection,[1] cites the example of Goldbach's conjecture that every even number greater than two is the sum of two primes. Though this conjecture has been confirmed so far as it has been

[1] *Probability and Induction*, pp. 79 ff.

tested, no one yet knows for certain whether it is true or false: no proof has been discovered either way. All the same, if it is true, it is necessarily true, and if it is false, it is necessarily false. Suppose that it should turn out to be false. We surely should not be prepared to say that what Goldbach had conjectured to be true was actually inconceivable. Yet we should have found it to be the contradictory of a necessary proposition. If we insist that this does prove it to be inconceivable, we find ourselves in the strange position of having to hold that one of two alternatives is inconceivable, without our knowing which.

I think that Professor Kneale makes his case: but I do not think that it is an answer to Hume. For Hume is not primarily concerned with showing that a given set of propositions, which have been taken to be necessary, are not so really. This is only a possible consequence of his fundamental point that 'there is no object which implies the existence of any other if we consider these objects in themselves, and never look beyond the idea which we form of them',[1] in short, that to say that events are distinct is incompatible with saying that they are logically related. And against this Professor Kneale's objection has no force at all. The most that it could prove is that, in the case of the particular examples that he gives, Hume might be mistaken in supposing that the events in question really were distinct: in spite of the appearances to the contrary, an expression which he interpreted as referring to only one of them might really be used in such a way that it included a reference to the other.

But is it not possible that Hume was always so mistaken; that the events, or properties, which are coupled by the laws of nature never are distinct? This question is complicated by the fact that once a generalization is accepted as a law of nature it tends to change its status. The meanings

[1] *A Treatise of Human Nature*, i, iii, vi.

which we attach to our expressions are not completely constant: if we are firmly convinced that every object of a kind which is designated by a certain term has some property which the term does not originally cover, we tend to include the property in the designation; we extend the definition of the object, with or without altering the words which refer to it. Thus, it was an empirical discovery that loadstones attract iron and steel: for someone who uses the word 'loadstone' only to refer to an object which has a certain physical appearance and constitution, the fact that it behaves in this way is not formally deducible. But, as the word is now generally used, the proposition that loadstones attract iron and steel is analytically true: an object which did not do this would not properly be called a loadstone. In the same way, it may have become a necessary truth that water has the chemical composition H_2O. But what then of heavy water which has the composition D_2O? Is it not really water? Clearly this question is quite trivial. If it suits us to regard heavy water as a species of water, then we must not make it necessary that water consists of H_2O. Otherwise, we may. We are free to settle the matter whichever way we please.

Not all questions of this sort are so trivial as this. What, for example, is the status in Newtonian physics of the principle that the acceleration of a body is equal to the force which is acting on it divided by its mass? If we go by the text-books in which 'force' is defined as the product of mass and acceleration, we shall conclude that the principle is evidently analytic. But are there not other ways of defining force which allow this principle to be empirical? In fact there are, but as Henri Poincaré has shown,[1] we may then find ourselves obliged to treat some other Newtonian principle as a convention. It would appear that in a system of this kind there is likely to be a conventional

[1] Cf. *La Science et l'hypothèse*, pp. 119-29.

element, but that, within limits, we can situate it where we choose. What is put to the test of experience is the system as a whole.

This is to concede that some of the propositions which pass for laws of nature are logically necessary, while implying that it is not true of all of them. But one might go much further. It is at any rate conceivable that at a certain stage the science of physics should become so unified that it could be wholly axiomatized: it would attain the status of a geometry in which all the generalizations were regarded as necessarily true. It is harder to envisage any such development in the science of biology, let alone the social sciences, but it is not theoretically impossible that it should come about there too. It would be characteristic of such systems that no experience could falsify them, but their security might be sterile. What would take the place of their being falsified would be the discovery that they had no empirical application.

The important point to notice is that, whatever may be the practical or aesthetic advantages of turning scientific laws into logically necessary truths, it does not advance our knowledge, or in any way add to the security of our beliefs. For what we gain in one way, we lose in another. If we make it a matter of definition that there are just so many million molecules in every gram of hydrogen, then we can indeed be certain that every gram of hydrogen will contain that number of molecules: but we must become correspondingly more doubtful, in any given case, whether what we take to be a gram of hydrogen really is so. The more we put into our definitions, the more uncertain it becomes whether anything satisfies them: this is the price that we pay for diminishing the risk of our laws being falsified. And if it ever came to the point where all the 'laws' were made completely secure by being treated as logically necessary, the whole weight of doubt would fall upon the statement that our system had application. Having deprived ourselves of the power of expressing empirical generalizations, we should have to make our existential statements do the work instead.

If such a stage were reached, I am inclined to say that we should no longer have a use for the expression 'laws of nature', as it is now understood. In a sense, the tenure of such laws would still be asserted : they would be smuggled into the existential propositions. But there would be nothing in the system that would count as a law of nature : for I take it to be characteristic of a law of nature that the proposition which expresses it is not logically true. In this respect, however, our usage is not entirely clear-cut. In a case where a sentence has originally expressed an empirical generalization, which we reckon to be a law of nature, we are inclined to say that it still expresses a law of nature, even when its meaning has been so modified that it has come to express an analytic truth. And we are encouraged in this by the fact that it is often very difficult to tell whether this modification has taken place or not. Also, in the case where some of the propositions in a scientific system play the rôle of definitions, but we have some freedom in deciding which they are to be, we tend to apply the expression 'laws of nature' to any of the constituent propositions of the system, whether or not they are analytically true. But here it is essential that the system as a whole should be empirical. If we allow the analytic propositions to count as laws of nature, it is because they are carried by the rest.

Thus to object to Hume that he may be wrong in assuming that the events between which his causal relations hold are 'distinct existences' is merely to make the point that it is possible for a science to develop in such a way that axiomatic systems take the place of natural laws. But this was not true of the propositions with which Hume was concerned, nor is it true, in the main, of the sciences of to-day. And in any case Hume is right in saying that we cannot have the best of both worlds; if we want our generalizations to have empirical content, they cannot be logically secure; if we make them logically secure, we rob them of their empirical content. The relations which hold between things, or events, or properties, cannot be both factual and logical. Hume himself spoke only of causal relations, but his argument applies to any of the relations that science establishes, indeed to any relations whatsoever.

It should perhaps be remarked that those philosophers who still wish to hold that the laws of nature are 'principles of necessitation' [1] would not agree that this came down to saying that the propositions which expressed them were analytic. They would maintain that we are dealing here with relations of objective necessity, which are not to be identified with logical entailments, though the two are in certain respects akin. But what are these relations of objective necessity supposed to be? No explanation is given except that they are just the relations that hold between events, or properties, when they are connected by some natural law. But this is simply to restate the problem; not even to attempt to solve it. It is not as if this talk of objective necessity enabled us to detect any laws of nature. On the contrary it is only *ex post facto*, when the existence of some connection has been empirically tested, that philosophers claim to see that it has this mysterious property of being necessary. And very often what they do 'see' to be necessary is shown by further observation to be false. This does not itself prove that the events which are brought together by a law of nature do not stand in some unique relation. If all attempts at its analysis fail, we may be reduced to saying that it is *sui generis*. But why then describe it in a way which leads to its confusion with the relation of logical necessity?

[1] Cf. Kneale, *op. cit.*

A further attempt to link natural with logical necessity is to be found in the suggestion that two events E and I are to be regarded as necessarily connected when there is some well-established universal statement U, from which, in conjunction with the proposition *i*, affirming the existence of I, a proposition *e*, affirming the existence of E, is formally deducible.[1] This suggestion has the merit of bringing out the fact that any necessity that there may be in the connection of two distinct events comes only through a law. The proposition which describes 'the initial conditions' does not by itself entail the proposition which describes the 'effect': it does so only when it is combined with a causal law. But this does not allow us to say that the law itself is necessary. We can give a similar meaning to saying that the law is necessary by stipulating that it follows, either directly or with the help of certain further premisses, from some more general principle. But then what is the status of these more general principles? The question what constitutes a law of nature remains, on this view, without an answer.

II

Once we are rid of the confusion between logical and factual relations, what seems the obvious course is to hold that a proposition expresses a law of nature when it states what invariably happens. Thus, to say that unsupported bodies fall, assuming this to be a law of nature, is to say that there is not, never has been, and never will be a body that being unsupported does not fall. The 'necessity' of a law consists, on this view, simply in the fact that there are no exceptions to it.

It will be seen that this interpretation can also be extended to statistical laws. For they too may be represented

[1] Cf. K. Popper, 'What Can Logic Do For Philosophy?', *Supplementary Proceedings of the Aristotelian Society*, vol. xxii: and papers in the same volume by W. C. Kneale and myself.

as stating the existence of certain constancies in nature: only, in their case, what is held to be constant is the proportion of instances in which one property is conjoined with another or, to put it in a different way, the proportion of the members of one class that are also members of another. Thus it is a statistical law that when there are two genes determining a hereditary property, say the colour of a certain type of flower, the proportion of individuals in the second generation that display the dominant attribute, say the colour white as opposed to the colour red, is three quarters. There is, however, the difficulty that one does not expect the proportion to be maintained in every sample. As Professor R. B. Braithwaite has pointed out, 'when we say that the proportion (in a non-literal sense) of the male births among births is 51 per cent, we are not saying of any particular class of births that 51 per cent are births of males, for the actual proportion might differ very widely from 51 per cent in a particular class of births, or in a number of particular classes of births, without our wishing to reject the proposition that the proportion (in the non-literal sense) is 51 per cent.'[1] All the same the 'non-literal' use of the word 'proportion' is very close to the literal use. If the law holds, the proportion must remain in the neighbourhood of 51 per cent, for any sufficiently large class of cases: and the deviations from it which are found in selected sub-classes must be such as the application of the calculus of probability would lead one to expect. Admittedly, the question what constitutes a sufficiently large class of cases is hard to answer. It would seem that the class must be finite, but the choice of any particular finite number for it would seem also to be arbitrary. I shall not, however, attempt to pursue this question here. The only point that I here wish to make is that a statistical law is no less 'lawlike' than a causal law. Indeed, if the propositions

[1] *Scientific Explanation*, pp. 118-19.

which express causal laws are simply statements of what invariably happens, they can themselves be taken as expressing statistical laws, with ratios of 100 per cent. Since a 100 per cent ratio, if it really holds, must hold in every sample, these 'limiting cases' of statistical laws escape the difficulty which we have just remarked on. If henceforth we confine our attention to them, it is because the analysis of 'normal' statistical laws brings in complications which are foreign to our purpose. They do not affect the question of what makes a proposition lawlike: and it is in this that we are mainly interested.

On the view which we have now to consider, all that is required for there to be laws in nature is the existence of *de facto* constancies. In the most straightforward case, the constancy consists in the fact that events, or properties, or processes of different types are invariably conjoined with one another. The attraction of this view lies in its simplicity: but it may be too simple. There are objections to it which are not easily met.

In the first place, we have to avoid saddling ourselves with vacuous laws. If we interpret statements of the form 'All S is P' as being equivalent, in Russell's notation, to general implications of the form '$(x)\,\Phi x \supset \Psi x$', we face the difficulty that such implications are considered to be true in all cases in which their antecedent is false. Thus we shall have to take it as a universal truth both that all winged horses are spirited and that all winged horses are tame; for assuming, as I think we may, that there never have been or will be any winged horses, it is true both that there never have been or will be any that are not spirited, and that there never have been or will be any that are not tame. And the same will hold for any other property that we care to choose. But surely we do not wish to regard the ascription of any property whatsoever to winged horses as the expression of a law of nature.

The obvious way out of this difficulty is to stipulate that the class to which we are referring should not be empty. If statements of the form 'All S is P' are used to express laws of nature, they must be construed as entailing that there are S's. They are to be treated as the equivalent, in Russell's notation, of the conjunction of the propositions '$(x)\ \Phi x \supset \Psi x$ and $(\exists x)\ \Phi x$'. But this condition may be too strong. For there are certain cases in which we do wish to take general implications as expressing laws of nature, even though their antecedents are not satisfied. Consider, for example, the Newtonian law that a body on which no forces are acting continues at rest or in uniform motion along a straight line. It might be argued that this proposition was vacuously true, on the ground that there are in fact no bodies on which no forces are acting; but it is not for this reason that it is taken as expressing a law. It is not interpreted as being vacuous. But how then does it fit into the scheme? How can it be held to be descriptive of what actually happens?

What we want to say is that if there *were* any bodies on which no forces were acting then they *would* behave in the way that Newton's law prescribes. But we have not made any provision for such hypothetical cases: according to the view which we are now examining, statements of law cover only what is actual, not what is merely possible. There is, however, a way in which we can still fit in such 'non-instantial' laws. As Professor C. D. Broad has suggested,[1] we can treat them as referring not to hypothetical objects, or events, but only to the hypothetical consequences of instantial laws. Our Newtonian law can then be construed as implying that there are instantial laws, in this case laws about the behaviour of bodies on which forces are acting, which are such that when combined with the

[1] 'Mechanical and Teleological Causation', *Supplementary Proceedings of the Aristotelian Society*, vol. xiv, pp. 98 ff.

proposition that there are bodies on which no forces are acting, they entail the conclusion that these bodies continue at rest, or in uniform motion along a straight line. The proposition that there are such bodies is false, and so, if it is interpreted existentially, is the conclusion, but that does not matter. As Broad puts it, 'what we are concerned to assert is that this false conclusion is a necessary consequence of the conjunction of a certain false instantial supposition with certain true instantial laws of nature'.

This solution of the present difficulty is commendably ingenious, though I am not sure that it would always be possible to find the instantial laws which it requires. But even if we accept it, our troubles are not over. For, as Broad himself points out, there is one important class of cases in which it does not help us. These cases are those in which one measurable quantity is said to depend upon another, cases like that of the law connecting the volume and temperature of a gas under a given pressure, in which there is a mathematical function which enables one to calculate the numerical value of either quantity from the value of the other. Such laws have the form '$x = Fy$', where the range of the variable y covers all possible values of the quantity in question. But now it is not to be supposed that all these values are actually to be found in nature. Even if the number of different temperatures which specimens of gases have or will acquire is infinite, there still must be an infinite number missing. How then are we to interpret such a law? As being the compendious assertion of all its actual instances? But the formulation of the law in no way indicates which the actual instances are. It would be absurd to construe a general formula about the functional dependence of one quantity on another as committing us to the assertion that just these values of the quantity are actually realized. As asserting that for a value n of y, which is in fact not realized, the proposition that it is realized, in conjunction with the set of propositions describing all the actual cases, entails the proposition that there is a corresponding value m of x? But this is open to the same objection, with the further drawback that the entailment would not hold. As asserting with regard to any given value n of y that either n is not realized or that there is a corresponding value m of x? This is the most plausible alternative, but it makes the law trivial for all the values of y which happen not to be realized. It is hard to escape the conclusion that what we really mean to assert when we formulate such a law is that there is a corresponding value of x to every *possible* value of y.

Another reason for bringing in possibilities is that there seems to be no other way of accounting for the difference between generalizations of law and generalizations of fact. To revert to our earlier examples, it is a generalization of fact that all the Presidents of the Third French Republic are male, or that all the cigarettes that are now in my cigarette case are made of Virginian tobacco. It is a generalization of law that the planets of our solar system move in elliptical orbits, but a generalization of fact that, counting the earth as Terra, they all have Latin names. Some philosophers refer to these generalizations of fact as 'accidental generalizations', but this use of the word 'accidental' may be misleading. It is not suggested that these generalizations are true by accident, in the sense that there is no causal explanation of their truth, but only that they are not themselves the expression of natural laws.

But how is this distinction to be made? The formula '$(x)\ \Phi x \supset \Psi x$' holds equally in both cases. Whether the generalization be one of fact or of law, it will state at least that there is nothing which has the property Φ but lacks the property Ψ. In this sense, the generality is perfect in both cases, so long as the statements are true. Yet there seems to be a sense in which the generality of what we are calling generalizations of fact is less complete. They seem to be restricted in a way that generalizations of law are not. Either they involve some spatio-temporal restriction, as in the example of the cigarettes *now* in my cigarette case, or they refer to particular individuals, as in the example of the presidents of France. When I say that all the planets have Latin names, I am referring definitely to a certain set of individuals, Jupiter, Venus, Mercury, and so on, but when I say that the planets move in elliptical orbits I am referring indefinitely to anything that has the properties that constitute being a planet in this solar system. But it will not do to say that generalizations of fact are simply conjunctions of particular statements, which definitely refer to individuals ; for in asserting that the planets have Latin names, I do not individually identify them : I may know that they have Latin names without being able to list them all. Neither can we mark off generalizations of law by insisting that their expression is not to include any reference to specific places or times. For with a little ingenuity, generalizations of fact can always be made to satisfy this condition. Instead of referring to the cigarettes that are now in my cigarette case, I can find out some general property which only these cigarettes happen to possess, say the property of being contained in a cigarette case with such and such markings which is owned at such and such a period of his life by a person of such and such a sort, where the descriptions are so chosen that the description of the person is in fact satisfied only by me and the description of the cigarette case, if I possess more than one of them, only by the one in question. In certain instances these descriptions might have to be rather complicated, but usually they would not : and anyhow the question of complexity is not here at issue. But this means that, with the help of these 'individuating' predicates, generalizations of fact can be expressed in just as universal a form as generalizations of law. And conversely, as Professor Nelson Goodman has pointed out, generalizations of law can themselves be expressed in such a way that they contain a reference to particular individuals, or to specific places and times. For, as he remarks, 'even the hypothesis "All grass is green" has as an equivalent "All grass in London or elsewhere is green"'.[1] Admittedly, this assimilation of the two types of statement looks like a dodge; but the fact that the dodge works shows that we cannot found the distinction on a difference in the ways in which the statement can be expressed. Again, what we want to say is that whereas generalizations of fact cover only actual instances, generalizations of law cover possible instances as well. But this notion of possible, as opposed to actual, instances has not yet been made clear.

If generalizations of law do cover possible as well as actual instances, their range must be infinite; for while the number of objects which do throughout the course of time possess a certain property may be finite, there can be no limit to the number of objects which might possibly possess it: for once we enter the realm of possibility we are not confined even to such objects as actually exist. And this shows how far removed these generalizations are from being conjunctions: not simply because their range is infinite, which might be true even if it were confined to actual instances, but because there is something absurd about trying to list all the possible instances. One can imagine an angel's undertaking the task of naming or describing all the men that there ever have been or will be, even if their number were infinite, but how would he set about naming, or describing, all the possible men? This point is developed by F. P. Ramsey who remarks that the variable hypothetical '$(x)\,\Phi x$' resembles a conjunction (*a*) in that it contains all lesser, *i.e.* here all finite conjunctions, and appears as a sort of infinite product. (*b*) When we ask

[1] *Fact, Fiction and Forecast*, p. 78.

what would make it true, we inevitably answer that it is true if and only if every x has Φ; *i.e.* when we regard it as a proposition capable of the two cases truth and falsity, we are forced to make it a conjunction which we cannot express for lack of symbolic power'.[1] But, he goes on, 'what we can't say we can't say, and we can't whistle it either', and he concludes that the variable hypothetical is not a conjunction and that 'if it is not a conjunction, it is not a proposition at all'. Similarly, Professor Ryle, without explicitly denying that generalizations of law are propositions, describes them as 'seasonal inference warrants',[2] on the analogy of season railway-tickets, which implies that they are not so much propositions as rules. Professor Schlick also held that they were rules, arguing that they could not be propositions because they were not conclusively verifiable; but this is a poor argument, since it is doubtful if any propositions are conclusively verifiable, except possibly those that describe the subject's immediate experiences.

Now to say that generalizations of law are not propositions does have the merit of bringing out their peculiarity. It is one way of emphasizing the difference between them and generalizations of fact. But I think that it emphasizes it too strongly. After all, as Ramsey himself acknowledges, we do want to say that generalizations of law are either true or false. And they are tested in the way that other propositions are, by the examination of actual instances. A contrary instance refutes a generalization of law in the same way as it refutes a generalization of fact. A positive instance confirms them both. Admittedly, there is the difference that if all the actual instances are favourable, their conjunction entails the generalization of fact, whereas it does not entail the generalization of law: but still there

[1] *Foundations of Mathematics*, p. 238.

[2] '"If", "So", and "Because"', *Philosophical Analysis* (Essays edited by Max Black), p. 332.

is no better way of confirming a generalization of law than by finding favourable instances. To say that lawlike statements function as seasonal inference warrants is indeed illuminating, but what it comes to is that the inferences in question are warranted by the facts. There would be no point in issuing season tickets if the trains did not actually run.

To say that generalizations of law cover possible as well as actual cases is to say that they entail subjunctive conditionals. If it is a law of nature that the planets move in elliptical orbits, then it must not only be true that the actual planets move in elliptical orbits; it must also be true that if anything were a planet it would move in an elliptical orbit: and here 'being a planet' must be construed as a matter of having certain properties, not just as being identical with one of the planets that there are. It is not indeed a peculiarity of statements which one takes as expressing laws of nature that they entail subjunctive conditionals: for the same will be true of any statement that contains a dispositional predicate. To say, for example, that this rubber band is elastic is to say not merely that it will resume its normal size when it has been stretched, but that it would do so if ever it were stretched: an object may be elastic without ever in fact being stretched at all. Even the statement that this is a white piece of paper may be taken as implying not only how the piece of paper does look but also how it would look under certain conditions, which may or may not be fulfilled. Thus one cannot say that generalizations of fact do not entail subjunctive conditionals, for they may very well contain dispositional predicates: indeed they are more likely to do so than not: but they will not entail the subjunctive conditionals which are entailed by the corresponding statements of law. To say that all the planets have Latin names may be to make a dispositional statement, in the sense that it implies not so much that people do always call them by such names but that they would so call them if they were speaking correctly. It does not, however, imply with regard to anything whatsoever that if it were a planet it would be called by a Latin name. And for this reason it is not a generalization of law, but only a generalization of fact.

There are many philosophers who are content to leave the matter there. They explain the 'necessity' of natural laws as consisting in the fact that they hold for all possible, as well as actual, instances : and they distinguish generalizations of law from generalizations of fact by bringing out the differences in their entailment of subjunctive conditionals. But while this is correct so far as it goes, I doubt if it goes far enough. Neither the notion of possible, as opposed to actual, instances nor that of the subjunctive conditional is so pellucid that these references to them can be regarded as bringing all our difficulties to an end. It will be well to try to take our analysis a little further if we can.

The theory which I am going to sketch will not avoid all talk of dispositions ; but it will confine it to people's attitudes. My suggestion is that the difference between our two types of generalization lies not so much on the side of the facts which make them true or false, as in the attitude of those who put them forward. The factual information which is expressed by a statement of the form 'for all x, if x has Φ then x has Ψ', is the same whichever way it is interpreted. For if the two interpretations differ only with respect to the possible, as opposed to the actual values of x, they do not differ with respect to anything that actually happens. Now I do not wish to say that a difference in regard to mere possibilities is not a genuine difference, or that it is to be equated with a difference in the attitude of those who do the interpreting. But I do think that it can best be elucidated by referring to such differences of attitude. In short I propose to explain the distinction between generalizations of law and generalizations of fact, and thereby to give some account of what a law of nature is, by the indirect method of analysing the distinction between treating a generalization as a statement of law and treating it as a statement of fact.

If someone accepts a statement of the form '$(x)\ \Phi x \supset \Psi x$' as a true generalization of fact, he will not in fact believe that anything which has the property Φ has any other property that leads to its not having Ψ. For since he believes that everything that has Φ has Ψ, he must believe that whatever other properties a given value of x may have they are not such as to prevent its having Ψ. It may be even that he knows this to be so. But now let us suppose that he believes such a generalization to be true, without knowing it for certain. In that case there will be various properties X, X_1 . . such that if he were to learn, with respect to any value of a of x, that a had one or more of these properties as well as Φ, it would destroy, or seriously weaken his belief that a had Ψ. Thus I believe that all the cigarettes in my case are made of Virginian tobacco, but this belief would be destroyed if I were informed that I had absent-mindedly just filled my case from a box in which I keep only Turkish cigarettes. On the other hand, if I took it to be a law of nature that all the cigarettes in this case were made of Virginian tobacco, say on the ground that the case had some curious physical property which had the effect of changing any other tobacco that was put into it into Virginian, then my belief would not be weakened in this way.

Now if our laws of nature were causally independent of each other, and if, as Mill thought, the propositions which expressed them were always put forward as being unconditionally true, the analysis could proceed quite simply. We could then say that a person A was treating a statement of the form 'for all x, if Φx then Ψx' as expressing a law of nature, if and only if there was no property X which was such that the information that a value α of x had X as well as Φ would weaken his belief that α had Ψ. And here we should have to admit the proviso that X did not logically entail not-Ψ, and also, I suppose, that its presence was not regarded as a manifestation of not-Ψ; for we do not wish to make it incompatible with treating a statement as the expression of a law that one should acknowledge a negative instance if it arises. But the actual position is not so simple. For one may believe that a statement of the form 'for all x, if Φx then Ψx' expresses a law of nature while also believing, because of one's belief in other laws, that if something were to have the property X as well as Φ it would not have Ψ. Thus one's belief in the proposition that an object which one took to be a loadstone attracted iron might be weakened or destroyed by the information that the physical composition of the supposed loadstone was very different from what one had thought it to be. I think, however, that in all such cases, the information which would impair one's belief that the object in question had the property Ψ would also be such that, independently of other considerations, it would seriously weaken one's belief that the object ever had the property Φ. And if this is so, we can meet the difficulty by stipulating that the range of properties which someone who treats 'for all x, if Φx then Ψx' as a law must be willing to conjoin with Φ, without his belief in the consequent being weakened, must not include those the knowledge of whose presence would in itself seriously weaken his belief in the presence of Φ.

There remains the further difficulty that we do not normally regard the propositions which we take to express laws of nature as being unconditionally true. In stating them we imply the presence of certain conditions which we do not actually specify. Perhaps we could specify them if we chose, though we might find it difficult to make the list exhaustive. In this sense a generalization of law may be weaker than a generalization of fact, since it may admit exceptions to the generalization as it is stated. This does not mean, however, that the law allows for exceptions: if the exception is acknowledged to be genuine, the law is held to be refuted. What happens in the other cases is that the exception is regarded as having been tacitly provided for. We lay down a law about the boiling point of water, without bothering to mention that it does not hold for high altitudes. When this is pointed out to us, we say that this qualification was meant to be understood. And so in other instances. The statement that if anything has Φ it has Ψ was a loose formulation of the law: what we really meant was that if anything has Φ but not X, it has Ψ. Even in the case where the existence of the exception was not previously known, we often regard it as qualifying rather than refuting the law. We say, not that the generalization has been falsified, but that it was inexactly stated. Thus, it must be allowed that someone whose belief in the presence of Ψ, in a given instance, is destroyed by the belief that Φ is accompanied by X may still be treating '$(x)\ \Phi \supset \Psi x$' as expressing a law of nature if he is prepared to accept '$(x)\ \Phi x \cdot \sim X x \supset \Psi x$' as a more exact statement of the law.

Accordingly I suggest that for someone to treat a statement of the form 'if anything has Φ it has Ψ' as expressing a law of nature, it is sufficient (i) that subject to a willingness to explain away exceptions he believes that in a non-trivial sense everything which in fact has Φ has Ψ (ii) that his belief that something which has Φ has Ψ is not liable to be weakened by the discovery that the object in question also has some other property X, provided (*a*) that X does not logically entail not-Ψ (*b*) that X is not a manifestation of not-Ψ (*c*) that the discovery that something had X would not in itself seriously weaken his belief that it had Φ (*d*) that he does not regard the statement 'if anything has Φ and not-X it has Ψ' as a more exact statement of the generalization that he was intending to express.

I do not suggest that these conditions are necessary, both because I think it possible that they could be simplified and because they do not cover the whole field. For instance, no provision has been made for functional laws, where the reference to possible instances does not at present seem to me eliminable. Neither am I offering a definition of natural law. I do not claim that to say that some proposition expresses a law of nature entails saying that someone has a certain attitude towards it; for clearly it makes sense to say that there are laws of nature which remain unknown. But this is consistent with holding that the notion is to be explained in terms of people's attitudes. My explanation is indeed sketchy, but I think that the distinctions which I have tried to bring out are relevant and important: and I hope that I have done something towards making them clear.

9

FATALISM

WHAT will be will be. Either the Labour party will come to power in Britain within the next three years or it will not; and if it will, it will, and if it will not, it will not. But if it will, is it already true that it will? This is a strange question, just as it would be a strange question to ask whether it is still true that the Conservative party was in power three years ago. The reason why these questions are strange is that the truth of a statement is not a proper subject of temporal predicates. The state of affairs which makes an empirical statement true is locatable in time, but the truth of the statement is not. Thus the statement that the Battle of Hastings was fought in 1066 is made true by this historical occurrence, but the truth of this statement is not in its turn an event of history. We can ask for the date of a battle but, having learned when it was fought, we cannot then go on to ask for the date of its being fought at that date. There is a time at which a given event occurs, and a time, which may be the same or different, at which it is discovered to occur, but there is no second dimension of time in which its occurring at a time occurs. Correspondingly, there may be a time concerning which a statement is true, and a time, which may be the same or different, at which it is discovered to be true, but there is no time at which it is true and no stretch of time during which it is true. In this sense truth is timeless.

This is, indeed, a fact which it is fairly easy to overlook. One reason for this is that we do not always distinguish very clearly between predicating truth of statements and predicating truth of sentences. So we make remarks like 'It wasn't true when I told you that I had a headache, but it is true now', which seems to imply that truth, so far from being timeless, is subject to change. But this consequence follows only if we take truth to be a predicate, not of the statement which a given sentence is used to express, but of the sentence itself; and even then it holds only for a certain type of sentence, namely that in which the meaning of the sentence is dependent on the context of its utterance. Thus if we are going to attribute truth-value to sentences we shall have to allow that the truth-value of a sentence like 'I have a headache' may not be constant. Since its meaning varies according to the identity of the speaker and the time of its utterance, so may its truth-value. It is, however, plain that this conclusion is easily avoidable. Instead of saying that the sentence is true at one time and false at another, we can say that it is at one time used to make a statement which is timelessly true and at another time used to make a different statement which is timelessly false. And since we normally conceive of truth and falsehood as applying not to a sentence itself but rather to what the sentence serves to express, this is the course to be preferred.

Another source of confusion lies in the fact that except when we are practising some deception we do not pronounce a statement to be true unless we accept it; and commonly we do not accept a statement unless we have some good reason for thinking it to be true. The result is that some people talk of truth as though a statement's being true were just equivalent to its being accepted, and others limit the class of true statements to those that have been ascertained to be true. In the first case truth is again exposed to temporal change, for a statement which is accepted at one time may not be accepted at another; in the second case it acquires a temporal limitation; since no statement about the future can yet have been ascertained to be true, we arrive at the conclusion that statements about the future are neither true nor false. But both views are mistaken. Though the class of statements which I think to be true is indeed identical with the class of statements which I accept, it cannot be inferred from this that to say that a statement is true is to say no more than that it is accepted. Acceptance does not guarantee truth; the supposition that some false proposition is universally accepted is not formally self-contradictory. For much the same reason, we cannot equate being true with being ascertained to be true. To bring out the formal error, we need only ask what in that case it is supposed that the statement which is ascertained to be true is ascertained to be. One may lay down the rule that a statement should not be taken to be true until it has been verified, though even this goes too far if it forbids our relying upon indirect evidence; it still will not follow that the concept of verification can simply be substituted for the concept of truth.

So I maintain that if such and such an event is going to happen, then it is true that it is going to happen. It is not true at any special time, whether now or in the future, but just true. To ask *when* it is true is to put an improper question. And if it is true that the event is going to happen, it is also true that it will not be prevented. It will not be prevented, no matter what else happens. This is another point that is often overlooked, especially in works which trade on the idea of pre-cognition. Thus it is quite commonly suggested that if we had this power, it would be very helpful to us in commanding our destinies. If a man could foresee, for example, that he was going to be killed in a certain railway accident, then he would avoid taking that train. But if he does not take that train, he will not be killed in that railway accident, and if he will not be killed in that railway accident, then his being killed in it is not something that he pre-cognized; for to say that something is pre-cognized implies that it will in fact be so. If our man foresaw the accident he foresaw it incorrectly, since he wrongly included himself among the victims. But if he is to be among the victims, if it just is a fact with regard to that particular person and a particular train and a particular time that the person is killed in that train at that time, then no matter what else actually happens at that or any other time, the man will not be saved. This is indeed a logical triviality. There is a sense in which we can no more prevent the future than we can undo the past. This sense is just that if something is so, it is so, independently of the date at which it occurs. This is an application of the logical truism that if *p*, then *p*, no matter what proposition *p* may be. If it is true, it is true and that is all there is to it.

All the same, many people find it paradoxical to allow that there is any sense at all in which no future event can be prevented. And one reason for this may be that they take it to imply that we have no control over the future. They do not realize that to say that the future will be the same, will be what it will, no matter what we do, is not equivalent to saying that it would be the same no matter what we did. The result is that they are troubled by the sort of paradox that Professor Ryle mentions in his essay 'What Was To Be', the first of his *Dilemmas*, to which I shall be referring again later on. 'It is of no practical use for a sailor to learn to swim. For either he will die by drowning, or he will not. If he will not die by drowning, then so far as this goes his learning to swim will be a waste of time; if he will die by drowning, it will not save him.' Now clearly something is wrong here. And what is wrong is the tacit assumption that to say that he will not die by drowning, all other circumstances being in fact what they are, is equivalent to saying that he would not die by drowning, no matter what the other circumstances were. But these statements are not equivalent. We shall never make things other than they will be, but we do often make them other than they would have been, if we had acted differently or failed to act at all.

It is interesting to note that in this respect there is no distinction between the future and the past. The past has been what it has been, just as the future will be what it will. What is done cannot be undone. But just as the future would in many respects be different if we acted differently in the present, so would the past. For if we assume no more than that our present actions are, to some extent at least, the effects of past events, then it will often be reasonable to infer that if these present actions were not being performed, the past events which caused them would not have existed. This inference is indeed demonstrative in the cases in which the cause in question is a sufficient condition of a present action, but examples of sufficient conditions, at least in the field of human behaviour, are not easy to find. Even so, we do often make such judgements as 'It was only his quick reactions that saved him from being run over', from which it can be deduced that if he had at that moment been run over he would at an earlier moment have reacted more slowly. Admittedly we do not think that anything we did in the present could make the past other than what it would have been, because we take it for granted that our actions can affect only the present and future. We assume that the direction of causal agency must be from earlier to later in time, or at any rate not from later to earlier. It is not clear to me why we should assume this, unless one is content to say that this is just how we happen to use causal terms, but I do not want to pursue this question here. The point which I am here concerned to make is that it is not only future events that would be different if we acted differently now. This much at least is also true of events in the present and the past.

Returning to our sailor, let us assume that he will not in fact be drowned. Then if it is a fact that he will not be drowned, it must remain a fact whether or not it is also a fact that he learns to swim. This is the ground on which the paradox is constructed, but the construction is faulty. There is nothing wrong with the premiss, but all that it proves is that the propositions that the sailor will not be drowned and that he learns to swim are logically independent. Neither of them entails the truth or falsity of the other. It does not follow, however, that they are not causally connected. It may well be that there are occasions on which the sailor would be saved from drowning only by his having learned to swim. If we combine this proposition with the proposition that he will not be drowned, what we can infer is just that he does learn to swim.

Still, however differently things might turn out if we acted differently from the way we do, 'things and actions are what they are and the consequences of them will be what they will be'.[1] If the sailor will not be drowned, he will not be drowned. Does this mean then that it is certain that he will not be drowned ? Assuming it to be true that the Labour party will win the next General Election, is it certain that it will ? Is it certain that the sun will rise to-morrow ? The trouble with these questions is that there is more than one sense in which they can be taken. If certainty is being identified here with logical necessity, then the answer is that none of these propositions is certain ; their negations may be false but they are not self-contradictory. In a more liberal and indeed more proper sense of the word 'certain', there are, however, circumstances in which one might take it to be certain that the sailor was not going to be drowned, for example, if one found him dying from some other cause ; but such contexts would be excep-

[1] Bishop Butler, *Sermons*, 7, 16.

tional. Normally a prediction of this kind could not rightly be held to be certain, in any ordinary sense of the word. And surely it is not certain, though I hope that it is true, that the Labour party will win the next General Election. That is to say, no one is now in a position to claim that he knows for certain that it will win. There may be enthusiasts who feel certain of this, but if so they must be making more of their evidence than it warrants. On the other hand, I am inclined to say that it is certain that the sun will rise to-morrow. For here I think that the evidence is strong enough to give me the right to be sure. This is indeed to display great confidence in the laws of astronomy; but is it not reasonable to think that they have earned it?

Of course, if in saying that a future event was certain one implied that nothing could prevent its happening, then it would not be certain that the sun will rise to-morrow. I do not know exactly what would be required to prevent its rising, but some such cataclysm is conceivable, and if it is conceivable there is a sense in which it could happen. But when I claim it to be certain that the sun will rise to-morrow I am not saying that nothing could conceivably prevent its rising. I am saying that nothing will prevent it, and I imply, I think with sufficient reason, that I have the right to be sure of this.

This does not mean that I am claiming any more for the proposition that the sun will rise to-morrow than that it is deducible from a well-established scientific theory. I am not suggesting that it is logically necessary, or even that it follows from any set of propositions the truth of which can be assured by present observation. So if we were to side with those philosophers who hold that no proposition is certain unless it is either logically demonstrable or capable of being established by present observation, we should have to regard it as uncertain that the sun will rise to-morrow. By this reckoning, no proposition about the future can be held to be certain, nor indeed any proposition about the past, unless one takes the unsound view that memory and pre-cognition, if it ever occurs, are forms of present observation. However, there does not seem to be any good reason to restrict the use of the word 'certain' in this fashion. It is a departure from ordinary usage, and while I am not at all against breaking with ordinary usage if there is anything to be gained by it, I do not see what is to be gained in this case. Some philosophers, indeed, are stricter still and will call nothing certain unless it is impossible to be mistaken about it. But this has the consequence that nothing at all is certain, not even, as I now think, statements about one's present experiences, for they can be misdescribed; not even logically necessary statements, for people frequently make mistakes in mathematics and logic, and while this does not prove that they are not very often right, or even that they do not very often know that they are right, still the possibility of their being wrong must remain, however simple the proposition in question may be. But surely we do not want to use the word 'certain' in so strict a way that it has no application at all.

In general, however, I think that people's reluctance to say that any statement about the future is certain, no matter how strong the evidence for it may be, is due not to their giving the word 'certain' a philosophically strict sense, but to their being over-impressed by the fact that something may prevent, that it is always possible to imagine that something will prevent the future event in question from occurring. For this reason they are led to draw a sharp distinction between the future and the present or past. Thus, nothing can now prevent its being true that I began writing this essay so many hours ago, and nothing that subsequently happens can prevent its being true that I am writing these words now, but many things can prevent its being true that I shall write the last paragraph of it so many hours hence. I cannot even claim to know that none of these things will happen, though I hope and believe that none of them will. But even in a case where I might claim to know that the future event was going to occur, it might be in the power of nature to stage a surprise. On this account it comes to be thought that the future is uncertain in a way in which the present and past are not.

If I have understood it rightly, this is the line that Miss Anscombe takes in her very interesting paper on 'Aristotle and the Sea Battle'.[1] 'Could anything that can happen make it untrue that the sun rises to-morrow?'[2] asks one of the participants in her dialogue. 'No,' says the other, but the implication is that he is wrong. The light could go out of the world. On the other hand, nothing that can happen could make it untrue that there is daylight now. And presumably the same could be said about the past. Nothing that can happen could make it untrue that the sun rose this morning. The question is whether the same security could be claimed for anything in the future. Miss Anscombe considers an imaginary example which might lead one to think that it could. 'Every day I receive a letter from someone giving an accurate account of my actions and experiences from the time of posting to the time I received the letter. And whatever I do (I do random, absurd actions for example, to see if he will still have written a true account) the letter records it. Now, since we are dealing in what can be imagined and therefore can be supposed to happen, we must settle whether this would be knowledge of the future, and whether its certainty would be a proof that what I did I did necessarily.'[3]

There are two questions here which must be kept distinct. I shall argue later on that from the premiss that someone knows what I am going to do, it does not follow

[1] *Mind*, vol. lxv, no. 257, January 1956.
[2] *Op. cit.* p. 12. [3] *Op. cit.* p. 13.

that I do it necessarily, in any customary sense of this term. But before coming to this we must first consider the question whether the clairvoyant in Miss Anscombe's example would be displaying knowledge of the future, and to this Miss Anscombe herself gives the answer No. 'This letter about my actions would not have been knowledge, even if what it said was always right. However often and invariably it was verified, it would still not be certain, because the facts could go against it.'[1] On the other hand the facts could not go against anything that is happening or has already happened. It is as if future events were at sea, in danger of shipwreck, while present and past events are safely home in port. So '"A knows that *p*" makes sense for any *p* that describes a fact about the past and present',[2] but not, it is implied, for any *p* that describes a fact about the future. 'Does not make sense' because with regard to the future, there is no performance that is to be allowed to qualify as knowledge.

But let us look more closely at this expression 'the facts could go against it'. Assuredly, if something has happened, or is happening, nothing that subsequently happens can make it untrue that it has happened, or is happening. But so far as this goes the future is in no worse case than the present or past. If something is going to happen, nothing else that happens can make it untrue that it will happen. For if it is true that it will happen, it is true no matter what else is true. No doubt there are any number of things that *could* make it untrue, but equally there are any number of things that *could* make it untrue that something is happening now, or that something happened in the past, that I am now writing these words, for example, or that Miss Anscombe sent her article to *Mind*. Anything that is logically or causally incompatible with either of these propositions could make them untrue, and indeed would make

[1] *Op. cit.* p. 14. [2] *Op. cit.* p. 13.

them untrue, if it were true itself. But since the propositions which I have mentioned are in fact true, the ones which would make them untrue are themselves untrue. Since I am writing these words and since Miss Anscombe did send her article to *Mind*, we can safely infer that any propositions which are incompatible, whether logically or causally, with either of these facts are false. But equally if it is true that I shall finish this essay, or that the Labour party will win the next election, then any facts that could go against these things will not go against them ; or rather, to speak more accurately, there are no such facts. There are propositions the truth of which is incompatible with the truth of these propositions, but if these are true those that would go against them are false. So again, there seems to be no essential difference, in this respect, between the future and the present or past. What is so is so whenever it occurs, and if it is so, nothing that actually happens can make it not be so. This is not to deny that something *could* make it not be so, in the sense that it is possible to imagine events or situations which are inconsistent with its being so ; but again this applies *whenever* it occurs.

But surely there is this difference, that we know that the Labour party lost the last General Election and therefore know that no proposition which is inconsistent with its having lost it can be true ; whereas we do not know that the Labour party will win the next General Election, and therefore we do not know that there are not facts which will prevent its winning. Yes indeed : in this example there is this difference. But if you generalize from it and say that when it comes to the future we can never know that the facts do not prevent a given proposition from being true, you are begging the question. You are not using the premiss that 'the facts could go against it' to prove that the proposition about the future is uncertain ; you are using the premiss that all propositions about the future are uncertain in order to infer that the facts could go against them. But this premiss, which you are assuming, is what you are required to prove. As it is, someone who thinks that he does know some proposition about the future to be true will also claim to know, in consequence, that there are no facts that can go against it ; and he may very well be right. He must indeed allow that the facts could go against it, in the sense that we can imagine things that would be inconsistent with its truth, but in *this* sense, as we have seen, the facts *could* go against true propositions about the present or past.

Of course, it is not to be denied that we do in fact know a great deal more about the present and past than we know about the future. I myself should say that our knowledge of the future, at least the immediate or not very distant future, was quite considerable, but it is mostly negative. There are a great many things of which I am prepared to say that I know they will *not* happen to-morrow, as that no human being will fly to Saturn, that I shall not wake up to find that my weight has increased to sixteen stone, that none of my friends will run the mile in less than three minutes, or become chess champion of the world ; there are not so many things of which I am prepared to say that I know that they *will* happen to-morrow, other than that the sun will rise and that the tides will ebb and flow in the English Channel and that there will be a number of people still alive on the earth, and various other facts of similar sorts. On the other hand, there are a great many more positive facts and also more negative facts that I should claim to know about the present and past. The difference mainly depends on our being endowed with memory and not, or only in very rare instances, with the power of precognition. But it is only a difference of degree. It is not that we know nothing about the future and everything about the present and past. There must be a host of true propositions about the present and past that we are much further from knowing, that is, have much less strong evidence for, than we are from knowing many true propositions about the future.

Professor Ryle, in his lecture 'What Was To Be', to which I have already referred, also maintains that there is an important difference, other than the mere difference of tense, between what he calls 'anterior truths and posterior truths, or between prophecies and chronicles'. 'After 1815', he says, 'there could be true and false statements mentioning the Battle of Waterloo in the past tense. After 1900 there could be true and false statements in the present and past tenses mentioning me. But before 1815 and 1900 there could not be true or false statements giving individual mention to the Battle of Waterloo, or to me, and this not just because our names had not yet been given, nor yet just because no one happened to be well enough equipped to predict the future in very great detail, but for some more abstruse reason. The prediction of an event can, in principle, be as specific as you please. It does not matter if in fact no forecaster could know or reasonably believe his prediction to be true. If gifted with a lively imagination, he could freely concoct a story in the future tense with all sort of minutiae in it and this elaborate story might happen to come true. But one thing he could not do — logically and not merely epistemologically could not do. He could not get the future events themselves for the heroes or heroines of his story, since while it is still an askable question whether or not a battle will be fought at Waterloo in 1815, he cannot use with their normal force the phrase "the Battle of Waterloo" or the pronoun "it". While it is still an askable question whether my parents are going to have a fourth son, he cannot use as a name the name "Gilbert Ryle" or use as a pronoun designating their fourth son the pronoun "he". Roughly, statements in the future tense cannot convey singular, but only general propositions, while statements in the present and past tenses can convey both.' [1]

Now whatever force there may be in this argument it must be objected that the conclusion which Professor Ryle draws from it is much too sweeping. It is not even roughly true that statements in the future tense cannot convey singular propositions. To begin with the most obvious set of counter-examples, if a thing is already known to us to exist, we can make predictions about its future behaviour which are just as specific as any story that we can tell about its present or past. There is nothing in the least suspect about such singular propositions as 'this tree will bear fruit next summer', 'the London train will be half an hour late', 'Professor Ryle will be lecturing at 10 a.m. to-morrow morning'. By the same token, we can significantly refer to Professor Ryle's lecture, though it has not yet taken place. Our reference may fail, the lecture may be cancelled, but this does not mean that when we erroneously referred to it we failed to express a singular proposition. Neither are we limited in our power of future reference to attempts to continue the biography of things which already exist. We can refer without any logical difficulty to to-morrow's weather, or next autumn's harvest, or the Presidential election of 1968, or next year's Cup Final. Of course these references are made against a background of existing knowledge. We rely on the constancy of the astronomical relations which supply us with our method of dating or on the stability of a political system or on the regularity of sporting events. It remains true, however, that having such footholds we do significantly refer to things which are not yet known to exist.

I think, therefore, that Professor Ryle has been misled by his choice of examples, which do indeed lend plausibility

[1] *Dilemmas*, p. 27.

to his thesis. A situation might develop in which someone could attempt without absurdity to give a description of the next world war, predicting when and where the battles would occur and what their outcome would be. We should not expect him to be right in every detail, but we might be prepared for his getting at least the outline of the story right. Yet we should think that he was using language strangely if he referred to the battles by name. I should be thought rather odd if I were heard to speculate about the future of little Susan, and it turned out that little Susan was my unborn grandchild. Even if I do eventually have a grandchild and it is female and in fact called Susan, it would still be odd of me to talk in this way now. But what would make it odd is just that I do not know and cannot be expected to know that any of these things will be. So far as I can see, there is nothing more to Professor Ryle's argument than the point, which I have already conceded, that we happen to know a great deal more about the present and past than we do about the future. This is borne out by the fact that when we do know, or think we know, or even only believe or strongly hope that some future event will occur, we do very often allow ourselves to refer to it by name.

This applies even to Professor Ryle's examples. If the Duke of Wellington had decided the day before the battle to make his stand at Waterloo, there would be nothing very strange or logically improper in his referring in his despatches to the forthcoming Battle of Waterloo. There are parents who are so anxious that any son of theirs should go to an exclusive school that they enter the boy's name before he is born and sometimes, if they are very optimistic, before he is conceived. The name under which they enter him may fail in its reference, the person to whom it is intended to refer may never be born, but it may succeed. And if it does succeed, the use of the name before the child exists fulfils exactly the same function as its use after the child has come into existence. The risk of its failing in its reference is greater, but this does not make the usage incorrect.

I suppose that what Professor Ryle had in mind when he said that statements in the future tense could not convey singular, but only general propositions, was that the subject of a singular proposition must be something to which, in a sense, one could point, and that it was not possible to point to anything which did not yet exist. In the case of a prospective existent, the best we could do would be to predict that there would exist something of a certain sort, hence the generality. But, as I have argued, one can also try to point to future events and may succeed. Neither is there any force in the contention that our success is merely a matter of good fortune; that we cannot know whether the future event exists or not. For in the first place this is not true of all future events and secondly we do not have to know that things exist in the present or past in order to make them the subject of singular propositions. People apostrophize spectres, without knowing whether they exist. Was Odysseus a real man? Did the Argonauts steal the Golden Fleece? It may well be that these names denote nothing, yet someone who used them in the belief that he was recording historical facts would not be committing any logical fault. His statements would not be true, but they would be perfectly genuine. Indeed the meaning of the sentences which expressed them would be quite unaffected by the historical question whether or not they succeeded in their reference.

It is now time to pass to the second of Miss Anscombe's questions. Suppose that someone did know all about my future actions, that he correctly predicted, in some such fashion as she describes, everything that I was going to do. Would it follow that I was bound to do these things, that I was fated to do them, that I did them necessarily? I shall try to show that it would not. We have already seen that the fact that I shall do what I shall does not entail that I am bound to do whatever it is that I shall do. It entails that I cannot fail to do it, since if I fail to do it it is not something that I shall do, but not that I could not fail to do it. Whatever I shall in fact do, it is conceivable that I should act otherwise. But if the fact that I shall do what I shall does not entail that I could not act otherwise, it does not entail that my actions are necessary. They may still be necessary in the sense of being causally determined, but that is a different question. It is quite independent of the purely logical point that the future will be what it will. And though we shall have to say something about the issue of determinism, it is on the logical argument that the fatalist usually relies.

Now if the fact that I shall, for example, take a train to Oxford to-morrow does not entail that it is necessary that I shall, then the fact, if it be a fact, that somebody knows that I shall do this does not entail that my doing it is necessary either. It may be thought to be necessary, because of the argument that if he really knows this fact about me he cannot be mistaken ; if he could be mistaken he would not really know it. But this is a confusion. It is only for a verbal reason that if he knows, he cannot be mistaken. It is not that his knowing puts a spell upon the facts but simply that the verb 'to know' is used in such a way that if he is in fact mistaken it follows that he does not know. And this fact about the proper use of the verb 'to know' has no bearing whatever upon the necessity of anything. The man's knowing what I am going to do does not compel me to do it ; the point is merely that if I fail to do it he will have been wrong. His knowing what I am going to do does indeed come to more than his being successful in his prediction ; we shall not credit him with knowledge unless we think that he is entitled to be sure of this success. But even if he satisfies this requirement, it still does not follow that the event which he predicts is necessary. The only doubtful case is that in which the prediction of the event is a successful inference from a causal law. But even here the ground for saying that the event is necessary, in one sense of the term, is not that someone knows that it will occur, but just that it does fall under a causal law.

In fact, though we often have a pretty shrewd idea what people are going to do, it rather seldom amounts to knowledge; with respect to human actions, even more than other types of future events, such knowledge as we can claim to have is mostly negative. It has, however, been maintained that there is someone, namely God, who does know all that any of us is ever going to do. And this gives rise to the question whether those who hold this view are committed by it to regarding all human behaviour as predestined, whether they must infer that, in view of God's foreknowledge, they have no power to act otherwise than as they will. Of course not all those who accept the premiss do draw this inference from it: some do and more do not. The question is whether the inference is valid. I am not concerned here with the validity of the premiss, but only with the question whether this conclusion follows from it.

From what we have already said, I think it must be clear that it does not. If the fact that someone knew what I was going to do to-morrow would not make it necessary that I should do it, then the fact that someone knew what I was going to do, not only to-morrow but all the days of my life, would not make these actions necessary either. The extent of the supposed foreknowledge makes no difference to the argument. Neither does it make any difference whether the person to whom the foreknowledge is attributed is taken to be human or divine. If there is any sense in which we are free, then we remain free, no matter whether there is someone who has some knowledge of what we will in fact do, no matter how much knowledge he has, and no matter what sort of person he is. All these considerations are irrelevant.

The position becomes less clear, however, when it is assumed that there is a God who not only has foreknowledge of everything that is going to happen but also has foreordained it. And indeed it would seem that we need some such further assumption in order to give any substance to the doctrine of fatalism. The fact that what will be will be is incontestable, but also, as we have seen, innocuous. On the other hand, if it were the case that some agency, whether benevolent or not, had planned everything that was going to be, then there might be some ground for our regarding ourselves as puppets in its hands. Can those who believe in such an agency consistently regard themselves as free, in any interesting sense ?

Once more I am not concerned here with examining the status of this belief. I do not in fact think that there is any way in which it can be justified. I see no reason to regard the universe as a goal-directed system, neither do I think that the analogy which some natural theologians have attempted to draw between its workings and the workings of human artefacts is capable of supporting an argument from design. But the objections to this form of argument are well known, and I have nothing fresh to add to them. The question which I now wish to raise is whether it leads to fatalism. Even for those who disbelieve in the existence of an Arch-Designer, this question should be of theoretical interest, if only because of its historical bearing upon the stubborn problem of free-will.

One difficulty in answering this question is that the assumption which gives rise to it may take different forms. If it is held that everything that happens, including everything that any of us does, is planned in every detail, then

I do not see how it can be denied that if the responsibility for what we do can be assigned to anyone at all, it must ultimately fall upon the planner rather than ourselves. We may still make choices but, in the last resort, we are no more responsible for them, or for the actions which flow from them, than if we had been hypnotized. For someone who takes this view, the doctrine of predestination does seem irresistible; and even so it would appear rather unjust that we should be rewarded or punished simply for playing our allotted part.

On the other hand, it might be held that while the course of events was designed in the main, some elements were left to chance. If these elements included human actions, or human actions were dependent on them, then the responsibility for human actions could not be attributed to the deity. But could it be attributed to their agents either? If the actions are due, directly or indirectly, to chance, it would seem that no one is responsible.

I suppose, however, that the most prevalent view is neither of these. It is assumed that there is a grand design, but that it does not cover every detail. Some things happen, perhaps, by chance, and some are the result of the exercise of human will. There are, indeed, limitations to what can be achieved by the human will, but within these limits it operates freely. God gives us the power to do this or that, but whether we do it and how we do it is our own concern. Therefore, we are accountable for what we do not only to one another but to him.

Given its presuppositions, how far is this a tenable theory? It is not suggested that we act as we do by chance; for this would appear to imply that we are not responsible. It is held rather, that our actions proceed from our characters, and that our characters are to some extent of our own making. We start with certain dispositions for good or evil and it depends upon our own free choice which of these dispositions are actualized and to what degree. But how do we come to make these choices ? Through the exercise of our wills. But what does this mean ? The picture which is presented is that of the will as a sort of crane hovering over a storehouse of motives, shuffling them around, and picking one or other of them out. It operates on its own or else, perhaps, it is directed by a crane-man, called the self. Some of the instruments are more powerful than others, and some of the crane-men have a firmer hand upon the levers. But how does it come about that some of the instruments are more powerful or that some of their operators are more resolute and skilled ? Were they made so, or did it just happen ? If they were made so, the responsibility would seem to fall upon their maker. If it just happened, it would seem that no one is responsible.

It can now be seen that this problem goes beyond the theoretical framework in which I have so far presented it. It is possibly more acute for theists because it is a recognized ground for disclaiming responsibility that one has been no more than the instrument of another's will ; but even if I am right in thinking that we have no good reason to accept this idea of a Creator, the fatalistic argument can still be presented in a slightly different form. It again runs very simply. Either human actions are entirely governed by causal laws or they are not. If they are, then they are necessary : given our heredity and environment we could not act otherwise than as we do ; if they are not, then to the extent that they are not caused they must occur by chance : if they occur by chance they are indeed not necessary, but equally we have no control over them. In neither case can we help ourselves.

The response which many philosophers now make to this argument is that it presents a false dilemma. It is not true that the only alternative to explaining human actions in causal terms is to regard them as occurring by chance. To speak of an action as occurring by chance suggests that it is done at random. But what an action which is done at random is properly contrasted with is not an action which lacks a cause, in the sense of a sufficient condition, but an action which lacks a purpose. The alternative to explaining human actions in terms of their causes is to explain them in terms of the reasons for which they are done. What was the agent's intention ? What end did he have in view ? When we account for actions in this way, we do not have to conclude either that they are necessary or that they occur by chance.

I think that this answer makes an important point. We do normally explain people's actions in terms of reasons rather than in terms of causes, and it is a perfectly legitimate form of explanation. The distinction between reason and cause is tenable at this level, since the fact that the agent has such and such a motive or intention need not consist in his having some particular experience which would be a sufficient, or even a necessary condition of the action which ensued. Nevertheless, I doubt if this answer really opens up a way of escape between the horns of the dilemma. For it can still be asked how it comes about that the agent has these purposes, and how it comes about that he does or does not seek to realize them. If he inhibits them, we may say that he does so for a reason, but then again what supplies him with this reason, and how does it come to work more strongly on him than the purposes which it overrides ? Is there a causal explanation of these things, or do they just happen to be so ? In either case, it is tempting to conclude that in the last resort the agent is not responsible.

Considering the extent to which it goes against our habitual mode of thought, this is not a conclusion to be accepted lightly, and various means have been suggested which would enable us to avoid it. The course which I have hitherto favoured [1] is to argue that when we say that an action was done freely we are not implying that it cannot be given any sort of causal explanation. On this view, we have to distinguish between causation and constraint. To say that an action is subject to a causal law need mean no more than that it can be fitted into some regular pattern, that under conditions of this kind an action of this sort always does occur, and this in itself is not destructive of the agent's freedom. It is only if the cause is of a certain special type that the agent is constrained and so not responsible for what he does: if, for example, he is drugged or hypnotized or suffering from certain forms of mental disease. Generally speaking the cases in which he is not responsible are those in which his will is, as it were, by-passed. They are contrasted with the cases in which the agent's choice, though it can be accounted for in causal terms, is still itself a causal factor.

I still think that a theory of this kind may be tenable, but it is by no means so obviously true as some of its advocates have assumed. The main objections to it are that the boundaries of constraint are not at all easy to draw with any precision; and that even if they could be drawn at all precisely, the distinction for which they are needed seems rather arbitrary. Why should a man be praised or blamed if his actions are brought about in one way, and acquitted of all responsibility if they are brought about in another? In either case they are equally the product of his heredity and environment.

An answer which is sometimes given to this objection is that the distinction can be justified on utilitarian grounds. The cases in which we hold an agent responsible are those in which we judge that the stimulus of praise or blame,

[1] *Vide, e.g.*, the essay on 'Freedom and Necessity' in my *Philosophical Essays*.

reward or punishment, will have some effect upon him. If the action is one which we regard as socially undesirable, and the consequences of doing it are made painful to the agent, then we may hope that their effect on him will be such that his inclination to repeat the action will be inhibited. On the other hand, if the action is one that he has been constrained to do, these stimuli are likely to be ineffective. Given the constraining factor, the application of them would not cause him to act differently on a subsequent occasion. There is therefore no point in holding him responsible.

Again, I think that this view may be tenable. Though it might be rather difficult in practice to discriminate between the cases in which the stimulus of praise or blame would be effective and those in which it would not, the theoretical basis of the distinction is clear enough. At the same time I think it has to be admitted that this is not so much an analysis as a transformation of our ordinary notion of responsibility. It is true that when we have to decide how much or in what way we should reward or punish someone, we are influenced by considerations of utility. But the primary ground for rewarding or punishing a man at all is that he *deserves* it ; and this is understood to imply that the actions on which his merit is assessed were not necessitated. It is assumed that he need not have done them, not merely in the sense that he could, or would, have avoided doing them if the circumstances had been different, but that he could have avoided doing them, the circumstances being exactly as they were. Now the claim that our actions are avoidable in this sense is hard to interpret, let alone to justify, and it may well be false or even incoherent. In that case the ordinary notion of desert falls with it, and a great deal of our moral thinking will have to be revised. I do not say that this would be a bad thing, even on moral grounds, but only that it would be a much more far-reaching step than utilitarians commonly admit.

A quite different line of argument, which has recently come somewhat into favour, is that the teleological form of explanation, an explanation in terms of reasons rather than in terms of causes, is the only one that is appropriate to human conduct. The actions for which a man is held responsible are motivated, but not necessitated. He could have acted otherwise just in the sense that there is no causal law from which it follows, given the circumstances in question, that he must have acted as he did. How this could be is a question which we still have to examine. For the sake of argument, however, let us assume that it is so. What we must not then do is fall on the second horn of the dilemma by inferring that in that case it is just a matter of chance that the man acts for the reasons that he does. For not only are the actions of a rational agent not haphazard, his motives are not haphazard either. We can explain how he comes to have them, but the explanation will be in terms of the rational inter-connection of his purposes, and not in terms of their causal origin. His actions become intelligible to us in the light of our general understanding of his character, just as a work of art becomes intelligible to us when we grasp its general plan. To insist on asking whether or not it is a matter of chance that he has this character is beside the point, just as it would be beside the point to ask whether it was a matter of chance that Rembrandt painted his mother, or Beethoven composed his last quartets, in the manner that they did.

The difficulty with this view is that it is not at all clear why we should not be allowed to ask these questions. If we are anxious to understand a work of art, or even a person's character, it may not be very profitable to try to account for it in purely causal terms; but this is not to say that the attempt to do so is illegitimate. Neither is it clear why the problem of free-will should be solved merely through making the assumption that such an attempt is bound to be unsuccessful. And in any case what right have we to make this assumption ? How can we be so sure that the behaviour of a rational agent is not susceptible of a purely causal explanation ?

Let us begin, however, by approaching this question from the other side. What reasons are there for supposing that all human conduct is governed by causal laws ? Many people believe that this is so, but mostly, it would seem, on *a priori* grounds. That is, they deduce it from some general doctrine of determinism. Nowadays this most commonly takes the form of maintaining that every event, and in consequence every human action, is theoretically predictable. Admittedly, the number of human actions which we are in fact capable of predicting is very small : but this, it is claimed, is only because we do not know enough. The factors involved are so numerous and so complex that it is not practically possible to take account of them all. Nevertheless the fact remains that if we did know all the relevant initial conditions, and all the relevant laws, we could deduce exactly what any given person would think or feel or do ; and the same would apply of course, on the hypothesis of complete determinism, to every other type of event.

But let us consider what this claim amounts to. The first point to note is that it is not even logically possible that every event should actually be predicted, if only because this would lead to an infinite regress. The making of each prediction would itself have to be predicted and so *ad infinitum.* However, this does not exclude the possibility that every event is actually predictable in the sense that if one were required to predict some individual event, there is none of them that would not be a candidate. But even this is not certain. For it might be a necessary condition of the occurrence of certain events that they were not in fact predicted, or at any rate that they were not predicted by a given person. In one's own case, for example, there may well be actions which one would not in fact perform, if one had predicted that one was going to perform them. And here there is no refuge in the argument that to say that the action is foreseen entails that it will occur. For the point is just that there are actions which the agent cannot foresee. The mere fact that he made the prediction would ensure that it was false.

No doubt the determinist has a reply to this. He will argue that the most that such examples can prove is that it is causally impossible that certain actions should actually be predicted; it still does not follow that they are not predictable in principle, and this is all that he is claiming. But what is meant by saying that an event is predictable in principle? Presumably just that there are some events antecedent to it with which it is connected by a natural law; so that the materials which would permit it to be predicted are available, even if for some special reason the prediction cannot actually be made. But if this is what is being claimed, it is unnecessary, and indeed rather misleading, to couch it in terms of prediction. The thesis of determinism is just that every occurrence is governed by some natural law.

This sounds well enough, but what exactly does it come to? If the contention is merely that there is always some true generalization from which, given the appropriate initial conditions, the occurrence of a given event can be deduced, it is correct but trivial. For every set of events must fit into some pattern, if no restriction is placed upon its complexity; even if the event is of a type of which it is the only instance it can still be linked by a generalization to any other unique event; if each kind of event occurs only once, then, however they are spatio-temporally related, it will be universally true that no event of either kind occurs except in that relation to the other. It may indeed be objected that what we understand by a natural law is something stronger than a mere *de facto* generalization, but while there may be some ground for this distinction, it is not at all easy to see what it can be. My own view is that the difference does not lie in the character of the generalizations, so much as in our attitude towards them: the generalizations which we treat as natural laws are those which we are the most confident of being able to extrapolate successfully.[1] But, if this is correct, it is idle to speculate in the abstract about the subjection of events to natural laws. It is a truism that every event falls under some generalization or other; whether the generalization is one to which we should be prepared to accord the status of a natural law is a question to which there can be no answer unless we know what the generalization is.

The thesis of determinism has lived very largely on the credit of classical mechanics. Given that one knew the position and velocity of every physical particle in the universe at a given instant, the laws of classical mechanics enabled one to calculate exactly what would be the position and velocity of these particles at any other instant. The deterministic empire was then erected on the assumption that everything that happened could ultimately be accounted for in terms of the motion of these physical particles. If determinism is now said to have broken down in quantum physics, the reason is that one of the conditions which underlay its classical formulation cannot be fulfilled; it is not possible to fix exactly both the position and momentum of a microscopic particle at any given instant; indeed, the prevalent view is that it makes no sense to say of such particles that they simultaneously have an exact position and momentum. What this shows is that the causal scheme which was found to work in the domain of classical

[1] *Vide* 'What is a Law of Nature?'

mechanics cannot be simply transferred to the domain of quantum physics. It does not show that the behaviour of microscopic particles is entirely lawless, and it leaves it an open question what laws may hold in other fields. So, if we wish to discover how far human actions are subject to natural law, we have to pursue our investigations at the appropriate level.

To some extent this has already been done. The biological and social sciences do enable us to account for human actions to a certain extent. Admittedly the predictions which we draw from them are not very far-reaching and, for the most part, not very precise. We can foretell that a man will be angry if such and such things are said or done to him, but probably not the precise form that the expression of his anger will take; a psycho-analyst may predict in certain favourable circumstances that his patient will exhibit neurotic symptoms, a physiologist that as the result of a brain operation the patient's powers of perception or his moral character will deteriorate, but the range of behaviour which such predictions cover is wide: they come a long way short of pin-pointing the events which are said to verify them. We are rather more successful at explaining human conduct *ex post facto*, but still in a way that fits the facts rather loosely. Moreover the type of explanation which prevails in historical studies is that of explanation in terms of reasons rather than in terms of causes.

Nevertheless, I do not think that we can exclude the possibility of discovering a causal scheme into which human behaviour can be made to fit, not only in outline but even in detail. For example, it is believed by many physiologists that the sufficient condition of every conscious state or action is to be found in some state of the agent's body, and primarily in the functioning of his brain. They would, therefore, claim that every facet of human behaviour could be adequately accounted for in physiological terms. This is, indeed, only an ideal which is still very far from being fulfilled. Our knowledge of the mechanism of the brain is still imperfect, and no dictionary has been compiled which would serve to match variations in brain processes with variations in conscious states. It may be that such a dictionary never will be compiled, perhaps even that it never could be, on scientific grounds. On the other hand, there seems to be no logical reason why it should not be : so far as I can see, this is not a possibility that we are entitled to rule out *a priori*. I am, therefore, suspicious of any philosophical theory which is based on the assumption that a programme of this kind cannot be fulfilled.

Now suppose that it were fulfilled ; suppose that we had a physiological theory which gave content to the thesis that all human actions were determined, and that this theory were reasonably well established : how would this affect the problems which we have been discussing ? In particular how far would it lend support to any form of fatalism ?

In answering this question, we must distinguish between the practical consequences of applying such a theory and the logical consequences of the theory itself. If it came to the point where we had the means of knowing what was going on in a person's brain and could use this as a basis for predicting what he would do, and if this knowledge extended to our own future conduct, it is unlikely that our present view of life would remain the same. As I have remarked before, the making of these predictions would itself be a causal factor ; they would inhibit the emotional responses to an action which depend upon its being unexpected : in the long run certain forms of conduct would themselves be inhibited. But it is idle to pursue these speculations in the abstract, especially as the practical difficulties of applying such a theory would be so great that the predictions which it yielded would probably not be very far-reaching. And it is from our actual success in making such predictions that these consequences would result, rather than from the mere acceptance of the view that human action was physiologically determined.

One practical consequence which the acceptance of this view would itself be likely to have would be a weakening of our belief in the justice of retributive punishment, if only on the principle that the better we understand the more we are inclined to forgive. It might even be held that this was not merely a practical, but a logical consequence. For, as I have already said, it is at least very doubtful whether a deterministic view of this kind can be logically reconciled with our current notion of moral responsibility. As we have seen, this does not imply that we could not then operate with any notion of moral responsibility at all, but only that we should have to fall back upon a utilitarian notion which would differ, at least in one important respect, from that which most people now appear to have. The difference, as I have already suggested, would be that we should have to abandon, or at least to modify, the prevalent concept of moral desert. For if I am right in what I said about this concept, the conditions for its application would not be satisfied.

On the other hand, I do not think that the fact that human behaviour was governed by causal laws, in any such way as we have been imagining, would entail that human beings were merely puppets or that their aspirations were futile, or any fatalistic conclusion of that sort. A person is said to become a puppet when he is made the hapless instrument of another person's will, but unless we make certain theistic assumptions, for which there appears to be no reasonable warrant, our mere subjection to natural law would not put us in this position. Neither would it follow that our actions could not be purposive, or that our lives would pursue their courses independently of our purposes. The important point here is that acting for a reason is not incompatible with acting from a cause. The two forms of explanation are not exclusive. It does not cease to be true that an action is consciously directed towards an end, even if the agent's choice of the end in question and his selection of the means to attain it are explicable in purely causal terms.

An argument which is sometimes put forward against the hypothesis that all human behaviour is governed by causal laws is that it is self-defeating. For we ought not to accept a hypothesis unless we have some reason to believe it. But, it is argued, if this hypothesis were true, we could have no reason to believe it. We have reason to believe a hypothesis when we are able to see that it is supported by evidence which we also have reason to trust. But if the sort of hypothesis which we have been considering were true, whether or not we believed a hypothesis would depend simply on the condition of our brains, or whatever else was the determinant factor. It might indeed happen that the belief which so resulted was true, but this would be the fruit of one's good fortune, not of one's rational judgement: had one's brain been in a different condition one might just as inevitably have been led to a belief which was false. In neither case would the rational assessment of the evidence play any part.

I think that this argument is fallacious, just because it rests on the assumption that to act for a reason is incompatible with acting from a cause. The statement that one believes a given proposition on such and such rational grounds, and the statement that one believes it because such and such processes are occurring in one's brain can, both of them, be true. The word 'because' is used in a different sense in either case, but these senses are not destructive of each other. The fact that there was a causal explanation for my advancing these views, that I should, for example, be thinking differently if my brain were differently constituted, would not prove that I do not genuinely hold them, or that I hold them for any other *reasons* than the reasons which I give; neither would it have any bearing on the question whether the reasons are good or bad. This is illustrated even by the example of a calculating machine. The way the machine operates depends on the way in which it has been constructed, but it is also true that it operates in accordance with certain logical rules. From the fact that its operations are causally explicable it does not follow that they are not logically valid. However loose the analogy between human beings and machines, if this libertarian argument breaks down in the one case, it breaks down in the other.

I have not been maintaining that the case for regarding human conduct as causally determined has been made out: the most that I have tried to show is that it cannot be refuted on purely logical grounds. It is an empirical question which, in the present state of our knowledge, we are not in a position to decide. If we were able to decide it in favour of determinism, we might still attempt to avoid drawing a fatalistic conclusion. We might argue that the fact that our actions fitted into a causal pattern did not imply that they could not be purposive or that we had no command over our own fortunes. However they might be accounted for, our choices would still themselves be causal factors. It is true that if our actions are determined, there is a sense in which they are not avoidable. But from our own point of view as agents, this makes no more serious difference than the logical truism that the future will be what it will.

I think that this attitude could be maintained so long as the theory which was taken as justifying the belief in the causal determination of our actions was not one which we could easily employ to make concrete predictions. If its application were virtually limited to explaining human behaviour *ex post facto*, we should still be faced in practice with the responsibility of coming to decisions; and we should not cease to regard these decisions as being efficacious, even though we believed that they could all be given a physiological explanation. On the other hand, if the theory were actually used to predict human behaviour with a fair degree of precision, I think that our view of ourselves as agents might be radically changed. We should not have the same use for the concept of human action, if we had this scientific means of knowing what we were going to do and what the results would be. The important point here is not so much that our conduct would be foreseen, but that it would be foreseen without any account being taken of our intentions, except as the correlates of certain physiological states. If this were to happen, we might well come to think of ourselves, not as living our lives in the way we now do, but rather as spectators of a process over which we had no effective control. But while I think that this is a possibility, I do not think that it is one with which we have to reckon very seriously. For not only is the case for determinism, in respect of human behaviour, not yet established; but even if it were established, the practical consequences would not be likely to extend very far. The chances that we could actually use a physiological, or even a psychological, theory to plot the course of our destinies in detail appear very small.

INDEX

THE END

PRINTED BY R. & R. CLARK, LTD., EDINBURGH